THE GREAT CORONAVIRUS PANDEMIC AND MESSAGES FROM THE PROPHETS

THE GREAT CORONAVIRUS PANDEMIC AND MESSAGES FROM THE PROPHETS

Doman Lum

Foreword by Gerald C. Liu

RESOURCE *Publications* • Eugene, Oregon

THE GREAT CORONAVIRUS PANDEMIC
AND MESSAGES FROM THE PROPHETS

Copyright © 2021 Doman Lum. All rights reserved. Except for brief quotations in critical publications or reviews, no part of this book may be reproduced in any manner without prior written permission from the publisher. Write: Permissions, Wipf and Stock Publishers, 199 W. 8th Ave., Suite 3, Eugene, OR 97401.

Resource Publications
An Imprint of Wipf and Stock Publishers
199 W. 8th Ave., Suite 3
Eugene, OR 97401

www.wipfandstock.com

PAPERBACK ISBN: 978-1-7252-9088-4
HARDCOVER ISBN: 978-1-7252-9089-1
EBOOK ISBN: 978-1-7252-9090-7

02/11/21

This book is dedicated to the members and friends of The Chinese Community Church, Sacramento, California, who heard this preaching series, "Messages From The Prophets," during the height of the coronavirus pandemic and to my family: my wife, Joyce Wong Lum, who let me accept the responsibilities of pastoring this church and was with me every step of ministry and my children and grandchildren: Noel and Lori Domine and Riley and Alyssa; Jonathan and Lisa Lum and Evan, Brennen, and Trevor; Ross and Amy Sato and Jack, Joel, Jay, and Ally; and Matthew Lum who heard this Word of the Lord on various Sunday services.

CONTENTS

FOREWORD | xi
PREFACE | xiii
ACKNOWLEDGMENTS | xvii

INTRODUCTION
The Story of the Great Pandemic | 1

CHAPTER 1
GOOD AND EVIL
Amos 5:14–15 (April 19, 2020) | 12

CHAPTER 2
HOSEA'S WIFE AND GOD'S PROMISE
Hosea 1:1–11; 2:16–23 (April 26, 2020) | 19

CHAPTER 3
JUSTICE, KINDNESS, AND HUMILITY
Micah 6:8 (May 3, 2020) | 26

CHAPTER 4
A SINFUL NATION AND CHANGING SCARLET INTO SNOW
Isaiah 1:1–9, 16–18 (May 10, 2020) | 32

CHAPTER 5
HOLINESS AND HOLLOWNESS
Isaiah 6:1–13 (May 17, 2020) | 40

CHAPTER 6
FROM DARKNESS TO LIGHT
Isaiah 9:2–7 (May 24, 2020) | 48

CHAPTER 7
A SHOOT FROM JESSE AND THE SPIRIT OF THE LORD
Isaiah 11:1–10 (May 31, 2020) | 55

CHAPTER 8
WIPING AWAY THE TEARS
Isaiah 25:1-10 (June 14, 2020) | 62

CHAPTER 9
STRENGTH, TRUST, AND PEACE
Isaiah 26:1-15 (June 7, 2020) | 70

CHAPTER 10
GOD WILL DO AMAZING THINGS
Isaiah 29:13-24 (June 21. 2020) | 78

CHAPTER 11
THE PRAYERS OF HEZEKIAH AND THE ANSWER FROM GOD
Isaiah 37:14-20, 30-38; 38:1-8 (June 28, 2020) | 87

CHAPTER 12
A VOICE CRYING IN THE WILDERNESS
Isaiah 40:1-11 (July 5, 2020) | 96

CHAPTER 13
THE SUFFERING SERVANT
Isaiah 53:1-12 (July 12, 2020) | 103

CHAPTER 14
THIRST, MONEY, AND SEEKING THE LORD
Isaiah 55:1-11 (July 19, 2020) | 110

CHAPTER 15
I AM ONLY A BOY
Jeremiah 1:1-10 (August 2, 2020) | 117

CHAPTER 16
THE SPIRIT OF THE LORD IS UPON ME
Isaiah 61:1-4 (July 26, 2020) | 125

CHAPTER 17
THE POTTER AND THE CLAY
Jeremiah 18:1-12 (September 6, 2020) | 134

CHAPTER 18
THE NEW COVENANT
Jeremiah 31:31-34 (September 20, 2020) | 142

CHAPTER 19
ONE SHEPHERD, A COVENANT, AND VEGETATION
Ezekiel 34:23-31 (October 4, 2020) | 151

CHAPTER 20
FROM DRY BONES TO LIVE BONES
Ezekiel 37:1–14 (October 18, 2020) | 160

CHAPTER 21
JUDGEMENT AND CALLING ON THE NAME OF THE LORD
Joel 2:30–3:3; Malachi 3:1–4 (November 1, 2020) | 168

CHAPTER 22
LESSONS FROM THE CORONAVIRUS | 174

BIBLIOGRAPHY | 191

INDEX | 193

FOREWORD

Never in the history of modern homiletics have preachers faced the challenge of delivering a word during a pandemic as widespread as COVID-19. There have been other epidemics to be sure—typhus, smallpox, polio, cholera, dengue fever, West Nile Virus, SARS, Zika, and Ebola to name a few. North American preachers stand to learn much from fellow proclaimers around the world who have already produced messages in the face of outbreaks. Yet the challenges of the COVID-19 crisis have defined new conditions for Christian preaching everywhere and exponentially. Preachers have had to reinvent the art of proclamation outside the constants of sanctuary and pulpit. Upholding social distancing and quarantining have also prohibited preaching in the public square. Onscreen witness has been all that is available.

Where and how preaching occurs is more up for grabs in ways that stretch even the most homiletically creative minds. Is it best to film and post online, use social media, choose a software that facilitates group meeting, or make the most of the camera technology in a smartphone, and so forth? What if technological resources are in short supply or virtually nonexistent? What if parishioners do not have access to the technological tools that would allow them to access a message streamed on the internet? The digital divide has brought another cleavage in congregational life as access to technology and having the expertise to use it now complexify calculations regarding homiletic resourcefulness and the desire to share the message of Christ with wide invitation.

Preachers have also had to revisit questions of theodicy, where God is and how in the midst of human suffering. Wrestling with questions of hope, the exercise of expecting and enacting justice and mercy, has become more homiletically strenuous without an end to the pandemic in sight. Questions of eschatology, the belief in immediate and ultimate true and divine healing and redemption, with a virus outmaneuvering so many efforts at public health coupled with a scourge of national deadly racial and political violence assume another dimension that may scare away even the bravest of preachers.

Out of a cultural milieu that would make any preacher shudder, Doman Lum dares not only to name how God remains with us, but declares why our outcry is not unheard but helps lift us up to where Jesus is, and suggests how God is a potter shaping antiracist protests and molding the national upheaval into a better future headed toward the promise of a new creation. But he also provides a chronology of how an unwavering commitment to the preached Word, even in an unprecedented time, can make sense of high holy days and Mother's, Memorial, and Father's Days unlike any others that we have ever seen, as moments to remember that God comes to save. Salvation is also known and experienced in tangible acts of responsibility such as wearing a mask, working together to insist that Black Lives Matter, and to build covenants of peace with our civic and ecumenical neighbors that inform life within and beyond congregations. This includes all of us, even surprise wisdom from Lum's four-year-old granddaughter. Lum's focus upon drawing words of spiritual endurance and assurance from the prophetic literature of the Old Testament will show readers how one seasoned preacher shone light during the pandemic of 2020 and how the promises of God persist no matter how apocalyptic things seem.

Gerald C. Liu, PhD, Advent 2020
Assistant Professor of Worship and Preaching
Princeton Theological Seminary
Princeton, New Jersey

PREFACE

The COVID-19 pandemic has been the greatest public health problem that has faced the United States of America and the world since the Spanish Flu epidemic of 1918. Our country has lost over 346,346 victims (December 31, 2020) and has suffered economic loss, human suffering, and political and social upheaval. In the midst of this national crisis the Christian church faces the challenge of preaching the love and comfort of God to the world despite closing its doors because of the spread of the virus.

During this time it was my task to write weekly Sunday sermons for my church as the interim pastor in order to speak a relevant word to my congregation. I crafted twenty-one sermons from the books of Amos, Hosea, Micah, Isaiah, Jeremiah, Ezekiel, Joel, and Malachi and sought to apply them to the daily chronology of the coronavirus which affected the lives of American citizens. I thought that it would be important to share these sermons with a wider reading audience of pastors and parishioners. These sermons came from an exegetical understanding of various key passages from the prophets from Amos through Isaiah and Jeremiah to Malachi and sought to offer parallels to the daily happenings of the coronavirus facing the American public.

The Sunday sermon is the main feature of the Protestant Reformed Sunday worship service throughout the Christian church around the world. A sermon is a religious discourse given publicly by a minister during a religious service. In theological seminaries theological students take a homiletics course in order to learn how to compose a sermon and how to preach it effectively. Homiletics is the art of preaching and consists of sermon preparation, practice, and execution based on an exegetical analysis and understanding of a specific passage of scripture from the Old Testament and/or New Testament, a sharing of life experiences, illustrations, and practical applications to the congregation.

Phillips Brooks (1877) in the Lyman Beecher Lectures on Preaching at Yale Divinity School two centuries ago said that preaching was based on truth and personality.[1] Brooks asserted that the minister preaches the truth of the scriptures and conveys his/her personality as a channel of expressing the meaning of the sermon. Preaching is the proclamation of the Word of God and is emphasized in the theological understanding of the concept, Word of God, from Karl Barth's *Church Dogmatics*. Volume 1, Part 1.

Barth began his discussion of the meaning of the term *Word of God* by emphasizing the use of the Word of God as the *proclaiming Word of God* or *proclamation as preaching* as the primary emphasis. Barth boldly declared: "Preaching is such proclamation; i.e., the attempt, essayed by one called thereto in the church, to express in his own words in the form of an exposition of a portion of the Biblical testimony to revelation, and to make comprehensible to men of his day the promise of God's revelation, reconciliation and calling, as they are to be expected here and now."[2] Karl Barth was foremost a pastor and a preacher, a teacher of dogmatic theology, and a prolific writer of Biblical, systematic, and historical theological insights into the revelation of God in Jesus Christ. He remains the twentieth century model for how a theologian should act in the encounter with the issues of the world and speaking and doing the Word of God to others.

The Sunday sermons in this book reflected the careful analysis of Scripture and the connection to the life experiences of people who confronted the coronavirus pandemic. Preaching was done through virtual means (videos and internet) and feedback was encouraged by this preacher from the listeners and readers. The preaching series, "Messages From The Prophets," was conceived before the American outbreak of the COVID-19 erupted in March 2020, although the actual sermon series began in mid-April 2020. I started with this congregation a preaching series, "Great Leaders-Great Lives," in January 2020 which covered the lives of Abraham, Isaac, Jacob, and Joseph through Moses, Joshua, and the Judges to David. My purpose was to ground this church in the great leaders of the Old Testament in order to provide an adequate background to understand how the Old Testament interacted and connected with the New Testament.

The major and minor prophets of the Old Testament followed the Davidic kingship since the attention shifted from the kings of Israel and Judah to the role of the prophets who preached judgement and repentance to the rulers, clergy, the wealthy, middle class, and the poor of Israel. The prophets have been a source of personal interest and investigation for me

---

1. Brooks, *Lectures on Preaching*.
2. Barth, *Church Dogmatics, The Doctrine of the Word of God*, 61.

as a student of biblical studies. R. B. Y. Scott, Abraham J. Heschel, Gerhard von Rad, and Brevard S. Childs have written major books on the prophets.[3] I was familiar with their ideas, but I never had the opportunity to preach on the great passages from the Old Testament prophets during Sunday worship service. Now I was afforded the chance to preach on the themes of the prophets and to combine spiritual truths with the coronavirus pandemic facing our people and nation.

From my perspective I felt that it was important for me to provide in the preaching series a chronology of events and problem issues facing the American people in their daily struggle with the coronavirus and to explain how the messages of the prophets still speak to the issues of today's world of illness and threat of death. We are still not out of the woods and have not reached the end of the tunnel as this preaching series ends, but we as the Christian church are aware of the need to speak the Word of God and proclaim the salvation (healing and wholeness) of Christ to everyone who hears, listens, and responds to the good news of Jesus.

I want to thank the consistory, members, and friends of Chinese Community Church, Sacramento, California, who provided me the pulpit and the encouragement to preach on "Messages From The Prophets" as their interim pastor; my wife, Joyce, who allowed me to have this pastoral ministry opportunity after retiring as Professor Emeritus of Social Work, California State University, Sacramento; and my children, their spouses, and grandchildren who came to church to hear me preach during Sunday service (Noel and Lori Domine and Riley and Alyssa; Jonathan and Lisa Lum and Evan, Brennen, and Trevor; Ross and Amy Sato and Jack. Joel, Jay, and Ally; and Matthew Lum).

---

3. Scott, *The Relevance of the Prophets*; Heschel, *The Prophets*; von Rad, *The Message of the Prophets*; Childs, *Introduction to the Old Testament as Scripture*.

ACKNOWLEDGMENTS

I want to acknowledge many persons who have supported the publication of this book. Dr. Gerald C. Liu, Assistant Professor of Preaching and Worship at Princeton Theological Seminary, has been a support to me as a teacher, scholar, and writing colleague. When I asked him for the best book on homiletics, he immediately recommended Thomas G. Long, *The Witness of Preaching*,[4] which became a reference book for lay preaching and lay preachers' seminars in our church. I want to thank him for his gracious foreword to this book on sermons and preaching, the subjects which he teaches his students at Princeton Theological Seminary.

Much credit goes to the staff at Wipf and Stock Publishers who were kind enough to accept this book manuscript on the coronavirus pandemic and messages from the Old Testament prophets. Matt Wimer, Editorial Production Manager, shared with me the extensive materials that Wipf and Stock prepares for their authors. He answered my many questions and steered me through the stages of publishing this book with helpful suggestions to improve the finished product. I want to thank Joshua Little, Editorial Content Manager, who oversaw the content material of this book and improved its quality along the way and George Callihan, Editorial Administrative Assistant, who was the contact person for this publishing company. I would also like to thank Emily Callihan for her help in the book formatting, Zechariah Mickel for his careful copyediting, Ian Creeger for his fine typesetting work, Joe Delahanty for his marketing efforts, and Kyle Lundburg for the book cover.

Doman Lum, PhD, ThD, December 31, 2020
Interim Pastor, Chinese Community Church, Sacramento, California
Minister of The United Church of Christ,
Northern California-Nevada Conference
Professor Emeritus of Social Work, California State University, Sacramento

---

4. Third ed. (Louisville: Westminster John Knox, 2016).

INTRODUCTION
The Story of the Great Pandemic

This is the story of the Great Coronavirus Pandemic which invaded the United States of America slowly in the ending days of January 2020. It began with a man in his thirties from Washington state returning from Wuhan, China, who brought the coronavirus to the United States on January 21, 2020. Then China imposed a strict lockdown in Wuhan on January 23, 2020, and the World Health Organization (WHO) declared a global health emergency on January 30, 2020. The next day, January 31, 2020, President Trump blocked travel from China. It was first reported that the first COVID-19 death on February 28, 2020, was a man in his fifties in the Seattle area but later it was confirmed that two deaths attributed to coronavirus occurred on February 6 and 28, 2020, in Santa Clara County, California.[1]

President Trump and the White House staff were confident that America could handle a contained spread of this disease which was called COVID-19. Little did we know that the coronavirus would be the greatest public health threat to hit my generation of older Americans in over a hundred years.

THE IMPACT OF COVID-19

The coronavirus disease disrupted a strong economy and the sure reelection of Donald Trump as President of the United States. His chances for a second term were strong before the virus, but in the subsequent months after the first wave struck the country in March 2020, his election has gradually diminished in terms of a certain victory.

---

1. University of Minnesota, Center for Infectious Disease Research and Policy, April 22, 2020.

Due to the growing disease outbreak, the mounting death toll, and the threat of disaster, American businesses were forced to close which left millions of people without work and a steady income. State unemployment claims rose to sixty million and employment development departments were overwhelmed with applications. Lines of cars flooded food distribution centers and food banks which were barely able to keep up with the needs of hungry middle-class Americans. For the first time the average citizen was forced to seek help which was formerly reserved for the poor and the indigent.

The United States Congress responded with two separate trillion-dollar assistance programs to stabilize the income of unemployed workers until the economy could regain its momentum and get workers back to their jobs. Still millions who were previously employed are still without work. Their former employment vanished with cutbacks and no promise of rehiring.

The coronavirus called COVID-19 started with two hot spots: the state of Washington with a concentration in Seattle and a long-term care facility of elderly patients where many died and in New York City where thousands were affected and hospitals and ICU units were overwhelmed with coronavirus patients who died by the hundreds daily during March to June 2020. From there the coronavirus spread to major cities in the South and West Coast and then to the Midwest, Far West, and Upper Midwest states in April through October 2020. With the beginning of school in fall 2020 the coronavirus pandemic outbreak was seen in K-12 schools and universities where in-person learning occurred in the South, the East Coast, and Midwest. On September 2, 2020, CNN reported that twenty-five thousand college students in thirty-nine states had contracted the coronavirus while on their campuses for the fall semester.

The Presidential Coronavirus Task Force and the Centers for Disease Control endeavored to coordinate national and state efforts to cope with the spread and treatment of the disease. The national group became a clearing house to provide proper protective equipment, ventilators, treatment medications, and best practices and to spearhead the research and clinical trials of promising vaccines. Testing and contact tracing were initiated in major cities throughout the country. Citizens were advised to wear a mask, practice social distancing, wash hands, and avoid large gatherings in order to flatten the curve and spread of the disease.

During December 2020 the FDA approved the Pfizer vaccine on December 11, 2020, and the Moderna vaccine on December 18, 2020. The Trump administration projected that twenty million first-line workers and elderly persons would be vaccinated by the end of the year, but it is estimated that only three million have received their initial shots. During the last three weeks of December 2020 California, particularly Los Angeles County, became the epicenter for coronavirus outbreaks and deaths. On the average during December 2020 the daily death rate across the United States was 3,800. On December 3, 2020, it was reported that two cases in Colorado and California showed that the coronavirus variant, which was more contagious and originated in the United Kingdom earlier in December had reached the United States. Both patients were quarantined to prevent the spread of this new form of COVID-19 virus. By December 31, 2020, as the year came to an end, there were 20,231,000 cases of coronavirus illness, 1,200,000 new cases during a seven-day period (December 25–31, 2020), and 346,346 deaths in the United States.

PRESIDENT DONALD TRUMP

To complicate the control of the coronavirus after two months of sheltering at home, social distance, and the wearing or not wearing of masks, President Trump encouraged the opening of businesses in the various states in May 2020. By then the direct responsibility of controlling the spread of the virus was in the hands of state governors supported by state and county departments of health. President Trump was concerned about his reelection and calculated that he needed to restore the economy to some semblance of order between June 2020 and October 2020. He calculated that he must encourage people to return to work in order to claim that he saved millions of lives and restored millions of jobs before the November election.

He held rallies of large crowds in Tulsa, Oklahoma, Phoenix, Arizona, Mount Rushmore, and the White House East Lawn without social distancing and masks. Many of the White House staff and Secret Service agents from the Tulsa meeting contracted the COVID-19 virus and remained quarantined as a result of the trip. Later reports estimated that five hundred new cases of coronavirus were triggered from the Trump Tulsa meeting. Trump's messaging was on law and order, the vilifying of the radical left and demonstrators, and the protection of statues as part of our national heritage. He asserted that the coronavirus testing showed that 99 percent of persons tested were harmless and that the virus would fade away. Regarding the demonstrations he claimed that Black Lives Matter posed a threat, but he failed to address the killings of African Americans by local police in Georgia, Kentucky, Minnesota, and Colorado.

Because many states gradually lifted their restrictions prematurely after just two months of shut down, by July 2020 the United States was coping with a resurgence of the coronavirus which doubled and even tripled the number of cases in Florida, Texas, Arizona, Georgia, and California. By the beginning of July 2020 there were fifty-seven thousand new cases per day clustered in these five states. California reported an increase of the virus during the Fourth of July 2020 surge among a younger population of adults ages eighteen to forty-five years old. By the middle of July 2020 there were eighty thousand new cases per day reported throughout the country.

As a result governors rescinded their phased opening and ordered the wearing of masks and the reclosing of indoor businesses such as restaurant dining, bars, and other large gatherings of people. Unfortunately President Trump chose not to wear a face covering (he wore a mask when he visited Walter Reed Army Hospital in Washington, DC, during the second week of July 2020) and has conducted large-scale political rallies without the protection of masks and social distancing. However, by the end of July 2020 Trump realized that due to the coronavirus surge he could no longer hold large political gatherings. Despite this, as the Republican National Convention began during the week of August 24–27, 2020, President Trump spoke to three hundred delegates at his nomination in North Carolina where later it was reported that four tested positive for the coronavirus; a crowd of 1,500 where the majority did not wear masks or practiced social distancing on the South Lawn of the White House during his acceptance speech; and large crowds who were without masks and without social distance in campaign stops in New Hampshire, Wisconsin, North Carolina, and other places.

Previously during mid-July 2020 he ordered the opening of school for children in the fall in order to get parents back to offices and factories and revive the business economy so that he could highlight this in his reelection campaign. The President of the United States has no jurisdiction to order the opening of public schools. Rather state governors along with county boards and city mayors have control over the state and local school systems. He has not offered a national strategy and public health safety plan for schoolchildren and teachers. A few days later on July 10, 2020, he announced a presidential commutation for his friend and campaign staffer, Roger J. Stone Jr., which voided his three-year sentence for seven federal felonies. He was testing the waters to see whether the justice system and the American people would allow him to get away with this decision. Senator Mitt Romney called this "unprecedented historic corruption," Democratic leaders denounced the move, and the rest of the Republicans in the Senate and the House were silent on the matter. Attorney General William Barr who was instrumental in the reduction of Stone's sentence from eight years to three years said that he advised the President against making this move.

As the presidential election loomed closer by Labor Day, September 7, 2020, President Trump began to shift his attention toward campaigning against former Vice President Biden. Against this backdrop a number of issues occurred which affected the tone of the country. The new stimulus bill for those unemployed persons who lost their jobs due to the pandemic remained stalled in Congress while the Democrats and Republicans could not agree on funding levels for numerous programs. A deadline for agreement was set for the third week of October 2020 with the goal of providing relief to out-of-work recipients before the November third election. Meanwhile on September 26, 2020, President Trump nominated Judge Amy Coney Barrett to replace the late Ruth Bader Ginsberg for the vacancy on the United States Supreme Court. Then President Trump contracted the coronavirus on October 2, 2020, and was hospitalized at Walter Reed Medical Center for three days. He returned to the White House and shortly resumed his campaign on October 11, 2020. Senate Judiciary Committee hearings for Judge Barrett occurred on October 12-14, 2020, with Democrats highlighting the impact on the Affordable Care Act on medical clients if the conservative majority rule against it with Judge Barrett joining the conservative members, while Republicans praised her qualifications as a Supreme Court justice. Judge Amy Coney Barrett was confirmed by the Senate on October 26, 2020, and became the fifth woman on the United States Supreme Court. Meanwhile President Trump has held multiple rallies on a single day in the key battle ground states in the East, Midwest, and Western states much like he did when he campaigned in 2016.

On October 26, 2020, it was reported that five Pence staffers tested positive for coronavirus. Rather than self-quarantine Vice President Pence continued to travel to various states campaigning for President Trump. He was head of the Presidential Coronavirus Task Force and should have followed CDC guidelines, but the White House answered that Pence was an essential worker and could continue his duties under these circumstances. Throughout the campaign rallies President Trump maintained that we are rounding the turn as far as the coronavirus was concerned rather than confronting the reality of a COVID-19 surge. President Trump's election numbers were strong on election day, November 3, 2020. He held 215 electoral votes but his leads in battle states has dwindled on the following two days because states began to count mail-in and absentee early ballots. He decided to contest the election in states where he was losing on November 5, 2020, and charged voting fraud. On November 7, 2020, Joe Biden became the president-elect of the United States of America and Donald Trump will leave the office of the President on January 20, 2021, which is inauguration day. Since the results of the election President Trump has lost challenge cases in court, failed to concede the election, and has not been involved in the coronavirus outbreak prevention efforts. Rather he has pardoned several former campaign confidantes and Gerald Kushner's father.

AFRICAN AMERICAN KILLINGS AND SHOOTINGS

Parallel with the coronavirus and the economy downturn have been the killings and murders of African Americans in various parts of the country. Georgia, Kentucky, Minnesota, Colorado, and Wisconsin have been states which have featured shooting and killings of Black Americans by local police which are below the norms of good police practices. The police are in the community to serve and to protect all citizens. Breonna Taylor, a young African American emergency medical technician woman, was shot eight times early in the morning in her home by Louisville, Kentucky, police in a drug raid which targeted the wrong people on March 13, 2020. Two months later the flash point was the arrest and murder of George Floyd who was recorded on video slowly dying as he laid in the street next to a police car with four officers holding him to the ground and the supervising officer with his foot on Floyd's neck. George Floyd died with a plea: "I can't breathe, Mama, help me, I can't breathe," on Memorial Day, May 25, 2020.

As a result, thousands of citizens from all walks of life took to the streets and protested his murder and other African American killings. In some cases, property was destroyed and demonstrators were injured by police and National Guard troops who were called out to restore order. City mayors took to the media and pleaded for calm and peace. President Trump denounced the demonstrators as terrorists and had photo opportunities at two Washington, DC, churches. Black Lives Matter was painted on the street leading to the White House and on the street of New York City in front of Trump Tower.

Unfortunately three months after the death of George Floyd in Minneapolis, Minnesota, Jacob Blake, a young African American father, was shot seven times in the back by Kenosha, Wisconsin, police on August 23, 2020, after a domestic violence incident. More demonstrations took place in protest and the NBA and WNBA playoff games along with the Milwaukee Brewers-Cincinnati Reds game were postponed on August 26, 2020, due to the Blake shooting by police. American professional sports athletes have banded together to promote social justice coalitions and to identify ways to address the police brutality and the need for police reform as well as voting in the presidential election.

Moreover on September 2, 2020, a video was made public by a Prude family attorney of a mental health episode which occurred on March 23,

2020, regarding Daniel Prude, a forty-one-year-old African American man, who was visiting his brother, Joe Prude, in Rochester, New York, from Chicago. Daniel Prude died on March 30, 2020, while in the custody of seven Rochester, New York, police officers. He was handcuffed, had his head covered with a spit head because he said that he had COVID-19, and his head and chest were forced onto the pavement after he became agitated in front of police. The Monroe County Medical Examiner Office ruled Prude's death as a homicide involving "complication of asphyxia in the setting of physical restraint" with excited delirium and PCP drug intoxication (phencyclidine).

Seven Rochester police officers were suspended with pay by the Rochester mayor, Lovely Warren, who began a series of police department reforms to overhaul practices related to people suffering from mental illness. Both Warren and Rochester police chief, La'Ron Singletary, are African Americans. *The Washington Post's* database of police shootings (2015–2020) indicated that 22 percent of those shot and killed by police reported signs of mental illness. A mental health crisis team should have been dispatched by 911 responders in this case, which should be the standard protocol practice. Mayor Warren is working toward this reform. New York State Attorney General, Letitia James, who is also African American is investigating the death and has impaneled a grand jury to hear facts related to the case. There were nightly protests in Rochester, New York, with clashes between Rochester police and demonstrators.

Let us hope that as the Biden administration takes office that President Biden will bring the police chiefs and mayors of major cities together to formulate national policy, strategy, and program legislation and practices to reduce police brutality and promote police service and protection to all citizens.

THE 2020 PRESIDENTIAL ELECTION

President Trump has portrayed former Vice President Biden as a far left radical who will destroy America and condemned Democratic mayors whose cities are places of violence in an attempt to strike fear in the voting public. He saw himself as the leader of law and order, has praised the police for their work, and admitted that there are a few bad apples in the police who choke like missing a putt in a golf tournament. Vice President Biden has dismissed Trump's portrayal of being a radical, sees himself as a unifier who wants to bring people together, and is fighting for the soul of America. He has criticized Trump for his mishandling of the coronavirus and his lack of a national strategy of safety and standards to open schools in America.

Both visited Kenosha, Wisconsin: Trump surveyed the damage, condemned the violence, and praised the local police, while Biden brought comfort to the family of Jacob Blake and sought to bring the community together.

On September 3, 2020, an article in *The Atlantic* broke reporting that President Trump during a trip to France in 2018 to honor the American war dead during the hundred-year commemoration of World War I referred to our fallen soldiers as "suckers and losers." Citing four sources the author of the article, Jeffrey Goldberg, editor in chief of *The Atlantic*, was supported by the *New York Times* for the authenticity of his sources. The following day, September 4, 2020, President Trump denied the article's accusations, while former Vice President Biden whose son, Beau Biden, fought in Iraq forcefully criticized the President based on the article. Fallout from the article was apparent from the press and those from the ranks of the military both active and retired.

Less than a week later on September 9, 2020, CNN reported on the release of eighteen taped interview conversations between President Trump and Robert Woodward in early February until July 2020 for a book on the Trump presidency which was titled *Rage*. On taped interviews (February 7, 2020, and March 19, 2020) Trump admitted the seriousness of the coronavirus: that it was airborne, deadly to the elderly as well as children, and should be taken seriously. It was reported by CNN that Trump's National Security Advisor, Robert O'Brien, warned him on January 28, 2020, that the coronavirus was the greatest threat to his presidency and that the reports of the virus in China were gravely serious. However Trump sought to "play it down" publicly because he wanted to minimize panic and reiterated this same reasoning in a news conference on September 9, 2020. Publicly during the early months of the coronavirus Trump stated that the virus was on the same par as the common flu, minimized the wearing of masks, and held large campaign rallies without social distancing. He failed to warn about the serious nature of the virus and mobilize the nation with a strategic plan of action which resulted in the loss of 190,000 lives by September 9, 2020, argued his critics and particularly former Vice President Biden.

When Ruth Bader Ginsburg died from pancreatic cancer on September 18, 2020, America lost a legal pioneer for gender equality. She was the second woman to serve on the Unites States Supreme Court. A few days before her passing she dictated to her granddaughter the following statement: "My most fervent wish is that I will not be replaced until a new president is installed." When President Obama nominated Merrick Garland in 2016 eleven months before the presidential election the United States Senate refused to take up confirmation hearings because it was controlled by the Republicans. Their argument was that it was a presidential election year and it was up to the American people to decide. The next President should make the Supreme Court nomination. Ironically when Ruth Bader Ginsburg died several states were already voting in the 2020 presidential election and the Republican majority Senate was ready to receive President Trump's nomination for the Supreme Court vacancy, US Circuit Court of Appeals Judge Amy Coney Barrett, and to act on it before the November presidential election. The selection has shifted to the balance of power between liberals and conservatives on the Supreme Court and the implications for future decisions which will affect the lives of the American people. Moreover it has given President Trump a rallying cry to his base and away from the reality of the 200,000 lost lives due to the coronavirus and his handling of this public health crisis.

A September 27, 2020, *New York Times* article reported that President Trump paid $750 in federal income taxes for 2016 and again in 2017 during the first year of his presidency. There were no income taxes paid at all in ten of the previous fifteen years by Trump. This caused quite a stir during the first presidential debate between Trump and Biden on September 29, 2020, in Cleveland, Ohio.

By October 1, 2020, President Trump received a positive coronavirus test after returning from a fundraiser in Bedminster, New Jersey. The following afternoon, October 2, 2020, he was transported to Walter Reed National Military Medical Center for monitoring. Before leaving the White House he is given an antibody cocktail from Regenero, zinc, vitamin D, the heartburn drug famotidine, melatonin, and a daily aspirin. In the hospital he began a five-day course of the antiviral drug remdesivir. On October 3, 2020, Trump was prescribed the corticosteroid drug dexamethasone for COVID-19 and the following day, October 4, 2020, Trump briefly left the hospital with his security detail to ride in an SUV to wave to his supporters outside the hospital. On October 5, 2020, three days after being admitted to the hospital Trump was stabilized and was discharged back to the White House. Along with his coronavirus positive test, thirty-five key White House staff and Trump associates along with three Republican senators tested positive for the virus.

On Wednesday October 7, 2020, Trump resumed work in the Oval Office despite isolation rules and infection risks. It is the day of the vice presidential debate in Salt Lake City, Utah, between Vice President Mike Pence and Senator Kamala Harris. In a series of tweets Trump ended negotiations with the Democrats over an economic stimulus package and then wrote more tweets about resuming those negotiations. He appeared erratic from the effects of his medication treatment. By Thursday October 8, 2020, he criticized Senator Kamala Harris and her debate performance, calling her "a monster" and " a communist." Biden and Trump clashed over the second presidential debate format. Trump rejected a virtual debate and the second debate was cancelled on Saturday October 10, 2020. By this time Nancy Pelosi, Speaker of the House, questioned his fitness for office and proposed a commission to investigate his fitness for the job and whether he needed to be removed under the Constitution's twenty-fifth amendment. Trump announced plans to hold a White House lawn gathering and give a campaign speech on Sunday October 11, 2020, and a rally in Florida on Monday October 12, 2020.

During the last three weeks of the presidential campaign Trump and Biden crisscrossed the country from October 12, 2020, to November 3, 2020, and travelled to the battleground states of Florida, North Carolina, Georgia, Pennsylvania, Ohio, Michigan, Arizona, and Wisconsin. Trump held large crowd rallies at airports outdoors with the majority of attendees without masks and social distancing, while Biden observed the wearing of masks and social distancing with small audiences. Both candidates held separate town meetings. Biden's message centered on the coronavirus and the failed leadership of President Trump, while Trump criticized a series of persons, particularly Dr. Anthony Fauci, calling him a disaster and an idiot. In the final presidential debate on October 22, 2020, Trump did not communicate a coherent plan for the next four years in office, while Biden connected with the middle class problems of common people who are struggling to cope with the economic problems of living.

On election night, November 3, 2020, the election results revealed a strong showing for President Trump who swept most of the South including Florida and the midwestern states, particularly Ohio. However, on the following day the remaining states were counting early mail-in and absentee ballots which favored Democratic voters, especially in Nevada, Arizona, Georgia, Wisconsin, Michigan, and Pennsylvania. The election vote was slowly pivoting away from President Trump toward former Vice President Biden. On November 5, 2020, as President Trump's leads in votes began to decline in Pennsylvania, Georgia, and Nevada he announced that he would contest the election and go to court with election fraud charges. On the morning of November 7, 2020, it was projected that Vice President Joe Biden won the election (Biden 273 electoral votes, Trump 214 electoral votes) and will be the forty-sixth president of the United States.

Let us pray for President Joe Biden and Vice President Kamala Harris that they will unite the country, restore the soul of America, and curb the second wave of the coronavirus. May President Biden reach across the aisle and work with Democrats and Republican lawmakers to pass the necessary programs for the welfare of the country. May he bring governors and state health officials to craft a national strategy to control the coronavirus. May he bring police chiefs together to implement safe procedures and mental health workers to aid domestic violence and mentally ill persons and incidents. May he bring school officials together to formulate a national plan of safety and protection to reopen schools across the nation to control COVID-19. May the Biden administration bring integrity and honor to America in the eyes of the world.

PRELIMINARY THOUGHTS

The coronavirus crisis, African American shootings and killings, and the presidential election have caused a series of events which were not anticipated in the year 2020. In the midst of these events, the Christian church was forced to shut down Sunday worship services and small group meetings. Most churches have used Zoom media to hold virtual church services and small group Bible study groups. However, because of the pandemic local churches have remained relatively quiet as far as their visibility and proximity to the great struggles facing the country. There has been a lack of national leadership and condemnation among American ministers regarding the events which have taken place during this year. No Martin Luther King Jr. and The Southern Christian Leadership Council in the civil rights days of the sixties and no Billy Graham and the call to repentance and turning to Christ in the midst of conflict. Rather silence on the great issues facing America during these times of peril.

At the same time we look toward the beginning of the Biden administration that peace, resolution, and unity will return to the nation and that the coronavirus, the presidency, the killings and murders of African Americans, and the divisions among our citizens will be addressed and resolved in the coming months and years ahead. The coronavirus pandemic and the messages from the prophets of the Old Testament continue to speak to the public health, political, and social problems facing our nation. Just as the Word of the Lord and the prophets spoke to the rulers, nation, and people of Israel centuries ago, the truths of those messages apply to us in the twenty-first century. Let us hear and listen to the Word of God.

CHAPTER 1

GOOD AND EVIL
Amos 5:14–15 (April 19, 2020)

Scripture Reading: Seek good and not evil, that you may live; and so the LORD, the God of hosts, will be with you. Just as you have said. Hate evil and love good, and establish justice in the gate; it may be that the LORD, the God of hosts, will be gracious to the remnant of Joseph.

THE BEGINNING BATTLE OF MARCH 2020

We are in the midst of a battle which has invaded the United States of America with full force in mid-March 2020. New York and California are now under statewide shelter in home quarantine due to the onslaught of the coronavirus virus called COVID-19. The Presidential Taskforce on the Coronavirus headed by Vice President Mike Pence has held daily briefings on national television which have educated the American people on the dangers of this public health pandemic.

The Battle of the Coronavirus, like The Battle of Britain or The Battle of Midway, rages on in the United States and around the world. There have emerged two great American generals. On the Eastern Front stands Governor Andrew Cuomo who is fighting a defensive battle around New York City, which is besieged from all sides with hospitals overwhelmed, staff exhausted, and patients in the hallways. He daily rallies the troops to battle and charges forward with new words of encouragement, calm, and patience.

On the Western Front is Governor Gavin Newsom who wages an offensive campaign in California. He has ordered his citizens to shelter in place earlier than any governor in the country, has procured vast resources and supplies, and has issued orders to address the many points of attack that the virus can penetrate. He has enlisted eighty-five thousand California Health Corp soldiers, appealed to Silicon Valley companies, procured trailers and motel rooms for the homeless virus patients, and has a battle plan for all points of entry against COVID-19. Perhaps after the next four years these two governors will run for commander in chief of the United States.

What are your observations on the coronavirus? Has it peaked or is it still climbing and spreading in our country? How long will it last? Will children be able to return to school or is the rest of the school year lost? Will the pandemic last during the whole summer? Or will it continue until the end of 2020? Will we have a mail-in presidential election without a Democratic and Republican convention and a quiet fall election campaign throughout the country? These are questions which have yet to be answered and no one has a crystal ball large enough to see the future clearly.

How does the COVID-19 pandemic relate to the message of Amos? The prophet Amos has a concise warning about good and evil. The coronavirus is neither the result of the sins of the people nor a judgement of God. This public health outbreak is part of the natural order of the universe and the periodic illness patterns of disease which occur in the world. In the midst of this pandemic we should follow the prophetic commandment to avoid evil and do good as we relate to each other. Our normal behavior patterns are heightened by the increase of stress over illness, loss, and death. These events should bring us closer together as a family and as a nation. However, it should not diminish the injunction of Amos to practice good and shun evil.

GOOD AND EVIL

Good and evil are the oldest problem of the world. There are good people and evil people, good nations who are concerned about the welfare of others and evil nations who seek to dominate others. Movies and television dramas depict good and evil (the start: evil occurs; the middle: good investigates, a struggle ensues; and the end: good prevails over evil, resolution). A discussion involving good and evil often centers around the origin of evil: Where does evil come from? If God is God, why does he permit evil to exist in the world? Did this pandemic come from God or is it the result of the foibles of human beings?

Amos does not approach good and evil with this perspective. Rather Amos was concerned about the reality of evil when he looked at the lives of the people of Israel. Amos saw exploitation and inequity. He was upset over the absence of good as the haves interact with the have nots. He was compelled by God to speak and to denounce the evil that he saw in the lives of people who have took advantage of the poor and the oppressed.

Amos was the first of the prophets who preached between 760–750 BC. He was a shepherd and rancher of sycamore fruit trees. His job was to slice and pinch the fruit of the sycamores, which was part of the fig family (Amos 7: 14). Amos was not a trained theologian or biblical scholar. He was an ordinary man who was called by God to deliver a message to the nation of Israel. We want to examine Amos 5:14–15, which is the essence of his message: hate evil, seek good.

HATE EVIL

Amos was reacting to social injustice in Israel. The wealthy lived in expensive homes, while the peasants were in debt and were sold into slavery. The wealthy profited from the poor and foreclosed on their dwellings. There was also spiritual drought in the land. The priests and prophets were going through the motions. There was no Word from God. A decaying society was going from bad to worse. There was no sense of truth and morality. Rather there were corruption and unfaithfulness. People were ripe for judgment. (Amos 8:2). The Assyrian army was ready to invade Israel. The irresponsible prophets of this time repudiated God. Evil abounded in the land. This was the analysis of the social situation from Amos.

As we look at the moral and ethical condition of the United States, can we make a comparison to the life and times of Amos and current American life? Are we in a similar state of affairs? Is the distribution of wealth and financial resources equitable between the wealthy, the middle class, the blue collar workers, and the poor (the elderly, the disabled, and the disadvantaged)? Are the haves taking advantage and exploiting the have nots? In the coronavirus pandemic the case has been made that African Americans and Latino Americans have a higher rate of illness and death due to socioeconomic differences compared to White Americans. As a result the leaders of our cities and states have been discussing the need to shift funding to offset the healthcare, education, and social services differences.

What about the spiritual needs of people in the United States? Is America similar to the spiritual plateau that Amos described about the people of Israel when he said: ". . . for it is an evil time" (Amos 5: 13). Is there a spiritual decay in the land? Are there charismatic spiritual leaders (a Martin Luther King Jr., a Billy Graham) calling America to repentance and salvation and to social justice, fairness, civil rights, and freedom, or are the pulpits of our churches avoiding the real social issues confronting us? Are there external forces and nations who are seeking to sow discord and division in American society which keep us from uniting as a whole nation, "indivisible with liberty and justice for all"? Think about these questions. Compare the times of Amos and our current American socioeconomic and spiritual life and note the similarities and differences.

SEEK GOOD

Good is the highest goal in life. To be a good person, to do good on behalf of others, and to perform the general good of society in our community and nation are virtues that we strive for as Americans. Our family, education system, churches, and form of government consistently teach and advocate for this common good. Amos sought good from two perspectives: the vertical and the horizontal.

The vertical is our dealings with God. Amos was concerned about faithfulness and obedience to God and honoring the presence and graciousness of God. Reading the entire book of Amos uncovers the message of having this vertical understanding of who God is and what God asks of us. The king was consumed with his own self-grandeur. The priests and prophets were going through their spiritual rituals. The people of Israel were worshipping other gods rather than the LORD God. The nation was focused on itself rather than turning to the vertical and toward the God who created the heavens and the earth.

The horizontal is our dealing with each other. Amos was concerned about how we treat the other person, our neighbor. What is the good? How do we live the good out to others? How do we promote fairness and honesty? How do we execute and implement justice? According to John Rawls, an authority on distributive justice, the golden rule is: "the greatest good to the least advantaged."[1] This means that persons who are least advantaged (the elderly, the disabled, the mentally ill, the sick, and the poor) should be the primary recipients of our public resources (e.g., social programs, temporary financial assistance, public healthcare) in our society. Amos sought out these ethical and moral values for those people of Israel who were in need and exploited. Amos wanted to seek the good for them.

The coronavirus pandemic is a great opportunity for us to do good to each other. Doctors and nurses in hospitals are doing their best in the patient care of COVID-19 victims. There are so many stories of courage and

1. Rawls, *A Theory of Justice*.

sacrifice. Stricken family members have been comforted and cared for by their extended family. Recovered COVID-19 individuals have given blood plasma to those who are still in the hospitals and who are helped by the antibodies although both the patient and the donor are strangers to each other. Food donations by local farmers and grocery stores and food banks staffed by students and the National Guard have provided nutrition for those unemployed and hungry. These are examples of goodness which are emerging from this disease crisis.

These two verses in Amos summarized the essence of his mission as a prophetic voice for God. They contained a simple and modest message of advocating for good and avoiding evil. From a grammar standpoint these verses are "a contrasting simile" which is an English grammar structural form. Amos 5: 14–15 is a simile which is "a comparison of two unlike things." In this instance Amos was comparing good and evil. When Amos said: Seek good—not evil, he was urging direction (seek good) and rejection (not evil). Likewise when he said: Hate evil—love good, he was advocating rejection (hate evil) and direction (love good). It was a profound message yet powerful and succinctly stated by the prophet Amos. In short, seek good—hate evil. Remember these two verses from the prophet Amos. They will take us a long way in our dealings with people and issues of social justice.

LINCOLN AND MALICE VS. CHARITY

Abraham Lincoln, the sixteenth president of the United States, was one of America's greatest heroes. He was hailed as the savior of the Union ("the Union must be preserved") and the emancipator of slavery and slaves. Lincoln was a religious man. He believed in prayer and yet felt a profound sense of sadness over the Civil War and the death of his son, Willie. He lost his mother when he was nine years old and became alienated from his father. He was saved by his stepmother who was a strong and affectionate woman. Lincoln was a reader of the Bible and walked miles to borrow a book when he was a boy in rural Indiana. As a young man he became a day laborer, splitting wood for fire and rail fencing. Later Abe worked as a shop keeper, postmaster, and general store owner. He was a captain in the Black Hawk War of 1832. Lincoln taught himself law and became a lawyer in 1837. He was elected to Congress (1847–1849) and became president in 1860. Upon the firing on Fort Sumter, the Civil War started on April 12, 1861, and Abraham Lincoln became a wartime president.

Abraham Lincoln sought good and hated evil. The Civil War reflected the economic roots of difference between the industrial North and the agricultural South, which depended on slave labor. It became a moral conflict over the emancipation of the slaves and the abolition of slavery as an institution. On January 1, 1863, Lincoln signed the Emancipation Proclamation freeing the slaves.

In his second inaugural address as president, Abraham Lincoln said: "with malice (*evil*) toward none, with charity (*good*) for all, with firmness in the right as God gives us to see the right . . ." Amos and Lincoln saw eye to eye. They both hated evil and sought the good. They witnessed the shortcomings of their times and steered their nations toward the good in their fight to end evil. In our own modest and effective way we must have the same resolve: seek good—hate evil.

THE EVIL AND THE GOOD IN THE CORONAVIRUS

The warning of Amos in Amos 5:14–15 has implications as the United States of America battles the coronavirus. Does COVID-19 uncover the evil and affirm the good in our nation? Let me share some observations that come to mind. On the one hand, as the virus infects the people of America it is becoming apparent that this disease is having a disproportionate effect on African Americans and Latino Americans due to socioeconomic and healthcare differences. Social stratification, social class differences, racism, and unemployment play major factors in the rate of death from the coronavirus among Blacks and Latinos. In this sense these are the results of the evils of injustice and inequality facing these two ethnic groups in our nation.

On the other hand, there has been good which has come from the American healthcare workers who have worked diligently and faithfully around the clock caring for COVID-19 patients in ICU units across the hospitals and medical care centers of our country. These medical resources have been bolstered by the love and good will of the American people who have been good friends and neighbors to coronavirus patients who have been often family members and friends afflicted by this illness.

In the midst of this public health pandemic we have witnessed the evil and the good emerge as the news of the virus is reported to the American public in our newspapers and on the nightly television network news. May we as a nation resolve that we will seek good and reject evil.

PASTORAL PRAYER

O God our Heavenly Father we pray that you will prepare our country as it begins to meet the challenges posed by this coronavirus pandemic. Guide us through the dark days ahead as our leaders address the needs of the medical doctors and nurses and formulate a national and state strategy for coping with this crisis.

We are weak in this battle and yet we are strong as we pray to you. In the coming week as we face the uncertainty of the unknown, walk us through each hour and each day as we rise in the morning, prepare our meals, shelter with our families, walk and play together, and prepare for rest and sleep so that we may live another day.

Protect our loved ones who are living in other cities and guide our church which is closed. Reach beyond our building to the people who still love you and have faith and trust in you to guide them through the darkness and to see the light at the end of the tunnel.

In the name of the Father, the Son, and the Holy Spirit we pray, Amen.

CHAPTER 2

HOSEA'S WIFE AND GOD'S PROMISE
Hosea 1:1–11; 2:16–23 (April 26, 2020)

Scripture Reading. The word of the LORD that came to Hosea son of Beeri, in the days of Kings Uzziah, Jotham, Ahaz, and Hezekiah of Judah, and in the days of King Jeroboam son of Joash of Israel. When the LORD first spoke through Hosea; the LORD said to Hosea, "Go, take for yourself a wife of whoredom and have children of whoredom, for the land commits great whoredom by forsaking the LORD. So he went and took Gomer daughter of Diblaim, and she conceived and bore him a son. And the LORD said to him, "Name him Jezreel; for in a little while I will punish the house of Jehu for the blood of Jezreel, and I will put an end to the kingdom of the house of Israel. On that day I will break the bow of Israel in the valley of Jezreel.

She conceived again and bore a daughter. Then the LORD said to him, "Name her Lo-ruhamah, for I will no longer have pity on the house of Israel or forgive them. But I will have pity on the house of Judah, and I will save them by the LORD their God; I will not save them by bow, or by sword, or by war, or by horse, or by horsemen. When she had weaned Lo-ruhamah, she conceived and bore a son. Then the LORD said, "Name him Lo-ammi, for you are not my people and I am not your God.

Yet the number of the people of Israel shall be like the sand of the sea, which can be neither measured nor numbered; and in the place where it was said to them, "You are not my people," it shall be said to them, "Children of the living God." The people of Judah and the people of Israel shall be gathered together, and they shall appoint for themselves one head; and they shall take possession of the land, for great shall be the day of Jezreel.

On that day, says the LORD, you will call me, "My husband," and no longer will you call me, "My Baal." For I will remove the names of the Baals from her mouth, and they shall be mentioned by name no more. I will make for you a covenant on that day with the wild animals, the birds of the air, and the creeping things of the ground; and I will abolish the bow, the sword, and war from the land; and I will make you lie down in safety. And I will take you for my wife forever; I will take you for my wife in righteousness and in justice, in steadfast love, and in mercy. I will take you for my wife in faithfulness; and you shall know the LORD.

On that day I will answer, says the LORD, I will answer the heavens and they shall answer the earth; and the earth shall answer the grain, the wine, and the oil, and they shall answer Jezreel; and I will sow him for myself in the land. And I will have pity on Lo-ruhamah, and I will say to Lo-ammi, "You are my people"; and he shall say, "You are my God."

We are at the end of April and the coronavirus is still with us. How are we doing as a nation? As over twenty-two million Americans have filed for unemployment insurance the mental health of these workers and their families has been adversely affected by the loss of jobs. There is more depression, domestic violence, and youth suicide reported as a result. Psychiatrists, psychologists, social workers, and pastoral counselors are needed to help individuals and families cope with economic and mental illness stress. Use these resources through your healthcare plans and churches as the need arises. Be aware of family members and friends who are under stress. Channel them to these services as you see the signs of crisis.

Are our political leaders mobilizing the full resources of the federal and state governments as they seek to bring the public and private might of the American people to fight this invisible disease? Are you coping in your own situation and thriving as best as you can under the circumstances? I feel the spiritual power of the Scriptures, the Word of God, as I prepare these weekly sermons. I ask God to speak through the Bible so that I can understand the meaning of these messages from the prophets. It is a splendid opportunity for me to learn from these passages and to pass on spiritual truths to help you as we confront the coronavirus crisis daily in our lives.

HOSEA THE PROPHET

Hosea was a man of many talents: a baker, a farmer, a lover of the desert, and an expert on lions, panthers, and bears. He lived in the northern kingdom of Israel and began his prophetic ministry during the reign of Jeroboam II (786–746 BC) and was active until the fall of Samaria in 722 BC. We know little about why God chose him to be his prophet or why he possessed such a multitude of careers and interests. We know that Hosea lived in a period of political uncertainty where there were a number of weak and unstable kings who followed each other and two strong nations, Assyria to the north and Egypt in the south, which threatened and interfered in Israel's affairs. Instead of placing their trust in God, the leaders of Israel were courting the favor of Assyria and trying to bribe Egypt. Either course of action meant disaster in the end.

The religious leaders of Israel reflected the instability of the government. The worship of Jehovah was intermingled with the idolatry of the Canaanite religion and the worship of Baal which included temple prostitution. Priests were not firm in their sole worship of the LORD God but more concerned with their material prosperity and revenue from selling the sin offerings of the lambs left in the temple from worshippers

Into this immoral political and religious situation came the prophet Hosea. God needed to gain the attention of the people of Israel and he asked Hosea to perform a public demonstration before his country. It was a reenactment in Hosea's marital and family life which mirrored how the people of Israel related to God.

Hosea 1:1–11 is a Before Depiction of the relationship between God and Israel seen in the marriage of Hosea and his wife, Gomer, while Hosea 2:16–23 is an illustration of an After Depiction of how God forgives Israel for their transgressions if the people repent and return in faithfulness to God. In our sermon we will describe the before and after scenes, using the relationship between Hosea and Gomer. Once faithful to each other, Gomer became unfaithful to her husband and engaged in a series of affairs which led to three illegitimate children. This scenario is played out publicly to the people of Israel so that they can see what they have done to destroy their relationship to God.

THE UNFAITHFULNESS OF HOSEA AND GOMER

God spoke to Hosea the prophet in Hosea 1:1–11 and commanded him to perform an irrational act: marry Gomer and let her embarrass him by allowing her to be unfaithful with other men. In a normal love relationship, would you get engaged and marry a woman that you knew would break your marriage vows, have sex with others, and bring three illegitimate children into the family? How utterly insane. Yet God asked Hosea to allow this to happen and to go public with this arrangement to show the people of Israel that this was exactly the way that they were relating to God. Hosea and Gomer's marriage was a reenactment of the relationship between God and Israel. Hosea, a prophet of God, must have been totally humiliated by this spectacle. How could this happen to me? Why did God ask me to do this? Why didn't I stay home, mind my own business, and live a peaceful and happy life with a stable woman? Instead Hosea suffered misery and heartache.

Hosea was called the prophet of the sorrowful heart. His life was the story of a broken heart as he dutifully obeyed the command of God and engaged in his heartbreaking relationship with Gomer. Unhappy, dejected, and forlorn Hosea pushed ahead with the relationship in order to convey an object lesson to Israel. The names of the children offered a commentary on the nature of Gomer's actions. The first child, a son, was named Jezreel which means "God sows," pointing to the sins of the house of King Jehu who was unfaithful to God. The second child was a daughter named Lo-ruhamah (not pitied) which referred to God having no pity on the sins of Israel. Finally the third child, a son, was named Lo-ammi (not my people).

How would you feel if you were in Hosea's shoes or even if you were in the place of Gomer? In all probability you would have hesitated and decided that you could not be a party to this stressful relationship. But Hosea went through with this sorted marriage and as a result the people returned to the Lord. God was quick to forgive and restore people when they realized their self-centered ways and their allegiance to false gods. Hosea 1:10 says: ". . . and in the place where it was said to them, 'You are not my people,' It shall be said to them, 'Children of the living God.'" Hosea saw that the portrayal of unfaithfulness between Gomer and himself worked and the people of Israel were on the right track with God.

Does God call us to do foolish and unfathomable things in our lives so that there are lessons learned as a result? Sometimes God does this to demonstrate to others his message of faithfulness unto the Lord alone. I remember back in the eighth grade at Wilson Junior High School in Hamilton, Ohio, that I did a stupid and foolish thing. During lunch recess I was playing tag with another boy in the restroom, ran out the door, and smashed my right hand and arm through the glass which was part of the door. I went to the school office because my arm was bleeding profusely. Assisted by the vice principal, the health teacher, and the physical education coach I was rushed to nearby Fort Hamilton General Hospital for surgery. Two arteries and several nerves in my right arm were severely cut and I was in an arm cast for two months. Physical therapy on my arm lasted for a year. The news spread rapidly around the school and throughout the town. I remember saying the Lord's Prayer while the doctors were working on my arm in the ER and that afternoon I cried when my minister, Rev. Robert Douglass, came to visit me in the hospital. Forty-five years later when I returned to Hamilton, Ohio, for a school reunion, a guy pulled me aside, took my arm, and examined it to prove to himself that I was the boy who was involved in the accident. It was my badge of identification. Why did I commit such a stupid act in my early teenage years? As I look back, the accident brought me closer to God and settled my life. Afterwards I became more careful and thoughtful in my actions. To this day my right hand is numb and it is difficult to move my fingers sideways. This became a constant reminder to slow down, be more circumspect, and live a thoughtful life. It taught me to draw closer to God and to ask him for his wisdom and protection. You may have a similar or different story to share with me about what occurred in your life. But the story of Hosea and Gomer triggered this experience which happened to me many years ago.

THE RESTORATION BETWEEN HOSEA AND GOMER

The love story and marriage of Hosea and Gomer have a happy ending. Gomer realized that she has made mistakes, hurt her husband, Hosea, repented, and asked for forgiveness and reconciliation. Likewise, when Israel repented of her sins, cast away the god Baal, and returned to the Lord there was acceptance and restoration. Hosea 2:19 -20 declares: "And I will take you for my wife in righteousness and in justice, in steadfast love, and in mercy. I will take you for my wife in faithfulness; and you shall know the LORD." Moreover God accepted figuratively the children of Gomer as he welcomed back the people of Israel. Concerning Jezreel, Hosea 2:23 says: "and I will sow him for myself in the land." Regarding Lo-ruhamah, Hosea 2:23 states: "And I will have pity on Lo-ruhamah." Finally for Lo-ammi God granted full acceptance and identification with him: "I will say to Lo-ammi 'You are my people', and he shall say, 'You are my God'" (Hosea 2:23). Through the message of God to the children of Hosea and Gomer who have been restored in the sight of God, the Lord was issuing an invitation: full pardon and restoration to Israel as the people of God. Not only have the marriage and family of Hosea and Gomer been fully restored and made whole, but the children of Israel have achieved this status in the eyes of God. There was a dual message on the human and divine levels. This is the promise of God.

When I was the director of the Makiki Christian Counseling Center at Makiki Christian Church, Honolulu, Hawaii, I worked with a number of families conducting family therapy. There were principles of family therapy which were important guidelines:

- The negative behavior of a child is a symptom of a family with problems.
- The immediate goal is to focus and resolve the presenting problems of the child and to explore the relationship between the husband and wife (the spousal subsystem) as well as between the father, mother (the parental subsystem), and children (the sibling subsystem).
- The intermediate goal is to assess the husband and wife and to activate a positive relationship through mutual communication, social activities, and personal time with each other.
- The maximizing of positive family activities together with parents and children and the minimizing of negative words, emotions, and behavior within the family system are a guide in the intervention process of change and recovery. (I called this the mini-maxi principle of family therapy.)
- The exploration of past experiences of the father and mother with their own parents and previous events in their childhood often shed light on the present family problem situation.

If I was conducting family therapy with Hosea and Gomer and their three children, the above family principles would be my points of reference as I worked to help them with their problems.

How are your family relationships going as you grow as parents and as you raise your children? What have you found helpful along the way in successful and unsuccessful ways of relating as husband and wife, father and mother, and grandfather and grandmother with your children and grandchildren? Share your wisdom with others and your successes and failures. Tell us about your best practices as a family unit. What do you enjoy as husband and wife and as parents with children? The sermon on Hosea and Gomer opens an opportunity to explore family life together as individuals and church worshippers of Christ.

PASTORAL PRAYER

Dear God: In the quietness of this hour we pray for our family and our home life. We thank you for the lessons learned in the life of Hosea and Gomer and pray that we will always be faithful to you and to each other. Be with our governor, healthcare workers, and all those who care for others. Grant them your wisdom, protection, and strength as they continue to keep our state and nation safe.

We lift up all those who are heavy-burdened and need you. Be with our church as we worship you and look to you for help. Guide us in the days ahead. We pray all of this in the name of our Lord Jesus. Amen.

CHAPTER 3

JUSTICE, KINDNESS, AND HUMILITY
Micah 6:8 (May 3, 2020)

Scripture Reading. He has told you, O mortal, what is good; and what does the LORD require of you but to do justice; and to love kindness, and to walk humbly with your God.

After the first wave of the coronavirus the Presidential Task Force and the Centers for Disease Control are concerned about the need to gather more demographic data through testing in order to pinpoint hot spots of the disease and state by state clusters of disease patterns. Prevention and treatment programs such as follow-up contact tracing are the result of systematic large-scale testing. The COVID-19 pandemic has reached the stage where there is a need for more testing of the American population in order to determine disease trends and community patterns so that governors and state health directors can make determinations about opening the economy (businesses, employment, and jobs) safely in their states. May we be guided by the facts and research data rather than the anger and frustration of the moment. May people in need be provided food and money to meet their needs. Give us, O LORD, our daily bread.

Protect and give wisdom to our leaders as they plan ahead for the coming months of summer and fall. Public health advisers warn that during the winter of 2020–2021 both influenza and coronavirus may both appear again as disease outbreaks. If this happens, the CDC and FDA must anticipate these needs as Americans struggle with their own health and safety. Preparations for the coming fall when schools are scheduled to open and realistic requirements implementing safe school practices and procedures must be identified, discussed and agreed upon by local school and city leaders. The sermon on Micah 6:8 provides a platform to give us three guidelines about national, interpersonal, and personal spiritual perspectives as we cope with this pandemic which has affected our lives.

THE PROPHET MICAH

Micah was a farmer who lost his land due to foreclosure in the small town of Moresheth on the major highway to Jerusalem. Micah lived from 751–687 BC and saw a half of a century of peace ending with the advance of the Assyrian army into Israel. The signs of the time revealed corruption in the capital city, Jerusalem, where the wealthy were taking advantage of the middle class and poor.

Into this economic and spiritual crisis situation enters Micah with a message: What does the Lord require of you? God told him to ask this question to the king, the priests, the prophets, the wealthy, and the people of Israel. Micah was hesitant to confront these groups, but God gave him the necessary boldness and courage. Micah 6:8 summarizes the essence of his message: "He has told you, O mortal, what is good; and what does the LORD require of you but to do justice, and to love kindness, and to walk humbly with your God?" This single verse asks a question and gives three answers. We will preach on the national requirement (do justice), the interpersonal requirement (love kindness), and the personal requirement (walk humbly with your God).

THE NATIONAL REQUIREMENT: DO JUSTICE

There was national corruption in the nation of Israel. The king was allied with the wealthy both of which were taking advantage of the middle class and poor. Priests and prophets were going through their religious ritual motions. There was no message from the LORD God. As a result, the people of Israel were divided, alienated, and suffering the loss of economic, social, and spiritual security. Justice was absent from the national life of the country. To understand the injustice faced by Israel one must define the meanings of social justice, economic justice, and distributive justice.

Social justice focuses on how social institutions deal fairly or justly with the social needs of people. There are social rights and benefits to promote well-being governing nutrition, housing, employment, education, and healthcare. Social justice corrects abuses and establishes an equal playing field.

Economic justice are moral principles which create economic institutions so that a person can earn a living, exchange goods and services, and produce economic independence. Education, employment, and temporary welfare assistance are areas of economic justice concerns.

Distributive justice involves distributing monetary and program resources where the greatest resources should be given to the least advantaged (the elderly, poor, and disabled).

As a nation we must ask ourselves if we practice:

- Social justice (fairness to the social needs of people which promote the well-being of all people)
- Economic justice (helping people with education, employment, and financial independence)
- Distributive justice (distributing resources to those who need them the most)

These concepts applied to social injustice in Micah's time and in the year 2020. How can we maintain justice in the midst of the coronavirus?

We practice social justice by making sure that every sick person who is seriously stricken by the virus receives the best possible medical care in the hospitals and medical centers across the United States guaranteed by the federal government. We make sure that all necessary medical supplies and equipment are produced and distributed across the board by the federal government which ensures equity to all regions of our country. We ensure social justice in this pandemic.

Economic justice addresses employment needs and financial income and requires legislation to guarantee that all Americans have sufficient funds to help them when normal job patterns fail them due to this pandemic. Economic justice also addresses the retraining of unemployed citizens who may require career crossovers to jobs which require short-term education and the retooling of skills. It is important for us to investigate the Public Works Administration of the Roosevelt era where the unemployed were paid by the federal government to build roads, highway, municipal buildings, airport terminals, and other facilities. Millions of Americans were mobilized and given work to hold them over until the economy improved and people were able to assume normal employment.

Finally distributive justice holds that the greatest advantage should be given to the least advantaged as far as resource distribution of goods and services are concerned. Traditionally the elderly, poor, and disabled have been the benefactors of distributive justice, but in this time of a worldwide pandemic and high unemployment the middle class unemployed fall into the distributive justice category.

THE INTERPERSONAL REQUIREMENT: LOVE KINDNESS

Micah does not say "be kind." Rather he insists: "love kindness." Kindness is being helpful, sympathetic, respectful, thoughtful, supportive, and encouraging. Micah says "be kind" to the extent that we love kindness so passionately that we will demonstrate it in every situation which comes our way. In other words, love to do kindness to the fullest extent possible. How do we treat other people? Micah suggests that we lead by example from the top down. That is, from the president of the United States to the least person in society, we are kind to each other and love to do it. We must improve our interpersonal skills with each other: relating and getting along with people (our spouse, children, neighbors, and fellow workers). During the last four years American society seems to have lost its sense of decency and kindness for each other. As American neighbors we are our brother's and sister's keepers who must be vigilant and watchful over persons in our neighborhood and community.

We offer lovingkindness by visiting our seniors who are shut-ins and need help with groceries and cooking meals. We phone and email persons who are alone in their homes and who need a daily call of support and reassurance. We mobilize volunteers from churches to join an effort to help people in practical ways. We support families who have a loved one who is in the hospital due to COVID-19 illness. We perform unimaginable feats of kindness with our thoughts and actions.

THE PERSONAL REQUIREMENT: WALK HUMBLY WITH YOUR GOD

It is so important to have a personal walk with God. The Christian hymn, "In the Garden," says: "He walks with me and He talks with me and He tells me 'I am His Own'; And the Joy we share as we tarry there, None Other has ever Known." Friedrich Schleiermacher,[1] the great German liberal theologian of the nineteenth century, said that Christian faith is "total dependence on God." It is the recognition that you are dependent on God as a single person in a vast universe. Walk humbly with your God in a sense of humility

---

1. Schleiermacher, *Christian Faith*, vol. 1.

rather than arrogance, rudeness, and narcissism. Have this personal walk with God in the quietness of your home and yard and as you walk your neighborhood, greet your neighbors or a stranger who passes you on your street.

Walk humbly with your God, your spouse, your family, your community, and your nation. Be thankful for your health and safety. Be aware that God protects us and wants us to use our common sense: shelter at home, wear a mask, practice social distancing, and wash your hands. Obey humbly signs in our stores to cover our faces when entering a public place. Humility does not raise a commotion. Rather it recognizes that we must all cooperate and seek healthy behavior for the greater good.

Lift up a prayer to God for yourself and others in this time of crisis and uncertainty. Humbly ask God for the concern and comfort that you provide to others who are ill from this virus or who are afraid for the safety and health of loved ones. Be strong and wise as we practice the patience and forbearance that God gives us in this time of crisis. Be anxious for nothing but in due supplication, make your requests known unto God who is the source of life.

A MODERN-DAY MICAH

Barry Obama, the forty-fourth president of the United States, is a graduate of Punahou School, Honolulu, and a native son of Hawaii. As a high school student Barry was a likeable and popular guy who played basketball for Punahou. One of his teachers remarked that when Barry (he wanted to be called Barry rather than Barack) was in school he did not live up to his full potential. Rather he was regarded by his classmates as a friendly guy who was bright and wanted to be accepted by others. There was always a smile and an encouraging word that he communicated as he related to his fellow students and teachers.

He was raised in a single-parent family, rarely saw his father, and later when his mother moved to Indonesia where she married her second husband, Barry was brought up by his maternal grandparents who lived within walking distance of his high school. His grandmother worked in a bank. He left Hawaii, went to Occidental College in Los Angeles, and then to Columbia University where he completed his undergraduate education. Later he enrolled at Harvard Law School.

He was a community organizer in Chicago, taught Constitutional Law at the University of Chicago Law School as a part-time instructor, and met his wife, Michelle, who helped him ease into a law firm practice. He became a state senator for the Illinois legislature and ran for the US Senate. All of us know what happened when he became the first African American president of the United States. President Obama returns to Hawaii every Christmas vacation where his stepsister teaches at The Hawaii School for Girls. He is a member of the United Church of Christ, a denomination which traces its history to the Pilgrims of Massachusetts, of which I am an ordained minister.

Of all the recent presidents Barack Obama from my perspective embodies the message of Micah. We have seen him seek justice, love kindness, and walk humbly with God. We hope that the next president of the United States will portray the message of Micah as a servant of this country. May the peace and love of God be with you now and forever more. May God the Father, God the Son, and God the Holy Spirit protect you in the coming days ahead.

PASTORAL PRAYER

Our God and our Father, we have seen you work in the lives of people even before this coronavirus has afflicted us. We thank you for your loving care for all those who have been afflicted, for all who have lost loved ones, and for patients who have recovered from this sickness. We continue to pray for the doctors and nurses who work with their patients, for the medical researchers who are exploring medical science to find a vaccine, for the governors and mayors who are the front lines, for our president and his taskforce, and for all those who perform countless and simple acts of kindness. Be with us all in this time of crisis.

See us through this battle to victory. Guide our church and bring us together so that we will emerge with a stronger faith as you supply our daily needs. Stop our complaining and criticism of each other and increase our praise and support of those who serve you in our midst. May we speak the encouraging word and be wise in our acceptance of each other as a church. Guide the consistory as it plans ahead. Be mindful of our needs. Supply the people that we need to lead our church. Increase our faith and strength in you. May we shoulder the burdens of those in our midst.

In the coming weeks ahead we pray that we will see your healing power on our lives and in the lives of our fellow citizens, and even all those around the world. For those in our church and community who are ill and laid up may your comfort and power be in our hearts and lives. May all of us find our resting place in your presence. In the name of our Lord Jesus, we pray. Amen.

CHAPTER 4

A SINFUL NATION AND CHANGING SCARLET INTO SNOW

Isaiah 1:1–9, 16–18 (May 10, 2020)

Scripture Reading. The vision of Isaiah son of Amoz, which he saw concerning Judah and Jerusalem in the days of Uzziah, Jotham, Ahaz, and Hezekiah, kings of Judah. Hear, O heavens and listen, O earth; for the LORD has spoken: I reared children and brought them up, but they have rebelled against me. The ox knows it owner, and the donkey its master's crib; but Israel does not know, my people do not understand.

Ah, sinful nation, people laden with iniquity, offspring who do evil, children who deal corruptly, who have forsaken the LORD, who have despised the Holy One of Israel, who are utterly estranged! Why do you seek further beatings? Why do you continue to rebel? The whole head is sick and the whole heart is faint. From the sole of the foot even to the head. There is no soundness in it, but bruises and sores and bleeding wounds; they have not been drained, or bound up, or softened with oil.

Your country lies desolate, your cities are burned with fire; in your very presence aliens devour your land; it is desolate, as overthrown by foreigners. And daughter Zion is left like a booth in a vineyard, like a shelter in a cucumber field, like a besieged city. If the LORD of hosts had not left us a few survivors, we would have been like Sodom, and become like Gomorrah.

Wash yourselves, make yourselves clean; remove the evil of your doings from before my eyes; cease to do evil, learn to do good; seek justice, rescue the oppressed, defend the orphan, plead for the widow.

Come now, let us argue it out, says the LORD; though your sins are like scarlet, they shall be like snow; though they are red like crimson, they shall become like wool. If you are willing and obedient, you shall eat the good of the land.

Happy Mother's Day to all mothers. We love you and without you, all of us would not be here. You gave us life, nurtured us as babies, guarded and guided us as young children, fostered our learning during our school years, shared your wisdom during our growing-up years, listened to us and problem-solved with us, were with us in our high and low moments, congratulated us in our achievements, consoled us in our failures, brought us to church, helped us when we left home, and stayed with us in our work, marriage, and parenthood. Thanks, mom, for the countless acts of love that you performed every day for the rest of our lives.

Unfortunately this Mother's Day is different. With shelter-in-place orders and social distancing we are probably unable to get together for Mother's Day lunch or dinner. We leave our Mother's Day presents by the front door, call mom to wish her a happy Mother's Day, or send a card to her if we live in another city. But for those who are still children and live with our mothers and fathers we celebrate this important day with her and enjoy sharing our acts of love and gifts with our mom.

In our family we have a grandchild, Alyssa, who was born on Mother's Day which has been a real treat for our family. She has brightened the lives of her mother and grandmother and all of us who have seen her growing into a wonderful and precious young lady who is now eleven years old. Every Mother's Day we are mindful of her and thank the Lord for her.

In our sermon Isaiah mentions the need to wash and change your spiritual clothes. This is a task of mothers in the family: making sure that the children take baths, change their clothes when they are dirty, and wash and dry clothes weekly. Isaiah takes this family chore and adds spiritual meaning to this task. There is a connection between Mother's Day and the message of Isaiah.

LOOKING AHEAD

On this unusual Mother's Day, many states are opening up small businesses and business owners are practicing social distancing and wearing face mask. In California Governor Newsom is taking a cautious stance based on medical trend data and trying to balance this with the economic needs of businesses and the economic plight of unemployed Californians. By and large the economy is still shut down while the virus is plateauing or on the decline in certain parts of the country. As we approach the summer we are cautiously considering how to enjoy the warm weather. Shall we go hiking, swimming, or visiting a nearby resort? Or shall we stay home and venture out to places in the community?

What about the school children who are missing part of their education? Will schools open at the end of July or the beginning of August with safeguards in place to protect children and teachers from the virus? Will they catch up and reach grade level this fall or will school be forced to combine staggered class size and on online distance learning? What will happen to parents who remain unemployed? Will Congress appropriate funds to states in order to make up for the short fall in state income revenue? Will churches remain closed and lose members due to attrition? There are so many questions affecting families, communities, states, and the nation as a whole.

Franklin Delano Roosevelt faced similar questions when he became president in 1932 as the nation was in the midst of the Great Depression. Historians will look back on history and compare the dilemmas of the Great Depression and the Great Pandemic. Roosevelt faced an economic restoration task which took years of social programs and American ingenuity. The next president confronts a medical disease which might be controlled when there is a vaccine available for worldwide inoculation. The recovery of the American economy hinges on the discoveries in the medical laboratory manned by medical scientists, public health researchers, and doctors with expertise on pandemic diagnosis and treatment. There are promising drugs and potential vaccines which are in the pipeline and need medical clearance approval by the CDC and FDA. But full economic and healthcare recovery may take at least two years as long as COVID-19 hangs around the country. God save and protect us.

THE BOOK OF ISAIAH AND THE PROPHET ISAIAH

The book of Isaiah written by the prophet Isaiah stands alone in the Old Testament as the hallmark of all the writings of the people of Israel. Next to Genesis the book of Isaiah contains sixty-six chapters filled with the "Thus saith the Lord" pronouncements against the sins of Israel, the message of judgement and repentance, and the agony and pain of the Suffering Servant. Written in the priceless words and eloquence of the prophet Isaiah stands a man whose name means "Jehovah saves" or "Jehovah is my salvation." We do not know much of Isaiah's background, but some Old Testament scholars believe that he may have been a priest. If so, Isaiah studied the Torah (the Law) and knew the Old Testament Scriptures which are reflected in the depth and quality of his writings. Truly Isaiah lived out his name and his genius for speaking and writing as he brought his people face to face with their sinful ways in his messages from God.

Isaiah's ministry spans the reign of five kings of Judah, the southern kingdom, starting in 742 BC. The book of Isaiah has been critically analyzed by Old Testament scholars around its authorship, arguing that there were two or three separate authors who wrote the book rather than a single author, the prophet Isaiah himself. The unity of the book of Isaiah vs. Deutero- or Tri-Isaiahs.

No matter the critical scholarship on the book of Isaiah, the words of the prophet Isaiah will be a blessing to you as we spend eleven sermons on this fascinating book. You will be amazed at the heights and depths, the grandeur and excellence, and the spiritual insights of this prophet as he wrestles with the sins of Israel and points his people to the everlasting God of creation and the universe.

Isaiah 1:1–9, 16–18 is the opening salvo describing the body, Israel, which is clothed with iniquity. We want to focus on three points: the dirt, the washing, and the change.

THE DIRT

My four-year-old granddaughter, Ally, has a new word in her vocabulary: DIRTY. When she pronounces the word, dirty, she holds on to the syllables so that it sounds like DIR TEE. She learned the word, dirty, when her aunt Lisa noticed that her own six-year-old son, Trevor, dropped some fruit loops on the floor and quickly picked them up with his hands. Aunt Lisa said: "Trevor, the fruit loops are dirty!" Ally who was there in the room immediately said: "Trevor, DIR TEE." This was the beginning of hearing the word, dirty, from Ally which was video-recorded on the cell phone and sent to all the relatives in Sacramento, Pleasant Hill, and Los Angeles.

In Isaiah 1:1–9 the prophet is saying to the people of Israel that they are dirty with sin. He starts by saying that "the LORD has spoken" who declares that the animals are smarter than the people of Israel: "The ox knows his owner, and the donkey its master's crib; but Israel does not know, my people do not understand" (Isaiah 1:3). This is a kind insult from God regarding the stupidity of Israel and their sinful ways. His description of Israel is graphic in Isaiah 1:4–6: "a sinful nation, people laden with iniquity, offspring who do evil, children who deal corruptly, forsaken the LORD, despised the Holy

One of Israel, utterly estranged." Moreover, these accusations are followed by a spiritual diagnosis of the body (Israel): "The whole head is sick, and the whole heart faint. From the sole of the foot even to the head, there is no soundness in it, but bruises and sores and bleeding wounds" (Isaiah 1:5 and 6). God lays into Israel through the prophet Isaiah who does not hold back but preaches the full force of the Word of the LORD. From the image of the body Isaiah moves his audience to the nation of Israel. His portrait is equally severe in its criticism: "Your country lies desolate, your cities are burned with fire, aliens devour your land, a besieged city, a few survivors" (Isaiah 1:7–9). This is a message of doom and destruction. There is gloom on the horizon.

There will be those who will declare that the coronavirus is the judgement of God upon the sins of the world and the evils of mankind. If you hear this message, do not believe the message or the messenger. We are faced with a worldwide pandemic like the Black Plague of the Middle Ages. Without a vaccine the medical authorities can only issue a public health strategy of containment and isolation and wait out the virus until it peaks and declines on its own time. In this situation we turn to God. We do not need the message of Isaiah to recognize that we need the help and guidance of God in the midst of the coronavirus. Proverbs 3:5 and 6 remind us: "Trust in the LORD with all your heart, and do not rely on your own insight. In all your ways acknowledge him, and he will make straight your paths." The message is to trust in God as the coronavirus is in our midst, rely on him, and he will direct the way that we should go.

THE WASHING

Returning to the message of Isaiah that the people of Israel were indeed dirty from their own sins, Isaiah 1:16 urges: "Wash yourselves, make yourselves clean; remove the evil of your doings from before my eyes; cease to do evil." The analogy formulated by the prophet Isaiah is that the people of Isaiah have been dirty from sin and require a spiritual bath. Wash off the evil from your body. Cleanse yourself from sin. Get into the shower and carefully and meticulously wash yourself thoroughly.

When I was in seminary my roommate took a Saturday-night bath once a week. I would bathe every day until I was older and realized that too much bathing dried out my skin. I cleanse myself each day and shower three times a week. I know that I need a shower when my skin and hair begin to itch after three or four days. How good it feels when I step out of the shower, dry myself, and put on clean clothes. It is so refreshing and relaxing to feel clean from head to foot. The words of the hymn, "Have you been to Jesus for the cleansing power, Are you washed in the blood of the Lamb," remind us that we need to be cleansed from our sins through the saving power of the blood of Christ shed for us on the cross.

Isaiah says that after you wash and make yourself clean, you need to put on some new clothes: "learn to do good; seek justice, rescue the oppressed, defend the orphan, plead for the widow" (Isaiah 1:17). Put on the garments of goodness, justice, and concern for the oppressed, the helpless, and the vulnerable. These new clothes will definitely change your appearance and your behavior. You will walk down the street and be a different and more compassionate and spiritually sensitive person. Have you taken a spiritual bath recently? Have you been washed and cleansed by the blood of the Lamb, Jesus Christ? Have you dressed up in spiritual and moral clothes? Think about this and make some changes in your life.

THE CHANGE

Finally Isaiah 1:18 brings us together as an audience: "Come now, let us reason together, says the LORD; though your sins are like scarlet, they shall be like snow; though they are red like crimson, they shall be like wool." The verse is an alliteration (the repetition of a phrase with two or more ways of expressing the same thought). How can scarlet be turned into snow? Or how can crimson be changed into wool? How can red be turned into white? Colors remain the same or can be changed into other colors when they are combined together. But red cannot be transformed into white. Isaiah is speaking figuratively and spiritually when he is talking about this color transformation. He is saying to the people of Israel: If you turn away from your sinful ways, God transforms your life and performs an impossible spiritual color change: from red to white (from sin to sanctification which is being set aside wholly for God).

I am amazed at the message of Isaiah. He was blunt and bold with the people of Israel. He insulted them and got their attention. He warned them about the judgement of God and their sinful lifestyle. He used the analogy of being dirty, washing away your sins, changing yourself and putting on the clothes of righteousness from the LORD. If Isaiah were alive today and employed as a minister in a large church, he probably would have been terminated by the church board. His message was hard to handle and filled with criticism about the behavior and lives of the people. Yet Isaiah spoke the Word of the LORD and was heeded by the people of Israel who turned from their selfish ways and returned to God in repentance and forgiveness.

This was the only wish from God: to love the LORD God with all your heart, soul and mind and your neighbor as yourself.

In this time of worldwide crisis, be a change agent. Reach out to each other. Call your relatives, friends, and neighbors. You can be helpful and supportive over the phone and through emails. You can bridge the gap of isolation, loneliness, and boredom. You can uplift another person with meaningful conversation (a story, a joke, a suggestion) which can go a long way to calm and make another person feel that their day was enriched by you. This is a creative time to show and communicate Christian love even though we are physically separated from each other. Make a contact and connection today. Brighten another person in the name of Christ. Uplift each other with loving thoughtfulness and kindness.

NEEDED CHANGES

We need a change in our nation much like Isaiah preached in Isaiah 1:1–18. We have been rolling around in the dirt of division and political discord for nearly four years. Americans have been pitted against Americans. We need to wash ourselves morally and spiritually and change our dirty clothes. As Isaiah said, we need to put on the garments of goodness, justice, and care for the most vulnerable in our society. When we undergo this cleansing, we will be transformed by the power of God. Yes, our sins which are crimson shall be turned as white as snow. We will feel a purity that will be refreshing and wholesome.

Will this change happen after we vote in the 2020 presidential election? Will a change in presidential leadership help in the healing of the great divide that we now face? Will we experience unification and a coming together with more compassion and understanding and with more wisdom and insight to know how to solve the multitude of problems facing the American people? Change and healing take time. Old feelings and disagreements have a way of working themselves out. Turning the page with new and fresh leadership often aids in this process of slowly coming to compromise and resolve our differences. I believe in the whole Pledge of Allegiance and particularly where we declare ". . . One Nation, Under God, Indivisible, With Liberty and Justice for All." God bless the United States of America. Amen.

PASTORAL PRAYER

Dear God: We thank you for all the mothers of the world and for our own mother who gave us life and love. We are grateful for the message from Isaiah. Help us to wash away our sins and put on the clothes of righteousness which you freely gave us through the death and resurrection of your Son, Jesus Christ our Lord. Keep us in your loving care. Help us to reach out to a person in need who is lonely, depressed, alienated, afraid, hungry, and in need. Give us a sense to know what to do to help this person. May the Word of God become our words of comfort and reassurance to that person who is in need of you. May we bind that person with your love and our love during this time of uncertainty and fear. May that person understand that love casts out fear as the Bible proclaims.

We remember our church and the needs of our congregation. For those who thrive and are vibrant we give you thanks. For those who are sick we ask your healing on them. For those who are young and still finding their way in school and growing mature we ask for your guidance and wisdom. For those who are parents and grandparents, help us to make a contribution to our children and grandchildren that you gave us to love and to raise. For the elderly who need your strength to face each day, may they rest in the shadow of your peace and care. For those who lead our church: the consistory, the Bible study leaders, the church school staff, the administrative assistant, the maintenance crew, the cooks in our kitchen, and all those who support and contribute to the ministry of our church, we ask your blessing and your endurance as they seek to serve you in so many ways. Above all be with our mothers this day. Guard and guide them. Grant them your strength and health as they serve and care for their families.

In the name of the Father, the Son, and the Holy Spirit we pray, Amen.

CHAPTER 5

HOLINESS AND HOLLOWNESS
Isaiah 6:1–13 (May 17, 2020)

Scripture Reading. In the year that King Uzziah died, I saw the Lord sitting on a throne, high and lofty; and the hem of his robe filled the temple. Seraphs were in attendance above him; each had six wings; with two they covered their faces, and with two they covered their feet, and with two they flew. And one called to another and said: "Holy, holy, holy is the LORD of hosts; the whole earth is full of his glory." The pivots on the threshold shook at the voices of those who called, and the house filled with smoke. And I said: "Woe is me! I am lost, for I am a man of unclean lips, and I live among a people of unclean lips; yet my eyes have seen the King, the LORD of hosts!"

Then one of the seraphs flew to me, holding a live coal that had been taken from the altar with a pair of tongs. The seraph touched my mouth with it and said: "How that this has touched your lips, your guilt has departed and your sin is blotted out." Then I heard the voice of the Lord saying, whom shall I send, and who will go for us?" And I said, "Here I am; send me!" and he said, "Go and say to this people: 'Keep listening, but do not comprehend; keep looking, but do not understand.' Make the mind of this people dull, and stop their ears, and shut their eyes, so that they may not look with their eyes, and listen with their ears, and comprehend with their minds, and turn and be healed."

Then I said, "How long, O Lord?" And he said: "Until the cities lie waste without inhabitant, and houses without people, and the land is utterly desolate; until the LORD sends everyone far away, and vast is the emptiness in the midst of the land. Even if a tenth part remain in it, it will be burned again, like a terebinth or an oak whose stump remains standing when it is felled." The holy seed is its stump.

As each state begins to open various business segments, there is a note of careful caution which must be followed: protecting the health of employees and the public as they venture out and mingle together. Social distancing, face masks, and limited numbers admitted to a business must be practiced by all. Accurate statistical data on disease onset after opening should be gathered along with contact tracing analysis. Regional states and their governors and public health directors should work together, coordinate strategies, and share information in order to minimize the risks and maximize the opportunities.

Large public gatherings such as church services, sporting events, and concert entertainment are likely not to happen in the near future. Churches must devise new ways to minister to the needs of their congregations, and denominations are offering their ministers and churches helpful information on how to work with church members during the COVID-19 crisis. Zoom conferencing for worship services, church meetings, and study groups are current ways to reach people. Emailing worship sermons and pastoral prayers help the congregation to read and meditate on Scripture and sermon messages.

All of us are getting familiar with an alternative solitude. This is an opportunity to reflect, think, plan, and imagine new ways of listening to ourselves and others. After our rushed and hurried life style, take this crisis as a gift of visualizing the holiness of God (Isa 6:1–13).

ISAIAH'S VISION

No one has seen God at any time, but in the Old Testament Jacob wrestled with God, Moses communed with God on Mount Sinai when he received the Ten Commandments, and Isaiah had a vision of God. Isaiah's experience is comparable to the visions of John in the book of Revelation. However, this passage recorded the calling of Isaiah by God to his prophetic ministry with the people of Israel. This event happened in the year of the death of King Uzziah who was a reform monarch and brought himself and his people back to faithfulness to God. King Uzziah removed the idolatry that was rampant in the land, brought justice and equality back to the people, and set an example in his personal worship of the LORD. Upon his death God called Isaiah to ensure that the reforms of Uzziah and the messages from God would continue and flourish throughout the nation of Israel.

As we read this famous passage, Isaiah 6:1–13, these familiar words have been used throughout the centuries to describe the holiness of God, the sinfulness of human beings, and the calling of many ministers and rabbis in ordination services throughout the Judeo-Christian tradition. We approach this Scripture with reverence and awe because of its wide usage and profound thoughts. We want to focus on three major points from Isaiah 6:1–13: the holiness of the experience, the herald of the calling, and the hollowness of the situation. In this time of battling the coronavirus as an individual, family, community, and nation, the words of Isaiah 6:1–13 are a comforting message to us.

THE HOLINESS OF THE EXPERIENCE

In September 2019 it was my privilege to visit Rome, Italy, and go to the Vatican to see St. Peter's Church and Square and the Sistine Chapel which houses the famous murals of Michelangelo. I thought that it would invoke a sense of holiness in me, but the grandeur and beauty of these religious sites failed to move me. I found myself reacting as a tourist who was visiting man-made religious monuments.

Isaiah's vision of God's holiness was a wholly other experience. Isaiah said that he saw the Lord and the angels, heard the seraphs (six winged angels standing in the presence of God) chanting their praise of holiness to God, and was burnt on his lips as a symbolic act that his guilt and sin were removed in the sight of God (Isa 6: 1–7). "Holy, holy, holy is the LORD of hosts; the whole earth is full of his glory" (Isa 6: 3). "Woe is me! I am lost, for I am a man of unclean lips, and I live among a people of unclean lips; yet my eyes have seen the King, the LORD of hosts!" (Isa 6: 5). His description of seeing the holiness of God and his own sinfulness matches no other human experience in the Old Testament. It is simply priceless and awe inspiring.

Can we experience such a vision of the holiness of God, perhaps a preview of our heavenly experience with God after we leave this earthly existence? One could call this "a mountaintop experience" where we scale the highest summit in the world, see the heavens and the earth from a new perspective, and feel the presence of God from the heights of the world. Will we ever realize our sinfulness in contrast to the holiness of God as Isaiah confesses that he is "a man of unclean lips who lives among a people of unclean lips"? Yet the angel burned his lips to purify them. I must confess that I have never had such an experience of holiness like Isaiah. The words of the hymn, "Holy, Holy, Holy," are comforting to me and raise my vision of God:

"Holy, Holy, Holy. LORD God Almighty. Early in the morning our songs will rise to Thee. Holy, Holy, Holy, Merciful and Mighty, God in Three Persons, Blessed Trinity." Let us dwell on the holiness (the wholly otherness) of God and our own contrast as sinners saved by the grace of God in Christ. Remember the vision of Isaiah regarding the holiness of God. May we have a similar vision and realize our own shortcomings and God's wonderful salvation for us in Christ.

THE HERALD OF THE CALLING

In ancient times the herald would run from city to city to bring news to the people. After a battle the herald would be dispatched by the general to announce to the people that there was a great victory won. God was preparing Isaiah to be the herald who was sent by him. Isaiah 6:8: "Then I heard the voice of the Lord saying, 'Whom shall I send, and who will go for us?' And I said, 'Here am I, send me!'" It is interesting to note that God does not command Isaiah. Rather he asks the question and leaves the door open for Isaiah's answer. "Whom shall I send?" might have been answered by Isaiah who could have mentioned a number of qualified persons. Perhaps God wanted Isaiah to volunteer his services rather than force his will on him. Nevertheless Isaiah readily said: "Here am I, send me!" in modesty and willingness to serve the LORD God Almighty.

I remember that it was cool to hire a person with music talent to come to a home, sing the Happy Birthday song, and present the person with a special birthday gift from a loved one. It was a novel idea to enhance the birthday celebration of the person. The person hired was a herald of good news. Likewise in time of war a spouse or a family received a formal visit from members of the armed forces accompanied by a military chaplain regarding the death of a loved one who was killed in action. These heralders were bearers of bad news. We like to receive good news: a great report card from our child, a letter of acceptance from our first-choice university, a telephone call from a company informing us that we have been hired for a new job, news of the birth of a baby, and a medical report that our vitals are in the normal healthy range. Let us be heralds of our calling in Christ. Philippians 3:13 and 14 encourage us: "Beloved, I do not consider that I have made it my own; but this one thing I do: forgetting what lies behind and straining forward to what lies ahead, I press on toward the goal for the prize of the heavenly call of God in Christ Jesus." Keep this in mind in the days ahead.

God calls us to serve Christ and his kingdom because of the great need that confronts the church at the present moment. He asks us: whom shall

I send or who can I send? God is looking for us to serve as heralds of good news. Serve the LORD with gladness in your family, church, and community. Think of innovative ways to do this in the midst of the coronavirus.

THE HOLLOWNESS OF THE SITUATION

God gives a message to Isaiah and asks him to transmit it to the people of Israel. This is a difficult task for Isaiah because the people were not listening to God. Their minds (their ears to hear and their hearts to open) were closed to God's prophetic message through Isaiah. Their lack of comprehension points to the hollowness of their mind, sight, and perception. God said: "Keep listening, but do not comprehend; keep looking, but do not understand. Make the mind of this people dull, and stop their ears, and shut their eyes, so that they may not look with their eyes, and listen with their ears, and comprehend with their minds, and turn and be healed" (Isa 6:9–10). A person does not want to listen, understand, and see the coming judgement of God. On the horizon was the defeat of Israel, the destruction of Jerusalem and the Temple, and the Babylonian Captivity which encompassed years of exile in a foreign land and a painful return to the ruins of Jerusalem and the rest of Judah and Israel. Isaiah 6:12 predicted: "until the LORD sends everyone away, and vast is the emptiness in the midst of the land." Figuratively speaking all that was left was the stump of an oak tree, a symbol of the remnant of the few returnees from exile (Isa 6:13). The people of Israel did not want to face the hard reality of the coming judgement of God and their hardness of heart.

This is the bad news for the people of Israel. Sometimes there is bad news mixed with good news. I recently saw a video from Daniel Dae Kim who began his acting career on *Hawaii Five-O*. He moved from this program to produce the television series, *The Good Doctor*, which is one of my favorite programs. In his video Daniel shares the news that after filming a guest spot on *New Amsterdam*, another favorite program of mine about a New York City hospital, he was on a plane back to Honolulu when he experienced some symptoms as he landed from his flight. He immediately consulted with his doctor in Honolulu and a few days later he was tested for the coronavirus. The test came back positive and he went into self-quarantine in his home. Members of his home were also tested and the results were negative. Daniel got medication from his doctor, got plenty of bed rest, and felt much better. He wanted to send this video to his friends and fans to stress the importance of this pandemic and to offer words of warning and encouragement. He was very concerned that Asian Americans, particularly Chinese Americans, were not blamed for the coronavirus.

Daniel's story grabbed our attention and heightened our senses of watching out for the invisible coronavirus. Unlike the hollowness of the situation confronting Israel, we are responsive to the medical crisis facing us. This pandemic struck home when actors like Daniel Dae Kim, Tom Hanks, and Rita Wilson were victims of the virus and were recovering from it. When COVID-19 strikes us our hardness and hollowness fall away and we are at the mercy and grace of God and those who treat and heal us. Let us be wise, careful, and prudent in the days ahead. Our hollowness turns into wholeness as we heed the Word of the Lord. Let us listen to him and obey his voice.

THE CALL AND THE RESPONSE

The calling of Isaiah as a prophet of God despite the hollowness of the people's hollowness reminds us that we face a major problem in the Christian church today. We need prophetic voices in the church of Jesus Christ today. Unfortunately less men and women are answering the call to full-time ministry than in previous generations. Theological education is in retrenchment. Several theological seminaries have closed their doors and most theological graduate programs have reduced their program centers and are offering online distance learning for the Master of Divinity degree. Many small churches cannot afford a full-time pastor. Church salaries for ministers are generally lower than public school teachers. Church employment is hard to find since there are fewer churches with openings. Retired ministers are unable to live on their small pensions. Christian college students can make higher salaries with degrees in computer science, economics, and engineering and with graduate degrees in medicine, law, and business. We need to turn this tide toward making the Christian ministry an attractive alternative career path for the brightest and the best of our Christian college students today.

How do you attract qualified candidates for the ministry in today's world? What is the payoff? Are there job advancements, opportunities for church administration and theological education positions, and job security? Or is there quick burnout, disillusionment, and career change? The Christian church needs to address these concerns today in light of the decline of the American churches and ministers. We have ducked these issues for a long time. The last major study of theological education was conducted over fifty years ago by Niebuhr, Williams, and Gustafson.[1] No attempt has been made to formulate a plan of action. There should be a national effort to address these problems with a blueprint for action which theological educators and denominational leaders put into action. A call for a national planning and strategy conference of all Christian leaders in the major denominations together with key seminary presidents and prominent Christian laity with business, political, and financial resources should address and deal with the crisis of ministry person power facing us in the third decade of the twenty-first century. The Christian church needs prophets like Isaiah. We have lost our Martin Luther King Jr.s, our Billy Grahams, and our Karl Barths and must nurture a new generation of ministers to become the socially conscious prophets, the fervent evangelists, and the theological thinkers and writers of this century who are new and fresh spiritual voices.

These concerns are the responsibility of the local church, denominations, theological seminaries, and administrative leaders (bishops, presidents) working together to construct a recruitment strategy for new ministry in the twenty-first century. We need to light the torch again, pass on the fire of the Word of God, and ignite the power of new prophets to preach and proclaim Christ.

PASTORAL PRAYER

Dear God, we thank you for the vision of your holiness that you gave to Isaiah many centuries ago and we pray that you will grant us a vision of your holiness as we face a grave crisis. We thank you that Isaiah said "Here am I, send me" when he heard your call. We pray for those who are being called by you into ministry that you will grant them the courage to respond. We pray for our churches that you will strengthen them and help them to provide openings for ministers who want to serve you. May you provide for the many needs of our ministers and may churches be sensitive and generous to meet these areas. May our churches take good care of their pastors who endure to serve you and feed their flock. May we play a significant role to be sensitive to the needs of our ministers, provide for their material and spiritual needs, and care for their spouses and families. May you strengthen our denominations, grow our theological seminaries, challenge our theologians who write and teach our future ministers, and increase our evangelists and social justice advocates who are on the frontlines of service.

Be with those who are in charge of our nation and our states that you will grant them wisdom to govern and to direct the lives of people in health

---

1. Niebuhr et al., *The Advancement of Theological Education*.

and safety. Help those who are restless and afraid and who face unemployment, hunger, and lack of funds to find peace and comfort in your presence. Provide for their needs as they face nothingness. Continue to be with our healthcare workers and researchers as they treat patients and work toward a cure for this virus. Help us to explore new ways of living. Continue to be with our church. Preserve us in this time of crisis and isolation. Draw us closer together. Be with our sick and elderly. Help our church leaders as they move forward. Grow us into maturity. Strengthen our numbers. See us through this pandemic. Increase our faith in this process of survival. Let us see the Light of the World, Jesus Christ, at the end of the tunnel.

We ask all of these prayers in the name of your Son, Jesus Christ our Lord, Amen.

CHAPTER 6

FROM DARKNESS TO LIGHT
Isaiah 9:2–7 (May 24, 2020)

Scripture Reading. The people who walk in darkness have seen a great light; those who lived in a land of deep darkness—on them light has shined. You have multiplied the nation, you have increased its joy; they rejoice before you as with joy before the harvest, as people exult when dividing plunder. For the yoke of their burden, and the bar across their shoulders, the rod of their oppressor, you have broken as on the day of Midian. For all the boots of the trampling warriors and all the garments rolled in blood shall be burned as fuel for the fire.

For a child has been born for us, a son given to us; authority rests upon his shoulders; and he is named Wonderful Counselor, Mighty God, Everlasting Father, Prince of Peace. His authority shall grow continually, and there shall be endless peace for the throne of David and his kingdom. He will establish and uphold it with justice and with righteousness from this time onward and forevermore. The zeal of the LORD of hosts will do this.

Tomorrow, May 25, 2020, is Memorial Day, a time to remember all military personnel who died serving in the United States Armed Forces. Some claim that President Abraham Lincoln was the founder of Memorial Day when he gave the Gettysburg Address in 1863. Others say that General John A. Logan, commander of the Grand Army of the Republic (head of the Union soldiers who were veterans of the Civil War), proclaimed the day on May 30, 1868, to honor soldiers who died in the Civil War. Originally called Decoration Day to decorate the graves of all soldiers, it was renamed

Memorial Day in 1967 by Congress. Today we remember all those who gave their lives fighting for the United States of America and especially those who have been killed recently in the wars of the Middle East which are still raging today with American troops stationed there.

In the midst of these wars we are fighting a battle with COVID-19 in our country. We pause to remember not only those who gave their lives for our nation but also for the nearly ninety-seven thousand Americans who have died from the coronavirus since March 2020. Our sermon on Isa 9:2–7 is about the people of Israel who go from darkness to light, from despair to hope, light and joy, liberation and peace, and good news. In the midst of the COVID-19 disease we need stability, certainty, and normalcy in our lives.

WE NEED HOPE

Hope is an encouraging word. It means that a desire or expectation will be fulfilled in the not too distant future. From a biblical viewpoint faith is "unseen hope" (Heb 11: 1). We need hope in the midst of the COVID-19 pandemic. Hope that there will be a vaccine to deal with this disease. Hope that we will get through this and shall overcome. Hope that we will recover economically, morally, and spiritually and be on a higher plane. The Bible gives us three gifts: faith, hope, and love. First Corinthians 13:13 states: ". . . faith, hope and love abide, these three, and the greatest of these is love." We need all three in the coming days. Faith in the Lord whom we trust. Hope in God who promises us a better tomorrow. Love for God and for each other in unity and support.

Of the three Christian concepts, hope has emerged as an important theological theme. Jürgen Moltmann, professor emeritus of systematic theology, University of Tübingen, Germany, wrote his famous book, *Theology of Hope*,[1] and caught the attention of the Christian world. Moltmann was a young seventeen-year-old who was drafted into the German air force during the last days of World War II and surrendered in his first battle with the Allied forces. Imprisoned for three years as a POW, young Jürgen was given a Bible by a US Army chaplain and became a Christian believer. He moved to three different POW camps where his detail worked to restore bombed out businesses which were destroyed by the German Luftwaffe. He later met several YMCA workers who befriended him and who shared their Christian faith with him. Returning to Germany, Moltmann finished his university degrees and became a church pastor and later returned to graduate school to complete his Doctor of Theology degree. He became the

---

1. Moltmann, *Theology of Hope*.

leading authority on the theology of hope, remembered the American army chaplain who led him to Christ, and taught at Emory University, Candler School of Theology, Atlanta, Georgia, for five years in gratitude to America for his conversion to Christianity.

Moltmann said: "But in faith and in hope we participate here already in the 'power of the new world'. For this reason Christ becomes for believers the focus of an all-embracing hope for the new world in which God dwells."[2] Hope is the theme of Isa 9:2–9 which announced new hope and good news for the people of Israel. Isaiah proclaimed a positive message from God for his people. We will preach our sermon on three themes: light and joy, liberation and peace, and birth of a child and hope.

LIGHT AND JOY

Three passages in the Old and New Testaments describe darkness and light: Gen 1:1–5 where God creates light from darkness, this passage in Isa 9, and John 1:1–5 where the Word (Jesus Christ) is "the light of all people" and is so powerful that darkness cannot overcome it. Isaiah 9:2 proclaims in amazement: "The people who walked in darkness have seen a great light. Those who lived in a land of deep darkness—on them light has shined." Analyzing this verse we have an alliteration (a grammar form which states a thought twice and adds more details in the second part of the sentence). There is darkness and the people have seen a light but also the light in the midst of darkness in the land has illumined the people who live there.

What is this light? Where does the light originate? Who is shining the light upon the people? The answer is God who casts light on the darkened paths of the people of Israel. If you ever tried to walk in your house when it is completely dark, you know that it is easy to stumble into furniture and fall down and hurt yourself. However, if you use a flashlight or open the light switch in the room, you have an easy time navigating around your house. We need light to see, read, and guide our paths. Isaiah said to his people that they have been wandering and have strayed from God in the darkness of their own lives. But now God has shined the light on them to find and return to him. Are you stumbling around in spiritual darkness? Go to the light, Jesus Christ, who will brighten your path and help you to walk in the light of his glory and grace. The Christian hymn, "The Light of the World is Jesus," gives this message: "The whole world is lost in the darkness of sin, The light of the world is Jesus; Come to the light, Tis shining on thee, sweetly the light has dawned upon me; Once I was blind but now I can see;

---

2. Moltmann. "Religion, Revelation, and The Future," 122.

The Light of the World is Jesus." Come to the light. Have Jesus shine in your life.

Isaiah 9:3 proclaims joy: "You have multiplied the nation, you have increased its joy; they rejoice before you as with joy at the harvest, as people exult when dividing plunder." This verse cites incidents of joy: when a baby is born and increases the population of the country, when there is a plentiful harvest of wheat and barley, and when soldiers seize the riches of another after a victory over the enemy. However, joy is fulfilled when people turn to God, when there is happiness in the household, and when the joy of the Lord is increased in faithfulness to him.

There is not much joy in the news that more people have been stricken by the coronavirus, particularly when Governor Gavin Newsom said that 56 percent of the people of California will contract the virus if no preventive measures are taken such as sheltering at home and social distancing. Can we find joy in the midst of this pandemic? A friend recently sent Stan Spencer, a lay leader of our church, a detailed list of community resources for those who need social services such as food distribution, medical care, and related areas. What a wonderful way to step up as good friends and neighbors to help each other with vital information. There is joy in this act of thoughtfulness and kindness. Think about how you bring joy and happiness to a friend or acquaintance who is sheltering at home.

LIBERATION AND PEACE

Isaiah 9:4–5 announces liberation and peace: "For the yoke of their burden, and the bar across their shoulders, the rod of their oppressor, you have broken as on the day of Midian. For all the boots of the tramping warriors and all the garments rolled in blood shall be burned as fuel for the fire." His message proclaims liberation from slavery and oppression and the cessation of war and the restoration of peace. Isaiah paints the picture of a people shackled by a yoke and bar around their neck and shoulder (like a pair of oxen plowing the field) captured and smitten by the Midianite enemy. This burden has been lifted. The captured people of Israel have been liberated from the oppressor. The people of Israel are now freed. War has ended. The warrior is no longer marching to battle and shedding blood. Killing has ceased and peace has been restored.

This is good news and brings hope to the people of the southern kingdom of Judah who saw their relatives and kinsmen of Israel slaughtered and captured by the Assyrians and the threat of invasion by the overwhelming enemy, the Babylonian army, camped on its border. The people craved for the assurance of liberation and peace.

In a way the sheer relief of the people of Israel to the announcement of liberation and peace mirrors the anxiety and uncertainty that we experience as we hear the news of the growing pandemic and the mounting statistics of the coronavirus which are affecting the American people and the rest of the world. When will it end? Will I be a victim of this sickness? Will I be spared from its grip? Isaiah 9:4–5 announces liberation and peace. Let us be patient, practice safety, maintain health, and wait it out. God is with us. Who can be against us?

THE BIRTH OF A CHILD AND HOPE

This prophetic announcement of the birth of a child, the Messiah, follows the preceding messages of Isaiah who proclaims good news. Old Testament scholars are in agreement that Isa 9:6–7 is a breaking into human events of salvation history: "For a child has been born for us, a son given to us, authority rests upon his shoulders; and he is named Wonderful Counselor, Mighty God, Everlasting Father, Prince of Peace. His authority shall grow continually, and there shall be endless peace for the throne of David and his kingdom. He will establish and uphold it with justice and with righteousness from this time onward and forevermore. The zeal of the LORD of hosts will do this." Picture the people of Israel in a large public square hearing the Word of the LORD through the prophet Isaiah. There is joy, relief, and conviction. A great cheer is heard throughout the kingdom. The announcement is seared in the hearts of the people. When will this happen? When will this come to pass? Where is this child who shall be God and who will establish the throne of David as a mighty conqueror and ruler of all nations?

Ministers preach from this text at Christmas. It is a majestic passage of Scripture filled with the birth of a child, Jesus, the Son of God given to us with the glorious names of Wonderful Counselor (the great listener and therapist), Mighty God (Emmanuel—God with us), Everlasting Father (God the Father, God the Son, God the Holy Spirit), Prince of Peace (peace on earth, good will to all men), the authority to rule and to ensure peace as did David and his kingdom, justice and righteousness forever, and the zeal and seal of the Lord as a promise of its fulfillment. How full and rich are these promises of God as we stand on fulfillment and completion!

Hope, anticipation, and expectation gripped the heart and life of every child of Israel from the time of Isaiah and every Christian believer from the time of Jesus to the present. The announcement of the birth of this child and the wonderful promises of God transcend the threat and terror of the coronavirus in the year of our LORD 2020 AD. When you experience a low point in your struggle against the coronavirus, turn to Isa 9:2–7. It will give you an uplift in your moment of despair and discouragement. Then return to your fight and vigilance against the disease. Protect yourself and others and share love and kindness today.

THE NEED FOR GOOD NEWS

Isaiah 9:2–7 is the good news of the book of Isaiah. Good news provides us hope, excitement, and promise. Good news is what we need as we cope with sheltering in place, practice social distancing, and venture out of our homes into the community for groceries, restaurant meals, haircuts, and mall shopping. Most of us leave our residences and practice caution. There is "the new normal" which includes adapting to the current news of COVID-19. Schools resume with half-size classes meeting in the morning or the afternoon combined with online distance learning assignments. Churches have spaced sitting in Sunday worship services and Zoom conferencing for meetings and study groups. Football, baseball, basketball, hockey, and soccer games are played without or with minimal fan spectators and viewed on television rather than in person. Elected officials conduct business via Zoom conferencing and virtual debates and voting rather than in a single chamber together. Is this good news or is this reality news? These are standard pandemic public health practices.

In the midst of anticipating good news about the virus, let us remember the good news about Jesus Christ who died for our sins and rose from the dead to celebrate his resurrection and the new life that he gives to us. Let us keep this gospel of good news with us as we anticipate the breakthrough vaccine which will cripple COVID-19 and bring peace and normalcy to the world and our nation. Let us renew our prayers for the medical researchers who are developing vaccines to cope with the virus that God will guide them in their efforts.

PASTORAL PRAYER

Our Father who art in heaven, we come to you on this Memorial Day to remember all those who gave their lives fighting for this country and for all those who have been victims of this coronavirus. We pray for your comfort and love to surround the families who are in sorrow and loss that you will be with them. We are thankful for all those who have been restored to health from this disease and for all those doctors and nurses who have cared for patients who have recovered. We uphold the public health leaders and researchers who are leading us in the paths of health and safety from this disease that you will grant them wisdom and good advice on how to reopen this country in a safe and sane way. We pray for our mayors, governors, and federal officials that they may seek your guidance and the counsel of medical experts for the health of the American people.

We pray that the spiritual lives of people will be drawn to the Solid Rock of Jesus Christ. May people confess that "on Christ the Solid Rock I stand, all other ground is sinking sand." We pray for our church this morning that you will keep it in the shelter of your everlasting arms. We ask that our church will lean on Jesus and that you will meet and satisfy their wishes and answer their prayers. Be with our Bible study leaders, our church school teachers, our consistory, our kitchen cooks, and those who serve you behind the scenes that they will be a blessing to others.

We pray all of these requests in the name of your Son, Jesus Christ our LORD, who loved us and gave himself for us. Amen.

CHAPTER 7

A SHOOT FROM JESSE AND THE SPIRIT OF THE LORD

Isaiah 11:1–10 (May 31, 2020)

Scripture Reading. A shoot shall come out from the stump of Jesse, and a branch shall grow out of his roots. The spirit of the LORD shall rest on him, the spirit of wisdom and understanding, the spirit of counsel and might, the spirit of knowledge and the fear of the LORD. His delight shall be in the fear of the LORD.

He shall not judge by what his eyes see, or decide by what his ears hear; but with righteousness he shall judge the poor, and decide with equity for the meek of the earth; he shall strike the earth with the rod of his mouth, and with the breath of his lips he shall kill the wicked. Righteousness shall be the belt around his waist, and faithfulness the belt around his loins.

The wolf shall live with the lamb, the leopard shall lie down with the kid, the calf and the lion and the fatling together, and a little child shall lead them. The cow and the bear shall graze, their young shall lie down together; and the lion shall eat straw like the ox. The nursing child shall play over the hole of the asp, and the weaned child shall put its hand on the adder's den. They will not hurt or destroy on all my holy mountain; for the earth will be full of the knowledge of the LORD as the waters cover the sea.

On that day the root of Jesse shall stand as a signal to the peoples; the nations shall inquire of him, and his dwelling shall be glorious.

We are facing a delicate balancing act: adhering to the latest medical science on the public health approach to COVID-19 and bringing the American economy and employment back from numbers that rival the Great Depression. How do we make use of both medical science and economy recovery without endangering the loss of more lives to the virus? The CDC predicted that by June 1, 2020, over 100,000 Americans will die from COVID-19. A national strategy plan involving both medicine and economics[1] should be devised and followed from the president of the United States through Congress and the governors and mayors down to the average citizen so that every American is adhering to the same guidelines.

The opening of public and private schools, initial and periodic coronavirus testing for returning employees and school children, regular public health inspection of businesses, the regulation of large gatherings (staggered attendance, social distancing), and mass vaccine inoculation are crucial factors which must be addressed to establish American behavioral boundaries. Uniformity, diversity, and flexibility among regions and states are required. The Trump administration in Washington, DC, seems unable to craft such a plan.

Isaiah 11:1–10 touches on the selection and the reign of the head of state, the leadership qualities of a leader, and the need for peace and harmony in the national life which are concerns of the American people in the November 2020 election.

ISAIAH AND THE MESSIAH

Isaiah was a former priest and a cousin of King Uzziah who ruled from 742 to 701 BC. He probably gained access to his relative who was a godly man. King Uzziah heeded the Word of the Lord and brought his people back to the worship of the only God of Israel. Isaiah may have spent time with Uzziah, was familiar with the workings of the royal court, and adept with the priestly duties and the study of the Old Testament Scriptures. As Isaiah began his ministry the northern kingdom of Israel was annexed to Assyria, while the southern kingdom of Judah was under threat of invasion from Babylonia. King Uzziah lived under this Babylonian shadow and was spared the onslaughts of the enemy. In the midst of this grim situation Isa 11:1–10 brings news of the Messiah who is portrayed as a Righteous Deliverer of Israel. Isaiah 11:1–10 describes the Coming Messiah promised to the

---

1. The state of New York has a planning and oversight task force which is balancing public health and economic stimulus concerns together for New York business enterprises.

people of Israel. Long quoted and remembered by those who followed in the prophetic path of Isaiah, this passage ranks as the finest description of the Davidic Messiah in the Old Testament.

Isaiah 11:1–10 is divided into three parts: a shoot from Jesse (Isa 11:1 and 11), the quality of his reign (Isa 11:2–5), and everlasting peace and harmony (Isa 11:6–9). The passage is a promise of a future event heeded eagerly by the people of Israel which is fulfilled in the coming of Jesus in the New Testament.

A SHOOT FROM JESSE, THE SPIRIT OF THE LORD, AND PENTECOST FOR ALL BELIEVERS

Isaiah 11:1–2 states: "A shoot shall come out from the stump of Jesse, and a branch shall grow out of his roots. The spirit of the LORD shall rest on him, the spirit of wisdom and understanding, the spirit of counsel and might, the spirit of knowledge and the fear of the LORD." A new shoot from the stump of Jesse refers to the coming of the Messiah who will have the Spirit of the LORD with him. When Jesus was baptized by John the Baptist the Holy Spirit descended on him (Matt 3:13–17). Later Jesus teaches his disciples about the coming of the Holy Spirit as the Advocate upon them as believers (John 14:25). The disciples were confused and disorganized after the death and resurrection of Jesus (John 21). But after they received the power of the Holy Spirit (Acts 1:8) at Pentecost they spoke with conviction and confidence about Jesus as Savior and LORD (Acts 2). Today is Pentecost Sunday when we remember the presence and gift of the Holy Spirit upon the lives of believers. Isaiah 11 discusses the presence of the Spirit and the coming of the Messiah which is fulfilled in the ministry of Jesus. Now the power of the Spirit is available to all believers to demonstrate the power of God in our lives.

But let us return to the shoot from the Jesse theme. If you have tried to grow a plant from seed to full bloom it is a time consuming process. First, one must buy a pot and soil, fertilizer, and the seedling. Choosing the particular seed involves careful research to select the plant species. Second, one must plant in a climate season and location. Third, protection from pests, watering cycle, and sun and shade are crucial for raising the seedling. The first shoot of the plant breaking through the soil triggers excitement to the grower. Likewise we read from the shoot of Jesse (Isa 11:1) comes the root of Jesse (Isa 11:10) which details the Davidic Messiah in the intervening verses.

Jesse is the father of King David. In Ruth 4:17 and Matt 1:5 Jesse is the son of Obed who was the son of Boaz, the kinsman redeemer, who married Ruth in the book of Ruth. Incidentally Ruth and Mary are the only two women mentioned in the genealogy of Matt 1. The prophet Samuel is sent by God to Jesse the Bethlehemite to select the future king of Israel in 1 Sam 16. He is commanded by God to anoint David as king of Israel. Jesse is from Bethlehem where Jesus is born. Later Paul quotes "The root of Jesse" in Rom 15:12 and mentions David, son of Jesse, in his sermon in the synagogue at Antioch (Acts 13:22). David is the son of Jesse and the shoot and root of Jesse is the Messiah, Jesus Christ, who comes from the line of Jesse, the father of David (Matt 1:5).

On Palm Sunday the crowd cries out "Hosanna (God save us) to the son of David" to Jesus (Matt 21:9). Isaiah 11:1 has been fulfilled: A shoot from Jesse has arrived, the Messiah has come! The message of Isaiah to the people of Israel is that although Israel is divided and conquered by outside nations there will be the coming of the Messiah who will restore the glory of Israel and establish the throne of David and the kingdom of Israel. How does this good news apply to the coronavirus crisis? At first glance there seems to be a wide gap between the coming of Jesus and the coronavirus. Can the promise and coming of Jesus, a shoot of Jesse, address the present situation that confront us?

A close examination of Isa 11:1 reveals these thoughts: ". . . a branch shall grow out of his roots" and "the root of Jesse shall stand as a signal to the peoples . . ." (Isa 11: 10). The ideas of life and growth and a signal are messages of promise and comfort to those who are stricken and suffering. Jesus gives life and growth and stands as a signal of hope and salvation to those who need help in time of need. Ponder these thoughts as we struggle to understand the depths of this pandemic.

THE QUALITY OF HIS REIGN

Isaiah 11:2–5 list the characteristics of the reign of the Messiah:

- Wisdom and Understanding
- Counsel and Might
- Knowledge and Fear of the Lord
- Judgement from an Inner Core of Righteousness
- Concern for the Poor and the Meek
- Ability to Take the Offense and to Attack the Problem

- Wearing the Badge of Righteousness and Faithfulness

The words of Isaiah point out a true leader of Israel. The Messiah has unique qualities: the spirit of the LORD rests upon him with wisdom and understanding, counsel and might, knowledge and the fear of the LORD, righteousness and equity and faithfulness. One discerns the nature of this strong and spiritual person. Israel lacked such a leader and God's promise of he that cometh was a prophecy that was fulfilled many centuries later in the person of Jesus Christ.

As we review these leadership qualities we see the human and spiritual features which comprise a true and proven leader in time of crisis. America faces a leadership crisis at the present time. Our nation desperately needs a person of integrity who brings us together for a single purpose. We have been divided and at odds with each other for a long time. As one nation under God we must mobilize our vast resources and fight a common enemy.

As we compare these biblical traits and the present American leaders we must ask: Who has proven to be a successful leader? Is Joe Biden ready to lead us for the next four years? Will Gavin Newsom and Andrew Cuomo be available after four years? The future is filled with many unknowns. We will make a major decision as we elect the next president of the United States. Let us pray that God will guide our country in this solemn task.

EVERLASTING PEACE AND HARMONY

Isaiah 11:6–9 portrays a picture of everlasting peace and harmony: the wolf and the lamb, the leopard and the kid, the calf and the lion, the cow and the bear, and the lion and the ox will live together as friends. At the forefront of this peace and harmony is a little child as the leader. The passage alludes to young David and also foresees Jesus as a child with a special knowledge of God. Recall Luke 2:48 and 49 when the parents of Jesus asked: "Child, why have you treated us like this?" Jesus answered: "Did you not know that I must be in my Father's house?" A child will lead them. How ironic that this is often true when we observe the actions of children.

The birth of a baby brings people together (the birth parents, grandparents, aunts and uncles, cousins, neighbors, and friends) who want to adore this newborn. As the baby grows to be a child, we see glimpses of leadership. My six-year-old grandson, Evan, defended me as my wife criticized my poor driving several years ago. He said: "Ying Ying (grandma in Chinese on the father's side), Yeh Yeh (grandpa in Chinese on the father's side) is just obeying the rules of the road!" Or Alyssa, age eleven, recently taught herself on the violin the song, "I Can't Help Falling in Love with You." Her mother and our daughter Lori recently sent us a video cellphone recording of Alyssa playing this song accompanied by her father, Noel, who was playing a countermelody on the cello. Children soon grow up into teenage and young adult years where they assume career leadership roles. Before we know it, they are making the major decisions and we are sitting on the sidelines. A child will lead them and the government will be on his shoulders, and the Spirit of the Lord will descend upon him.

There will be peace and harmony. People will get along with each other and live together in mutual understanding. There will be no more war. Disease will be eradicated. Salvation and deliverance will come to all. The new heaven and the new earth will descend from the clouds on high. The kingdom of God is here!

WAITING AND COMING

There is a stage play named *Waiting for Godot* where people are waiting for Godot who never comes. Waiting for the Messiah is the reality for Israel. In the fullness of time Jesus comes as the Son of God (the Word became flesh and dwelt among us and we beheld Him, the only begotten of the Father, full of grace and truth [John 1: 14]). In 1953 I was in the ninth grade at Stevenson Intermediate School, Honolulu, Hawaii. We were excused from class and lined the highway near our school to see President-elect Dwight David Eisenhower who passed by us on his way to laying a wreath at Punchbowl National Cemetery of the Pacific which was above our campus. The Korean War armistice had just been signed and Eisenhower was on his way to South Korea to visit the American troops. I caught a glimpse of the president-elect of the United States for a moment as his motorcade drove by. The coming of a president and the coming of the Messiah are two different events. Both comings were to bring peace. However, the coming of Jesus was to bring salvation through his death and resurrection.

PASTORAL PRAYER

Dear God, As summer begins please guard and guide the people of America. May they exercise wisdom and caution as they enjoy their vacation and leisure time. May they be aware of the health and safety of others near them. May you protect each of us as the virus is still in our midst. Give wisdom to our governors and mayors and may they lead us as examples of the citizens that we need to become in this pandemic. Help us to enjoy this summer of fun and relaxation. Free us to relax but help us to maintain our vigilance about our health and safety. Guide our church as we continue to worship you and to affirm our love and support to our fellow believers in Christ and to those who need to hear and believe in the good news of Jesus and his love. May the Spirit of the LORD descend upon our nation, giving each person a sense of purpose and love for their family and neighbor.

Be with our medical scientists and our business economists that they may truly work together as a team for the American people. Guide our president and Congress that they may harness the wisdom of these two disciplines and create a national strategy and program which will bring healing to our people and the restoration of jobs and businesses in the coming months and years ahead. We know that the tasks are difficult and challenging and that real change is slow and careful. Grant us the patience of mind and heart and the discipline and purpose of democratic and freedom-loving people. Give us the victory and the power of your might. Continue to be with our congregation and their needs. Help us to pull together with a single purpose and goal for Christ and his kingdom.

We pray for Risa who is recovering from a stroke and for her doctor's care, for Jan that your grace will be her strength each day, for Melanie and her heart condition, for Lorrie and her long-term recovery from her stroke, and for all those who are at home from illness and pain that your presence, love, and comfort will be with them. Bless all caregivers who daily minister to our seniors who need protection, food, and daily living needs. Be with all children who watch over their elderly parents.

We pray all of this in the name of our LORD and Savior Jesus Christ who taught us to pray and to love one another. Amen.

CHAPTER 8

WIPING AWAY THE TEARS
Isaiah 25:1–10 (June 14, 2020)

Scripture Reading. O LORD, you are my God; I will exalt you, I will praise your name; for you have done wonderful things, plans formed of old, faithful and sure. For you have made the city a heap, the fortified city a ruin; the palace of aliens is a city no more, it will never be rebuilt. Therefore strong people will glorify you; cities of ruthless nations will fear you.

For you have been a refuge to the poor, a refuge to the needy in their distress, a shelter from the rainstorm and a shade from the heat. When the blast of the ruthless was like a winter rainstorm, the noise of aliens like heat in a dry place, you subdued the heat with the shade of clouds; the song of the ruthless was stilled.

On this mountain the LORD of hosts will make for all peoples a feast of rich food, a feast of well-aged wines, of rich food filled with marrow, of well-aged wines strained clear. And he will destroy on this mountain the shroud that is cast over all peoples, the sheet that is spread over all nations; he will swallow up death forever.

Then the Lord GOD will wipe away he tears from all faces, and the disgrace of his people he will take away from all the earth, for the LORD has spoken. It will be said on that day, Lo, this is our God; we have waited for him, so that he might save us. This is the LORD for whom we have waited; let us be glad and rejoice in his salvation. For the hand of the LORD will rest on this mountain.

Today is Flag Day which honors the flag of the United States of America. Bernard Cigrand, a Wisconsin teacher, first proposed a Flag Day on June 14, 1885, and later President Woodrow Wilson officially proclaimed a national Flag Day honoring the flag on June 14, 1916. Our flag is a national symbol of unity incorporating all fifty states on a field of blue, with stars and red and white stripes of the thirteen original colonies. Our Pledge of Allegiance to the flag recalls our patriotism and honor to our country and the values that it stands for: "One Nation under God, with Liberty and Justice for All." On this Flag Day let us all rededicate ourselves to the truths of America and let us mourning all those who have been victims of the pandemic and racism, sexism, homophobia, and agism, no matter our race, color, or creed. We rejoice in the founding of America but cry for those who are no longer with us.

IT IS OKAY TO CRY

Crying is a powerful emotion and good for the soul. You can still maintain your manhood and have a good cry. Crying is a normal human emotion. Do women cry more easily than men? I have no research on this gender difference, but I have observed that women tend to share and show their feelings more readily than men. It is healthy and uplifting. As Americans we cry over the 100,000-plus lives which have been lost in our country and the many more around the world due to COVID-19. At the same time we cry tears of joy over the many more who have fought through this virus by self-quarantine and through the valiant efforts of doctors and nurses who have used the tools of medical science and treatment in the healthcare of patients. When this pandemic is finally over (and it may take years of medical research and worldwide inoculation) we will sit down and have a good cry. Yet at the same time when we view the destruction of our cities and the peaceful demonstrations over George Floyd, Breonna Taylor, and other African Americans we cry out for justice, sanity, and peace.

This sermon is titled "Wiping Away The Tears." Perhaps it is appropriate to have a sermon on crying and God wiping away the tears. The peoples of Israel and America faced similar situations of loss and grief. They mourned the loss of their cities and the lives of their family and friends in time of war and battle. We have seen the silent destruction of our economy and the loss of friends, neighbors, and city and small town dwellers due to a disease which knows no boundaries due to race, color or creed. This is a time to cry and lift up our voices to God in a prayer for comfort, strength, and guidance. It is a time for tears. It is okay to cry. Our manhood and womanhood are still intact when we express emotion.

Where are the tears in Isa 25:1–10? The tears part of the sermon comes at the end rather than the beginning. Isaiah 25:1–10 moves the reader from the problems of the cities to a mountaintop experience with God and that is when the tears will be wiped away by God. Isaiah has a video camera which pans the destruction of the cities and the survivors and trains his sights on a mountain hideaway where God will wipe away all tears. The American people in large and small cities are mourning the loss of lives and the need for justice and reform. We desperately need a leader who comforts, shows compassion, helps us to bind up our wounds, and promotes healing in the times of division and emerging unity. Isaiah 25:1–10 addresses: the destruction of the cities, the saving of the people, and the mountaintop experience with God.

THE DESTRUCTION OF THE CITIES

Isaiah 25:2 makes a dire prediction: The southern kingdom of Judah and the city of Jerusalem, the capital, will fall to the enemy and will be destroyed entirely. Isaiah says: "For you have made the city a heap, the fortified city a ruin; the palace of aliens is a city no more, it will never be rebuilt." God uses the Babylonian empire and the forces of Nebuchadnezzar to invade Jerusalem and defeat the Israelite forces in 587 BC. King Zedekiah of Judah was captured, blinded, and taken to Babylon where he later died. Jerusalem was torched and leveled to the ground. Its leading citizens were executed, many ordinary people were led into captivity, and the state of Judah ended forever. Isaiah's prophecy of judgment and destruction became a reality for the people of Judah.

At the beginning of the COVID-19 pandemic in March 2020 a friend sent me pictures of downtown San Francisco: empty scenes of familiar places due to the order of the governor of California for all citizens to remain in home shelter. KCRA Channel 3 Sacramento showed similar deserted streets in the center of our city. The bombed cities of England and Germany during World War II saw the death of citizens and destruction of London, Berlin, and Dresden. Similarly the coronavirus has crippled and compounded the lives of people who have lost their jobs, gone into survival mode, and suffered the loss of security, comfort, and health.

Historians will write a tragic chapter in the history of the United States: The coronavirus pandemic of 2019–2020 and the pandemic of racism. History books will describe the disease as it swept from China through Italy to the United States, the medical and political responses, and the efforts of medical research to find a vaccine for its cure. Widespread city populations were destroyed by this invisible illness and visible bigotry, but courageous individuals and groups stood up and made a difference in their communities. Decades after the coronavirus we will tell this story of sacrifice and courage to our children and grandchildren as survivors of this tragedy. But we will be witnesses to the goodness and mercy of God who saw us through our darkest moments.

THE SAVING OF THE PEOPLE

Judah's military forces, the intelligentsia (the leading thinkers and leaders) of the nation, and major landmarks of Jerusalem (the palace of the king and the temple of God) were wiped out by the invading enemy. Yet the common citizens were saved by the Lord, taken into exile and captivity, and later generations returned to their homeland. Isaiah 25:4 says: "For you have been a refuge to the poor, a refuge to the needy in their distress, a shelter from the rainstorm and a shade from the heat." A remnant of the people was saved from annihilation.

The saving of the people also applies to the coronavirus. A dear friend and high school classmate, Gladys Taketa, sent me an April 2020 email that her daughter received from a friend who lives in Bergano, Italy, the epicenter of the COVID-19 outbreak, with her husband and three children. Her name is Cristina Higgins. Gladys's daughter writes:

> The Italians were originally told that they would be out of lockdown by April third—this has been extended. Cristina believes that they will have another 6–8 weeks of lockdown. She is trying to warn us (again) of the steps we can really take to slow the curve. If we do not make these changes, we will end up in the same situation as she is in currently. This is not fear mongering but an opportunity to avoid the mistakes made by the Italians. Cristina believes that we are 10 days behind Italy.

This warning from Italy should strike a danger note in us. Saving the people from the outbreak of this virus is paramount in the thoughts and prayers of Americans and in the research and treatment of medical doctors and nurses. There are stories of medical first responders who have given their lives in the pursuit of caring for the health needs of people. We see them on the nightly news as they are the front lines of drive-through testing sites and the hospital rooms of medical centers in the United States and other countries.

We need to come to the cross and to Jesus but we have an incredible job to do as Americans: elect our president who stands as a model of what America is and should be, address our divisions and bring us all together as a nation with a common purpose "with liberty and justice for all," mobilize the unemployed as Roosevelt did in the Great Depression, reform our justice and police systems so that we truly "protect and serve" all citizens, marshal the medical and science research community to anticipate and prepare for future pandemics, and many more areas for Americans to explore together as citizen-leaders. We need to save our people from sin and redeem them through Christ, but we need to save our nation from self-destruction and the paths of strife, division, hatred, and political narcissism.

THE MOUNTAINTOP EXPERIENCE WITH GOD

Isaiah 25:7–10 describes a heavenly scene where God will serve us a banquet feast, destroy death, and wipe away our tears. Isaiah 25:9 promises: "It will be said on that day, Lo, this is our God; we have waited for him, so that he might save us. This is the LORD for whom we have waited; let us be glad and rejoice in his salvation." Heaven is a place where we will enjoy the presence of God and where there will be no more suffering, pain, and death. Isaiah describes heaven as a mountaintop experience with God. In contrast to the destruction of the cities and the saving of the people, Isaiah moves us toward the heavenly vision.

During the Middle Ages Saint Augustine,[1] a great theologian of his time, wrote a book, *City of God*, where he discusses the nature of man and the salvation of God. Augustine points us to heaven and the resting place of God. Likewise Isaiah turns the people toward heaven and God in the midst of their struggle.

There is a Christian hymn, "Turn Your Eyes Upon Jesus," which says: "O soul, are you weary and tired, no light in the darkness you see; there is light at the look of the Savior and Life more abundant and free; Turn your eyes upon Jesus, Look full in his wonderful face; and the things of earth will grow strangely dim, in the light of his Glory and Grace." We need to turn our eyes on Jesus in the midst of the coronavirus and look to him for guidance and strength. Isaiah 25:10 reassures us: "For the hand of the LORD rests on this mountain." God guarantees us a place on his mountain. He is saving a spot for us. Hebrews 12:1–2 exhorts us: "Therefore, since we

---

1. Saint Augustine, *City of God*.

are surrounded by so great a cloud of witnesses, let us also lay aside every weight and the sin that clings so closely and let us run with perseverance the race that is set before us, looking to Jesus the pioneer and perfecter of our faith, who for the sake of the joy that was set before him endured the cross, disregarding its shame, and has taken his seat at the right hand of the throne of God." We need this mindset as we battle the coronavirus as an individual, family, community, and nation in the coming days ahead. May God grant us strength and courage to fight the good fight.

Martin Luther King Jr. preached about "seeing The Promised Land where his eyes saw the Glory of the LORD, where there was neither black or white, and where the Coming of the LORD was a reality." He was talking about this mountaintop experience with God where "there is no longer Jew or Greek, there is no longer slave or free, there is no longer male and female; for all of you are one in Christ Jesus" (Gal 3:28). We long for that day and need to work toward the removal of these barriers so that all of us have that mountaintop experience with God and feel the breeze of love, caring, and togetherness.

COMFORT AND ASSURANCE

As we read and study Isaiah 25:1–10 we notice that the people of Israel have come through a great experience: the loss of their cities, nation, and way of life. But God has promised and performed two miracles: He has saved his people and has been their refuge, shelter, and shade and has promised them a mountaintop experience (a relief and rescue) from the destruction confronting them. God has given them a heavenly vision and a resting place from the harsh realities. The kingdom of God is in this age of the church in a partial manner and in the age to come when the kingdom of God will be fully established on this earth as promised in the closing chapters of Revelation. The apostle John calls this "the new heaven and the new earth" (Rev 21:1–4): "Then I saw a new heaven and a new earth; for the first heaven and the first earth had passed away, and the sea was no more. And I saw the holy city, the new Jerusalem, coming down out of heaven from God, prepared as a bride adorned for her husband, And I heard a loud voice from the throne saying, 'See, the home of God is among mortals. He will dwell with them; they will be his people, and God himself will be with them; he will wipe every tear from their eyes. Death will be no more; mourning and crying and pain will be no more, for the first things have passed away.'" This heavenly glimpse is prophesied in the mountaintop experience with God of Isa 25 which is a foretaste of Rev 21 where there is the full display of the kingdom of God on earth.

We continue to struggle with COVID-19 much like the people of Israel faced in the destruction of their cities and the loss of their citizens. But the promises of God stand for us as Christian believers. I remember singing the Christian anthem, "The Holy City": "Last night I lay asleeping, There came a dream so fair; I stood in old Jerusalem beside the Temple there; I heard the children singing and ever as they sang, Me thought the voice of angels from heaven in answer rang; Me thought the voice of angels from heaven in answer rang: Jerusalem, Jerusalem, Lift up your gates and sing; Hosanna to the highest, Hosanna to your King; And then me thought my dream was changed, The streets no longer rang, Hush were the glad Hosannas the little children sang. The sun drew dark with mystery, the morn was cold and chilled, As the shadow of the Cross arose along the lonely hill; And once again the scene was changed, New earth there seemed to be; I saw the Holy City beside the tideless sea; The Light of God was on its streets, The gates were open wide and all that who might enter, And no one was denied; No need of moon or stars by night or sun to shine by day; It was the New Jerusalem that would not fade away Jerusalem, Jerusalem, Sing for the night is o'er; Hosanna in the highest, Hosanna forever more." This sacred music composition was inspired by Isa 25 and Rev 21. May you find solace in the comfort of God who gives us a mountaintop experience and a heavenly vision in the midst of a virus which we are battling as individuals, communities, and citizens of the United States of America.

PASTORAL PRAYER

O God our Heavenly Father, We thank you in the midst of the coronavirus that you are with us. You have saved us and given us a holy city, a new Jerusalem which you have prepared for us. We sing "Hosanna to the Highest, Hosanna Forever More" with Isaiah and John who wrote about this in the Bible. This is our assurance no matter what befalls us, Jesus doeth all things well. He is our Savior who leads us all the way. Through life and death, in this life and in the next life he is with us. Help us to stand in the midst of this virus. Guard and guide us. Grant us your wisdom from above.

We come to you this morning aware of our needs and the needs of our nation and church. You have bought us through a grave pandemic and have taught us lessons of trust in you. Be with us this summer as we enjoy the warm weather and the freedom that summer vacation brings to us. Help us to be satisfied with the small and simple things of life rather than the big and expensive things of this world. May we have fun with our family and be satisfied with their presence. Bless our home as we enjoy the comforts of the simple life. As we walk around the neighborhood, help us to talk with those who are nearby and get to know them and their lives. May we appreciate the beautiful weather, the blue sky and the white clouds. We thank you for giving us another day to live and to enjoy. We thank you for the leaders of our community and state who are aware of the problems facing us and who act with our interest in mind.

Bless our church and those people who are in their homes and are our brothers and sisters in Christ. Keep them safe and happy and satisfied with their life. We remember Risa and her continual recovery from her stroke that you will be with her; Jan as she copes with her Parkinson's illness that you will help her to face each day with you as her Companion; Lorrie that you will strengthen her as she goes about her daily tasks; for Melanie and her heart condition and health needs; and for all seniors who are at home and who are ill and in pain that their families and loved ones will care for them. Continue to lead us in the path of righteousness. Nurture and feed us the Bread of Life. Equip us to fight the good fight. Turn our eyes upon Jesus. In his name we pray, Amen.

CHAPTER 9

STRENGTH, TRUST, AND PEACE
Isaiah 26:1–15 (June 7, 2020)

Scripture Reading. On that day this song will be sung in the land of Judah: We have a strong city; he sets up victory like walls and bulwarks. Open the gates, so that the righteous nation that keeps faith may enter in. Those of steadfast mind you keep in peace—in peace because they trust in you. Trust in the LORD forever, for in the LORD GOD you have an everlasting rock. For he has brought low the inhabitants of the height; the lofty city he lays low. He lays it low to the ground, casts it to the dust. The foot tramples it, the feet of the poor, the steps of the needy. The way of the righteous is level; O Just One, you make smooth the path of the righteous. In the path of your judgments, O LORD, we wait for you; your name and your renown are the soul's desire.

My soul yearns for you in the night, my spirit within me earnestly seeks you. For when your judgments are in the earth, the inhabitants of the world learn righteousness. If favor is shown to the wicked, they do not learn righteousness; in the land of uprightness they deal perversely and do not see the majesty of the LORD. O LORD, your hand is lifted up, but they do not see it. Let them see your zeal for your people, and be ashamed. Let the fire for your adversaries consume them. O LORD, you will ordain peace for us, for indeed, all that we have done, you have done for us. O LORD our God, other lords beside you have ruled over us, but we acknowledge your name alone. The dead do not live; shades do not rise—because you have punished and destroyed them, and wiped out all memory of them. But you have increased the nation, O LORD,

STRENGTH, TRUST, AND PEACE   71

you have increased the nation; you are glorified; you have enlarged all the border of the land.

On Memorial Day, May 25, 2020, in Minneapolis, Minnesota, George Floyd was murdered by now former police officer Derek Chauvin, which caused national protests in major cities across the country in the midst of the COVID-19 pandemic. Protesters took to the streets, confronted law enforcement officers, and voiced outrage at this happening. Businesses were looted and burned and properties were damaged and destroyed. Anger and frustration, anarchy and chaos, and threats and violence were traded back and forth. The president of the United States issued a series of tweets which revealed former threats and tactics used in the civil rights uprisings of the sixties. Rather than bringing the nation together in mourning, repentance, and healing, the actions of many furthered divided us into armed camps against each other.

Our sermon based on Isa 26:1–15 underscores the need of every citizen of the United States of America to kneel before Almighty God and to ask him for strength to endure this tragedy and trust in the goodness and mercy of the Lord. As the song says: Let there be peace on earth and let it begin with me. Can we exercise compassion? Can we come together? Can we bind up our wounds? Can we come to the cross? Can we rise up as one nation under God? Can we live out our pledge of allegiance? God, please can someone bring us together in the midst of this double tragedy of death and destruction? The American people are crying out for such a leader, guide, and friend. Let us remember George Floyd as we struggle with those we have lost to the pandemic. We mourn all who have left us.

THE MESSAGE AND THE MESSENGER

When the coronavirus started in Wuhan, China, in the closing days of 2019 it seemed to be a distant piece of news. Little did we know how the United States of America would be affected during January and February 2020 until it hit full force in the state of Washington and New York City in March 2020. In a period of ninety days during March, April, and May 2020, Americans realized that COVID-19 was a real killer which affected the health of millions of people and took the lives of over 100,000 victims. After sheltering in place and shutting down our economy we endured for ten weeks with medical treatment, isolation, and containment.

Americans are a restless and impatient people. There was a major push to reopen the economy and to find a cure for the virus. In the midst of this virus, what has been the message and who have been the messengers? The message has changed as the virus has progressed during the various stages of infection. There have been a host of messengers who have spoken to the American people: Governor Andrew Cuomo with his message of reality and grim warnings, Dr. Anthony Fauci with his message of medical science and public health facts, Governor Gavin Newsom and his message of needed programs and sane reopening procedures, and President Donald Trump with a plurality of messages from his task force and his sense of right and wrong.

What is the message that resonates to our senses? Who is the messenger that is believable to the American people? Who do we trust and follow in the midst of this pandemic which has stricken our nation? Who has proven to be a leader as this COVID-19 has unfolded in this country? Who has pointed the way and who will we follow in the coming months and years as we sort out and work through this virus? These are questions that we are still pondering and answering as the virus emerges in our country. In the midst of discovering the answers we turn to Isa 25:1-15, which preaches strength, trust, and peace. What a comforting message spoken by the prophet Isaiah many centuries ago to the people of Israel. This message and messenger still have relevance for us as a nation because we are still searching for answers during this crisis.

We need a leader who knows what to do, what to say, and how to say it. We think of Abraham Lincoln who set the goal of preserving the Union and Franklin Delano Roosevelt who talked about the real situation and explained what he was going to do to correct the wrongs and make things right to the American people in his fireside chats. Now Isaiah, a prophetic messenger of God, has a message which offers stability and certainty and speaks to our uncertain and instable times that we face today as we endeavor to cope with the virus. Listen to his comforting words and his message of strength, trust, and peace. Envision these concepts and apply them to your life and the problems facing the United States of America. Imagine how we can be strong, who we can trust, and how we can find peace. Be reassured that these ideals can be achieved and realized in our country.

COMFORTING WORDS

We need comfort and comforting words coming from our leaders and our churches. Several weeks ago it was reported by the Centers for Disease Control that the coronavirus death count could reach 100,000 by June 1 in the United States. This news turned me to Isa 26:1-15 for comfort and understanding. The message of this passage is: strength, trust, and peace. In the midst of this disease which has engulfed the United States far more than China and Italy we need such a message. Isaiah's words are spoken as if the prophet was aware of the present situation that we face in this country. However, his words are cast as Isaiah anticipated the immediate future. That is, the present may be dismal, but the future looks bright when you have faith in the Lord. This is the real meaning of hope: to understand the present and to be mindful of the reassurance from the Lord for the discernible future. Today we concentrate on the message from the prophet Isaiah in Isa 26:1–15: strength (26:1–2), trust (26:3–11), and peace (26:12–15). As we consider each of these traits, ask yourselves how we can weave these concepts into the fabric of our nation.

STRENGTH

Isaiah 26:1–2 opens with strength. He declares: "We have a strong city; he sets up victory like walls and bulwarks. Open the gates so that the righteous nation that keeps truth may enter in." Every city and nation wants strength in numbers, resources, and security. The ruler and people of Judah confidently declare that they have a strong city and a righteous nation. Strength is based on the righteousness of the people. As the seal of the state of Hawaii and the University of Hawaii motto declare: Ua Mau ka Eaoka ' I ka Pono ("The life of the land is perpetuated in righteousness."). Spiritual righteousness is the basis of strength, said Isaiah, and is reflected in the Hawaiian declaration which was influenced by the Christianity of early missionaries who brought the gospel of Christ in the mid-nineteenth century to the people of Hawaii.

The strength of an individual, family, community, and nation ultimately comes from God. We hear this from Isaiah, witness this in the history of Israel, and coin this on our American money: In God We Trust. Yet we are going through a major crisis in our nation which is beyond a world war, an economic spiral, and a natural disaster. We are facing a life-and-death health crisis which has engulfed the world and gravely affected our nation. Where is the strength that we need to face and cope with this challenge? Our strength cometh from the LORD who made heaven and earth, because the earth is the LORD's and the fullness thereof. We are strong because of the LORD God who daily strengthens us. Let us call on the LORD in this time of national crisis and ask for his strength and help.

Paul shares with the church at Philippi his "up and down" life. He is able to roll with the punches because of the strength that he has in Christ. He confesses: "I know what it is to have little, and I know what it is to have plenty. In any and all circumstances I have learned the secret of being well-fed and of going hungry, of having plenty and of being in need. I can do all things through him who strengthens me" (Phil 4:12). In the coronavirus outbreak facing us we may be able to say with the apostle Paul: I know what it is like to face the uncertainty of each day, afraid that I may contract the coronavirus and hearing the news that other people are infected with it. But there is one thing that I know: that whether I contract it or not, I can get though this crisis because Christ strengthens me every day.

TRUST

Trust means having confidence in the power of God. "Trust in the LORD forever" says Isa 26:4. Why should we trust in God? Isaiah gives the following reasons: "Trust in God because He will act against the inequity between the wealth and the lofty and the poor and the needy. He will bring judgement, righteousness, and justice to the land and will level the playing field against the wicked and the adversaries" (Isa 26:3–11).

Can we trust in the LORD to bring healing and wholeness to our land? Yes we can! The God who parted the Red Sea for the children of Israel and raised Christ from the dead to resurrection is the same God who can give us new hope and life in this time of coronavirus. Erik Erikson,[1] the Harvard psychologist, wrote a book about the eight stages of the life cycle. It was a masterpiece of knowledge in the literature of human development.

According to Erikson the first stage of the life cycle occurs at birth until eighteen months. Erikson describes this as a growth period when a baby experiences basic trust vs. mistrust. Trust is fostered as the parents of a young child along with a supportive and loving system communicate to the baby that "all is well" in the environment. Likewise mistrust occurs when there are negative vibes and a destructive environment generated in the life of the young child. Basic trust is the foundation for successful development as the person moves through the remaining seven stages of the life cycle. Along with human trust comes the importance of spiritual trust. This is the substance of what we can draw on as we face the daily struggle of maintaining our health in the face of disease and illness. Of course along with our spiritual strength from the Lord comes common sense knowledge of listening to our governor, our medical doctors, our public health officer, and our medical researchers. These health resources are there for us to help us through this crisis and to achieve a sense of health and safety.

---

1. Erikson, *Identity and the Life Cycle*.

I am amazed that across the nation medical schools and research centers are testing prototype vaccines and medicines to combat the coronavirus. The genius of American medicine and the prestige of Harvard Medical School and Harvard School of Public Health, the University of California Medical Schools at San Francisco, Los Angeles, Davis, Irvine, and San Diego, Stanford Medical School, the Mayo and Cleveland Clinics, and the research facilities of drug companies along with medical researchers around the world are cooperating and marshalling their resources and knowledge to find a vaccine to combat the effects of the coronavirus. Surely the hand of God is behind these efforts. We can trust in the LORD and in these human efforts by the best medical minds of the world to achieve a breakthrough cure in the end.

PEACE

Isaiah 26:12 starts: "O LORD, you will ordain peace for us . . ." and declares: ". . . you have increased the nation . . . you have enlarged all the borders of the land" (Isa 26:15). The importance of achieving peace and increasing the growth of a nation are underscored by Isaiah in these verses. In our perspective peace is the absence of war and our most desirable existence as a nation. The coronavirus has been considered a war against an invisible enemy without weaponry or defense. These are wartime conditions which demand around-the-clock production, vigilance, skilled talent, and common sense. I remember as a child during World War II that my family used ration coupons for food and gasoline, practiced air raid drills, and closed the lights during evenings. Likewise demands have been made for us during the coronavirus outbreak: sheltering at home, social distancing, no visitors, and washing hands. This is the price of peace and safety that we must pay to stay healthy and alive.

When the Second World War ended in Europe with the defeat of Nazi Germany there were celebrations in every town in the United States. I remember that our family went to the downtown of Hamilton, Ohio, and threw confetti, cheered, and hugged each other because we were all relieved that the war ended. So it will be when the coronavirus has been controlled and the governor gives the "all clear" directive that we can resume our normal living. We will be so relieved and happy when we will be able to worship again together as a congregation. There will be peace of mind and heart in the lives of people. There will be lessons learned and remembered. There will be peace with God and peace on earth, goodwill to men and women. As the Christian hymn says about peace: "When Peace like a river Attendeth my way; When Sorrow like sea billows row; Whatever my lot, Thou hast taught me to say, It is Well, It is Well, With my Soul; It is Well, With my Soul; It is Well. It is Well. With my Soul." We need the peace which passes all understanding, the peace which comes from God so that we can assure ourselves that all is well with our souls.

LEADERSHIP

Leadership is an important part of our local and national fabric. The year 2020 is important for our church and country. Our church is conducting a pastoral search to identify the next leader who will take the church to a new and higher level. Certainly the church needs a leader who can relate to children, youth, young adults, married couples, and seniors. It is also important to select a person who has biblical and theological insights and teaching knowledge, preaching skills to declare the Word of God in an interesting way and connect life experiences and biblical truths together, and pastoral care and counseling to work with individuals, married couples, and families. Yes, leadership with a vision is important in the development of an effective pastor.

At the same time we are beginning a presidential election with congressional seats and state and local races culminating in voting this coming November. We need leaders at the local, state, and national levels to guide us and move America toward recovery and greater levels of growth. Who will we elect as our president for 2020-2024? That person has the task to restore our economic stability, build public work jobs and educate and retrain the unemployed, reconnect us with other nations through treaties and alliances, maintain our healthcare treatment and research programs, pledge to be a person of truth and integrity, and provide for the general welfare of all Americans and all who seek to become citizens of this country.

This will be a moment of importance for the life of our church and nation. Be prepared to make your contribution and input into this process. Be ready to chose persons who believe in strength, trust, and peace. Select a leader and be a leader yourself.

PASTORAL PRAYER

Dear God, You have guided us so far on this journey of faith in the midst of disease and illness and we trust you to continue to be with us. We mourn the loss of life and the suffering and frustration that we have had to cope with in our community, state, and nation. We pray that you will free us in this time to relax, enjoy each other, and find gratitude in the small and simple life that we lead in our homes and neighborhood with our loved ones. Help us to call and communicate with our family, friends, relatives, and acquaintances scattered throughout the country. May our love for you and for them be foremost in our life and being. We know that we are finite and frail human beings but we ask that you will fill us with your love and care. Help us as we read the Bible. Show us passages from your written Word to help us as we walk our daily path. Encourage us to spend moments in prayer for our needs and the wants of others.

Help us in our daily chores: protect us as we shop in our grocery stores, pump the gas for our car, take our daily walk, and work around the yard. Help us to exercise and appreciate the small things of living. Help us to take a nap and to rest our body. Help us to read a good book or a favorite magazine. Be with us as we watch our TV programs to learn new information and to form a positive and insightful perspective on what is happening in our community and nation. Protect those who have been unjustly injured and save us from racism, sexism, homophobia, and agism. Help us to love others and care for them as we would love and care for ourselves and our family.

Be with our church. How we miss our brothers and sisters in Christ and long to see them. Help our church leaders to devise a plan of safety and health so that we can come together again and worship you in our church sanctuary. Continue to be with our members and friends. Watch over those who are ill and sick. We pray for Hazel that you will be with her in her struggle with cancer and that you will sustain her faith in you; for Risa that you will strengthen her as she copes with her stroke; for Jan and her struggle with Parkinson's disease; for Lorrie and her stroke recovery; and for Melanie and her heart condition. Be with their families who care for them.

Keep those in our church school and for the church school teachers who shepherd them. Bless our Bible study groups, our consistory, and our pastoral search committee and those who minister in our midst in the name of Christ. For the service that each one gives in cooking, cleaning, and giving we thank you for them. Be with our unmet needs and our future longings. In the name of Christ we pray. Amen.

CHAPTER 10

GOD WILL DO AMAZING THINGS
Isaiah 29:13–24 (June 21, 2020)

Scripture Reading. The Lord said: Because these people draw near with their mouths and honor me with their lips, while their hearts are far from me, and their worship of me is a human commandment learned by rote; so I will again do amazing things with this people, shocking and amazing. The wisdom of their wise shall perish, and the discernment of the discerning shall be hidden.

Ha! You who hide a plan too deep for the LORD, whose deeds are in the dark, and who say, "Who sees us? Who knows us?" You turn things upside down! Shall the potter be regarded as the clay? Shall the thing made say to its maker, "He did not make me," or the thing formed say of the one who formed it, "He has no understanding?"

Shall not Lebanon in a very little while become a fruitful field, and the fruitful field be regarded as a forest? On that day the deaf shall hear the words of a scroll, and out of their gloom and darkness the eyes of the blind shall see. The meek shall obtain fresh joy in the LORD, and the neediest of people shall exult in the Holy One of Israel. For the tyrant shall be no more, and the scoffer shall cease to be, all those alert to do evil shall be cut off—those who cause a person to lose a lawsuit, who set a trap for the arbiter in the gate, and without grounds deny justice to the one in the right.

Therefore thus says the LORD, who redeemed Abraham, concerning the house of Jacob; No longer shall Jacob be ashamed, no longer shall his face grow pale. For when he sees his children, the works of his hands, in his midst, they will sanctify his name; they will sanctify the Holy One

of Jacob, and will stand in awe of the God of Israel. And those who err in spirit will come to understanding, and those who grumble will accept instruction.

Today is Father's Day and we wish all the fathers and grandfathers a great day of celebration. Do you remember when you passed from husband to father? Was it the time when you heard that your wife was expecting a baby or the moment that you saw and held the newborn in the birthing room? What have been your high moments of fatherhood? Perhaps it was helping your wife make baby formula, changing diapers, and getting up in the early hours of the morning to comfort a crying child. Or was it when you saw your baby starting to crawl and later walk, speak the first words (was it "ma ma" or "da da"?), and eat on his/her own? Or can you remember when your child went to preschool, first grade, or graduated from elementary, middle, and high school? What about completing college, being at the wedding of your son or daughter, or repeating the cycle by becoming a grandfather?

For all of these wonderful milestones in life, we are thankful for being a father on this Father's Day 2020. However, this has been a difficult period for many fathers who may be out of work, depressed, and disillusioned by business closure, or taking a pay cut to keep a job in the midst of this economic shut down. This may be a down period for fathers who need encouragement, support, and reassurance. How can I be helpful as a retired grandfather when I know that even in my family my sons and sons-in-law are struggling with the economic realities of pandemic life? I can listen and give support to you. Perhaps we need grandfathers to help fathers in this economic downturn. Be a helpful hand, a listening ear, and a lender to those fathers who need help this Father's Day.

AMAZING GOD AND AMAZING GRACE

We have an amazing God! He created the heavens and the earth (Gen 1:1–5). How beautiful and majestic is God's creation for all of us to enjoy and marvel at the mountains, valleys, glaciers, and the oceans. He made man and woman "in his image," giving them spiritual awareness that there is a God who is vitally concerned about us (Gen 1:26). He was the God of Abraham, Isaac, and Jacob, who formed the nation of Israel from which came our Lord Jesus Christ. He freed the people of Israel from slavery and bondage out of Egypt and gave Moses the Ten Commandments and the Torah (the first five books of the Old Testament). He was with the judges and the kings of Israel and Judah and constantly called them back to faithfulness to himself.

His *hesed* (Hebrew word for lovingkindness and faithfulness) was always present as the people of Israel went astray from God and worshiped pagan idols. God was with the prophets from Amos and Micah through Isaiah and Jeremiah to Joel and Malachi who preached judgement and repentance and the promise of the Messiah. And the Word became flesh and dwelled among us, full of grace and truth (John 1:14).

This Jesus died for our sins and was raised from the dead and brought the church into this present age. He gathered Matthew, Mark, Luke, and John to write the Gospels; Paul, Peter, James, and John to pen the Epistles; and John to end the New Testament with the Revelation. He guided the early church fathers to keep the beliefs of the church, raised up Martin Luther and John Calvin to reform the church, formed theological seminaries to educate those called into ministry, and brought the gospel to Europe, England, and the Americas. This amazing God is still with us, hovering over the church, calling men and women into full-time ministry, sustaining our nation in its low moments and high points, and watching our small and strong congregation.

From this amazing God flows amazing grace. What is the grace of God? It is "God's free and unmerited favor and love toward us." We love him because he first loved us. This is why the grace of God is so amazing because he loves us with an everlasting love although we do not deserve his love. As the Christian hymn testifies: "Amazing Grace, How sweet the sound, that saved a wretch like me, I once was lost, but now am found, Was blind but now I see." Many centuries before John Newton wrote "Amazing Grace," the prophet Isaiah talked about this amazing God who can do amazing feats for the people of Israel. Isaiah 29:13–24 is a passage which promises that God will perform a makeover on the people of Israel. God says: ". . . I will again do amazing things with this people, shocking and amazing" (Isa 29:14). The scripture is divided into three parts: the actions of the people (Isa 29:13–16), the amazing acts of God (Isa 29:17–21), and the transformation of God's children (Isa 29:22–24). As you read this passage in Isaiah, you will be amazed at God and his grace.

THE ACTIONS OF THE PEOPLE

There is an old adage: You will know a person by his/her actions. For the people of Israel they were going through their religious motions but they were not sincere in their intentions. The actions of the people against God are reprehensible: pretending to honor God with their lips while their hearts are far away, going through the motions of worship, lacking wisdom and discernment, doing dark deeds, and placing one's self higher than God. Actions speak louder than words. The actions of the people of Israel were out of sync with the will of God. Israel was more unfaithful to the LORD than it was faithful to him (Isa 29:13). Isaiah called them on their pretense. Did they look at their behavior and realize that they were out of touch with God? Isaiah calls the people of Israel back to faithfulness to God (Isa 29:15 and 16). God is always faithful to us.

God is more faithful to us than we are to him. The hymn, "Great is Thy Faithfulness," reminds us: "Great is Thy Faithful, O God My Father, There is no shadow or turning with Thee, Thou changes not, Thy compassion they fail not, As thou hast been, Thou forever will be: Great is Thy Faithfulness, Great is Thy Faithfulness, Morning by morning, New Mercies I see, All that I need, Thy Hand hath provided, Great is Thy Faithfulness. LORD unto me." This inspiring song is a reminder that God is always faithful to us despite the fact that we forget his faithfulness unto us. I love this hymn. It is my favorite. It affirms the faithfulness of God through the seasons of life. I have sung it in my youth, my young adult years, my married life, my career as a teacher, counselor, and student of theology, and now in my later years.

God has been faithful to me although there are many times when I have forgotten God and gone my own way. Yet God has a plan for me and has organized my life so that there have been many amazing things that have happened to me. More than I could fathom and dream, God's faithfulness and blessings have been a part of my life.

How does the faithfulness of God apply to the COVID-19 crisis that we have been facing today? We have endured this coronavirus outbreak for four months (March–June 2020) as it has peaked to unprecedented heights. In the process each of us has known at least a single person who has been seriously ill or has died from this disease. In contrast to the people of Israel cited by Isa 29, the American people have responded to this crisis and the need for police reform with overwhelming faith in God, love of country, ingenuity of spirit, and creative solutions to these challenges posed by this medical emergency and police brutality and overreach crisis, with demonstrations, neighborly care, and thoughtfulness. A double crisis like this has brought people together, a nation united, a stronger faith and trust in the LORD, and messages and acts of love. Let us keep close to the LORD and not forget him. In times of plenty and times of want, in good times and bad times, may we forever remember and seek the LORD while he may be found.

THE AMAZING ACTS OF GOD

Despite our actions we have an amazing God who performs amazing acts. G. Ernest Wright,[1] Professor Emeritus of Old Testament at Harvard Divinity School, wrote a small monograph entitled *God Who Acts*. In his book Dr. Wright recalls the many actions of God who breaks into human history and performs the mighty acts of God which are a major part of the history of Israel. Isaiah reaffirms the acts of God for Israel. Isaiah 29:17–21 promises that God will act and remake the people of Israel from bad to good: Lebanon will become a fruitful field, the deaf shall hear and the blind will see, the meek shall obtain fresh joy from the Lord, the neediest people shall exult in God, the tyrant shall be no more and the scoffer shall cease to be, and the unjust shall be judged. In other words, there will be a total makeover of the people and nation. This is good news of which the people of Israel needed to hear from God through Isaiah.

The situation shall be transformed by God. Can God change the heart of a person and the situation of a country for the better? Is God powerful and strong to remake the life of a person, a community, and a nation? The prophet Isaiah believed it could be done when he wrote about the amazing acts of God in human history. Biblical theologians coin the German term, *Heilsgeschichte*, as salvation history, meaning the mighty acts of God breaking into human history. Can God break into history and alter the course of events? Perhaps God is doing this as we witness the progression of the coronavirus as it attacks the health of people simultaneously in different countries around the world and yet is met with the doctors, nurses, and medical researchers who are on the frontlines of the resistance. God is there fighting alongside with these healthcare workers who are battling this disease. His healing hands are present in the hospitals around the world. God's salvation history is here with us. If God is with us, who can be against us? We need to see the amazing acts of God through medical science which has saved thousands of people in this pandemic and yet we are in sorrow for the families who have lost loved ones at the same time.

THE TRANSFORMATION OF GOD'S CHILDREN

When the faithful God acts in amazing ways, the people will be transformed by the power and healing of God. Isaiah 29:23 and 24 says: "For when he sees his children, the work of my hands, in his midst, they will sanctify my name; they will sanctify the Holy One of Jacob, and will stand in awe of the

---

1. G. E. Wright, *God Who Acts*.

God of Israel, And those who err in spirit will come to understanding. And those who grumble will accept instruction." The key phrase in this verse is *the work of my hands*. That is, as the hands of God work in the lives of people, there will be an understanding and transformation. The prophet Isaiah sees the transformation and the change of the people at the sight and presence of God. No one has seen God at any time, so saith the Bible, but can we see the presence of God in the human healing acts of doctors and nurses during this pandemic?

Jesus said if you have done it unto the least of these my brethren, you have done it unto me. Is Jesus walking and ministering through these human agents of healing or am I stretching the message of the gospel of Christ and the meaning of salvation as wholeness and healing too far? Perhaps I am spreading heresy when I identify the acts of the Great Physician, Jesus Christ, with the countless acts of administering medications, bedside comfort, and placing ventilators on the faces of ill persons who are having a hard time breathing.

I hope that you see the connections that I am trying to make between these biblical truths and insights and the present coronavirus crisis that we are facing in the United States. When we get past this crisis we will be transformed by the power of God and the human sacrifice of these healthcare workers. Our country will never be the same. We will have an increased love for each other and an appreciation of living another day as a miracle and a privilege that is richer than the wealth of the world. In the end we will be a changed and transformed people who aspire to be the best and the finest and closer to the LORD.

GOD WILL DO AMAZING THINGS IN THE COMING DAYS AHEAD

Do you believe that God will do amazing things in the coming days ahead in your life, your family, your community, and your nation? Looking back on my life God brought a series of people into my life which influenced me in significant ways. There was Carol Chung Song, a Westmont College graduate, who was my Director of Religious Education at First Chinese Church of Christ, Honolulu, Hawaii, and who taught me how to study the Bible, how to lead a youth meeting, how to give a testimony, and how to sing in a choir. There was Merill F. Heiser, Professor of English, and Winfield Nagley, Professor of Philosophy, of the University of Hawaii, who gave me a broad background in literature and philosophy and undergirded my education. There was David Alan Hubbard, George Eldon Ladd, and Geoffrey

Bromiley of Fuller Theological Seminary who provided me with biblical and theological knowledge which helped me in my studies and preaching preparation. There was Howard J. Clinebell Jr and Joseph Hough of Claremont School of Theology who sharpened my pastoral counseling and psychology and theological ethics skills. There was Ted Ogoshi, pastor of Makiki Christian Church who was my pastoral counseling mentor and my own pastor. There was Arthur Blum and Gregory St. Lawrence O'Brien of Case Western Reserve University, Mandel School of Applied Social Sciences, who gave me expertise in social welfare and healthcare policy.

There was California State University, Sacramento, and the Council on Social Work Education which provided me an opportunity to teach cultural diversity and social policy, write my articles and books, and serve as a resource to accredit and guide social work programs across the country. There has been my wife, Joyce, and children (Lori, Jonathan, Amy, and Matthew) and grandchildren (Riley, Alyssa, Evan, Brennen, Trevor, Jack, Joel, Jay, and Ally) who have been with me in my achievements and crisis periods. My family has been my anchor. I have been amazed at the amazing grace of God who has performed amazing things in my life. I hope that you have experienced amazing acts of God in your life.

I am sure that each of us can point to people who have entered our life and have enriched our well-being. But beyond our own selves I believe that God has done, is doing, and will do amazing things in the life of our church, community, and nation. Recently Sacramento, California, mayor Darrell Steinberg proposed three areas to respond to the need for police reform: 1) an Inspector General in the City's Office of Public Safety to investigate police department use of force incidents that result in serious injury or death, 2) a Community Resource Corps composed of mental health and social work specialists who would respond to 911 calls that do not involve a crime, and 3) a clear delineation of duties for police officers. These ideas will go a long way to balance the overload placed on our police department.

This coronavirus pandemic has brought us together as one nation and as nations facing a common threat to civilization itself. Our doctors and nurses, president and governors, and our neighbors and friends have stepped up to meet this crisis in a marvelous way. We have seen the hands of God in our midst. God will do amazing things in the coming days ahead. The research and testing for a vaccine for COVID-19 have been fast tracked and we pray will be available in a safe and medically proven way. Surely the Lord God is behind these efforts. Yes, God will do amazing things.

PASTORAL PRAYER

Our Father who art in heaven, we thank you that you are an amazing God who has done amazing feats in our lives. You have created us from our mothers, given us life and growth, and watched over us from birth to maturity. You have blessed us along the way with the love and protection of our parents, with our brothers, sisters, cousins, and with grandparents, aunts, and uncles who have guided us and contributed to our well-being. You have blessed us with teachers who have filled our life with knowledge and skill and have prepared us to graduate to our careers. We look out upon this world and look to you to lead us as we make choices and decisions in our lives. As we look back to what has happened to us we see your amazing grace which has guided us and sense your amazing presence in our present moments of living. How truly thankful we are that you have been the amazing God of direction and that we can trust in the Lord who will direct our paths.

We thank you for our fathers who have provided for us and who have shared their wisdom and guidance along the way. Bless them on this Father's Day as they assume their role as protector and guide. Help our country as it continues to protest injustice and needless death and destruction of lives and property. Bring us to our senses. Raise up strong and compassionate leaders who are sensitive to the personal and social problems of people and who promote programs of help, assistance, and aid to their problems of living. Save us from racism, bigotry, and our egos. Move us together in the spirit of love of country and love for each other. Help our fathers who lead and protect our families that in their own way may lead and guide the present and the future of this great nation. May from the ranks of our fathers and mothers come men and woman who will become involved in the social, economic, and political problems of our communities, state, and nation. God, mobilize us to be better individuals and citizens of our country.

We think of our church on this Father's Day and thank you for the faith of our fathers who kept the faith and passed it down to us. May we spread this faith to our children and to others. Continue to watch over us and keep us in the shelter of your love. Be with those who strive to live in the simplicity of this time, who provide for their family, and strive to be good fathers and mothers, grandfathers and grandmothers. We pray for those who are elderly, who are ill, and who need aid and assistance. Please provide for their needs.

We want to remember the passing of our dear sister in Christ, Hazel, who died last Sunday from pancreatic cancer. Be with her three sons (Craig, Kent, and Scott) and their families in this time of loss. May they know your presence. We also want to uphold Baldwin and Patricia who lost his brother, Raymond, unexpectedly and suddenly to bacterial septic shock. Be with them and the rest of his extended family who grieved the loss of Baldwin's mother last October and his two aunts and now his brother in the last thirty days. Help them as they suffer the loss of all of these loved ones so closely together. In the name of Christ, we pray. Amen.

CHAPTER 11

THE PRAYERS OF HEZEKIAH AND THE ANSWER FROM GOD

Isaiah 37:14–20, 30–38; 38:1–8 (June 28, 2020)

Scripture Reading. Hezekiah received a letter from the hand of the messengers and read it; then Hezekiah went up to the house of the LORD and spread it before the LORD. And Hezekiah prayed to the LORD, saying: "O LORD of hosts, God of Israel, who are enthroned above the cherubim, you are God, you alone, of all the kingdoms of the earth, you have made heaven and earth. Incline your ear, O LORD, and hear; open your eyes, O LORD, and see; hear all the words of Sennacherib, which he has sent to mock the living God. Truly, O LORD, the kings of Assyria have laid waste all the nations and their lands, and have hurled their gods into the fire, though they were no gods, but the work of human hands—wood and stone—and so they were destroyed. So now, O LORD our God, save us from his hand, so that all the kingdoms of the earth may know that you alone are the LORD."

And this shall be the sign for you: This year eat what grows of itself, and in the second year what springs from that; then in the third year sow, reap, plant vineyards, and eat their fruit. The surviving remnant of the house of Judah shall again take root downward, and bear fruit upward; for from Jerusalem a remnant shall go out, and from Mount Zion a band of survivors. The zeal of the LORD of hosts will do this.

"Therefore thus says the LORD concerning the king of Assyria: He shall not come into this city, shoot an arrow there, come before it with a shield, or cast up a siege ramp against it. By the way that he came, by the same way he shall return; he shall not come into this city, says the LORD. For I will defend this city to save it, for my own sake and for the sake of my servant David."

Then the angel of the LORD set out and struck down one hundred eighty-five thousand in the camp of the Assyrians; when morning dawned, they were all dead bodies. Then King Sennacherib of Assyria left, went home, and lived at Nineveh. As he was worshiping in the house of his god Nisroch, his sons Adrammelech and Sharezer killed him with the sword, and they escaped into the land of Ararat. His son Esar-haddon succeeded him.

In those days Hezekiah became sick and was at the point of death. The prophet Isaiah son of Amoz came to him, and said to him, "Thus says the LORD: Set your house in order, for you shall die; you shall not recover." Then Hezekiah turned his face to the wall, and prayed to the LORD: "Remember now, O LORD, I implore you, how I have walked before you in faithfulness with a whole heart, and have done what is good in your sight." And Hezekiah wept bitterly.

Then the word of the LORD came to Isaiah: "Go and say to Hezekiah, thus says the LORD, The God of your ancestor David: I have heard your prayer. I have seen your tears; I will add fifteen years to your life. I will deliver you and this city out of the hand of the king of Assyria, and defend this city.

This is the sign to you from the LORD, that the LORD will do this thing that he has promised; See, I will make the shadow cast by the declining sun on the dial of Ahaz turn back ten steps." So the sun turned back on the dial the ten steps by which it had declined.

There is the separation of church and state in the United States of America so that no one religion can dominate the political and democratic scene. Yet every year there are presidential and governor prayer breakfasts which bring political and religious leaders together to talk about spiritual and national issues and to ask for prayer regarding these concerns. US currency says: "In God We Trust." The United States Senate has a chaplain who opens each session with a prayer and there are chaplains in many prisons and hospitals across the country.

Presidents have rarely declared a National Day of Prayer except in major events. I recall that President Roosevelt prayed a national prayer of deliverance and protection when Allied Forces stormed the Normandy beaches on D-Day in 1944. But these are not normal times. Rather these are unusual times when there is an international pandemic spreading across every nation and gravely affecting the United States of America.

In the midst of the 128,000 casualties, the valor of doctors, nurses, and other first responders, the essential workers who have held the frontlines, and the many acts of kindness between neighbors and communities, the president of the United States should soon declare a National Day of Prayer, asking Almighty God for deliverance, strength, and thanksgiving for the many acts of love and caring which the American people have given to those afflicted by this virus. Perhaps you can influence this to happen in our country. It seems appropriate for us to have a National Day of Prayer in light of the suffering borne by the people of this country.

PRAYER AND HOW TO PRAY

Prayer is a powerful force where we are able to talk to God. In the privacy and quietness of our homes we are able to communicate our feelings to the Lord. I believe that God listens and accepts the prayers of everyone. We come to God in prayer and thank him for the many blessings that he has given us. We make requests about ourselves and others who have needs and wants. We ask God to forgive us for the sins that we have committed in our lives. We pray constantly and daily. We have many prayers to pray to God regarding this coronavirus which is affecting the people that we know in our communities.

How should we pray? The disciples of Jesus asked him this question early in the New Testament. Jesus gives us a model for prayer when he taught us the Lord's Prayer. Protestants and Catholics pray the Lord's Prayer every Sunday in churches across this country. Let us analyze this prayer in order to learn how we pray (Matt 6:9–13):

- Our Father in heaven (focus on God the Father who guides, protects, and provides for us)
- Hallowed be your name (think about the holiness [sacredness and worthiness] of God)
- Your kingdom come (recognize that the kingdom of God is the reign of God in our lives and that one day God will establish his rule on earth)
- Your will be done, on earth as it is in heaven (admit that God's will often may not be our will and that God works in mysterious ways, his wonders to perform)

- Give us this day our daily bread (see that God nurtures and feeds us in many ways: our jobs, our food, and other provisions)
- Forgive us our debts (sins) as we also have forgiven our debtors (those who have sinned against us) (recognize that we need the forgiveness of our own sins and help to forgive those people who have violated us)
- Do not bring us to the time of trial (lead us not into temptation when we might commit an act of unkindness or a mistake that we will regret later)
- But rescue us from the evil one (don't let the Devil get the best of us but flee evil in every form)
- For thine is the kingdom and the power and the glory forever, Amen (thank God I have the resources of the kingdom of God and the power of God motivating me and the glory of God to shine a light on my path forever and forever; Hallelujah [praise God], Amen [so be it God])

Now that we have learned how to pray, we turn our attention on the two prayers that King Hezekiah prayed to the Lord in Isa 37 and 38 and the answer from God.

THE FIRST PRAYER OF KING HEZEKIAH AND THE ANSWER FROM GOD

King Hezekiah (his name means "God is my strength") was twenty-five years old when he became king of Judah (701 BC) and reigned for twenty-nine years. He was a just and religious leader who respected the Lord. In Isa 37:14–20 Hezekiah receives a letter from King Tirhakah of Ethiopia warning Hezekiah of imminent invasion by King Sennacherib of Assyria. The Assyrian forces were fighting and defeating the neighboring countries surrounding Israel. King Hezekiah knew that his nation would be the next country to be invaded by Sennacherib, a brutal foe who totally would destroy Israel. What did Hezekiah do? He went to the house of the Lord, spread himself on the ground, and prayed to the Lord for guidance and mercy.

Listen to his prayer: "O LORD of hosts, God of Israel, who are enthroned above the cherubim, you are God, you alone, of all the kingdoms of the earth. Incline your ear, O LORD, and hear; open your eyes, O LORD, and see; hear all the words of Sennacherib, which he has sent to mock the living God. Truly, O LORD, the kings of Assyria have laid waste all the nations and their lands, and have hurled their gods into the fire, though they were no gods, but the work of human hands—wood and stone—and so they were destroyed. So now, O LORD our God, save us from his hands, so that all the kingdoms of the earth may know that you alone are the LORD" (Isa 37:16–20).

King Hezekiah's prayer is focused on the personhood of God, particularly the majesty and splendor of the LORD. In contrast to the human images of the gods of the Assyrians, the LORD our God is above all other gods. Hezekiah has only one thought: to save Judah so that all nations will know that the LORD is God. This single request for salvation from the enemy is the essence of Hezekiah's prayer.

Does God answer the request of his prayer? Yes, God does. He offers a sign for the people of Judah: a plentiful harvest for three years. He promises that Judah will survive the threat as a band of survivors and pledges that the king of Assyria and his forces will not set foot in Jerusalem. God will defend and save the people and the city for his sake and for the sake of David. (Isa 37:30–35).

What does God do? The angel of the LORD strikes down 185,000 Assyrian soldiers. King Sennacherib of Assyria withdraws and returns to his country where he is killed by his two sons and is no longer a menace for King Hezekiah and Judah. God answers the prayer of Hezekiah in the face of danger and an enemy (Isa 37:36–38).

What does the first prayer of Hezekiah and the answer of God say to the coronavirus, our enemy, in our present situation? Think of the virus as a multi-prone invasion force like the threatening forces of Sennacherib who destroyed the neighboring nations around Judah and who was poised to attack King Hezekiah and his nation shortly. The real truth is that the coronavirus has already pierced the United States as an attacking force in a number of places: first the Northwest (the state of Washington), then the Northeast (specifically New York City), next the South (New Orleans), and finally the Pacific Coast (particularly Los Angeles and Southern California).

There is a surge of the virus in Southern and Western states (e.g., Florida, Texas, Oklahoma, and Arizona). Medical personnel, medical facilities, and medical supplies are marshalled at these key attack points to stem the tide and to offer a defensive strategy. Our offensive strategy is the useful discovery of existing medicines and the development of a vaccine which will inoculate the body. The invasion has begun. The battle is raging. There have been mounting casualties. The fighting supplies are dwindling and yet holding. It is all-out war. Victory is not yet in sight.

Like King Hezekiah we need to go to the house of the LORD, spread ourselves on the ground, and pray to the LORD for salvation. As Hezekiah prayed: save us (Isa 37:20), so we the people of America and the world pray: Save us, dear LORD, God of Abraham, Isaac, and Jacob, God the Father,

God the Son, and God the Holy Spirit. God answered the first prayer of Hezekiah, killed the enemy, and averted defeat and destruction. God can do it again for America although we have suffered casualties. Let us pray to the Lord. May this coronavirus falter and die. Give our nation the victory and salvation from you.

THE SECOND PRAYER OF KING HEZEKIAH AND THE ANSWER FROM GOD

King Hezekiah faced another threat after the near-missed invasion of Assyria. He became sick and was at the point of death (Isa 38:1). Even the prophet Isaiah came to the king and said: "Set your house in order, for you shall die; you shall not recover" (Isa 38:2). Facing a terminal illness and death, what did Hezekiah do? He prayed to the LORD a short prayer: "Remember now, O LORD, I implore you, how I have walked before you in faithfulness with a whole heart, and have done what is good in your sight" (Isa 38:3). His remarkable prayer brought a swift response from the LORD: "I have heard your prayer, I have seen your tears; I will add fifteen years to your life. I will deliver you and this city . . . and defend this city" (Isa 38:5 and 6). As a sign of God's promise to this answered prayer, God moves the sun back on the sundial ten steps backwards (Isa 38:7 and 8).

How remarkable and marvelous God was toward Hezekiah to grant him extra years of his life in the face of death because he turned to prayer and reminded God that he was a faithful man of God who served him with his whole heart and did what was good in the sight of the LORD. Perhaps God gives us borrowed time in our lives. Every new dawning of a day is a gift from God for us to treasure and enjoy. As the Westminster Catechism declares: What is the chief end of man? The chief end of man is to love God and to enjoy him forever.

Have you been spared from the coronavirus? Was it by chance? Did you take extra precautions? Did you catch the virus and recover from it? Why were you healed? Why were you saved? These questions come to mind as we read about King Hezekiah's reprieve from God.

If you are a survivor of this virus, make it your goal to do something good and pleasing in the sight of God for another person, your church and community, and your nation. Think of a creative way that you can give back for the blessings that you received: a healthy body and healing and wholeness in your life. There are so many wonderful ways that we can turn the tragedy of this disease into an opportunity for life and living. Do something today to make a difference for America.

PRAYER REQUESTS

We have called for a National Day of Prayer, explained what is prayer, analyzed the Lord's Prayer, and examined the two prayer requests and God's answers to King Hezekiah. What are some of your prayer requests that you consider important during this time? Let me give you space to write them down:

Worldwide Prayer Requests and National Prayer Requests

Community Prayer Requests and Neighborhood Prayer Requests

Family Prayer Requests and Personal Prayer Requests

Miscellaneous Prayer Requests and Prayers of Thanksgiving

Prayers of Confession and Forgiveness and Prayers of Praise to God

Prayers for Special Persons in our Lives and Prayers for our Leaders

PASTORAL PRAYER

Dear God, We thank you that we can come to you in prayer. We thank you for your goodness and mercy. We praise you for your Son, Jesus Christ our LORD, who came to save us from our sins and who died on the cross as the redeeming atonement for us. We pray that you will see us through this coronavirus pandemic and that you will keep us safe and healthy. We thank you for the lessons of prayer which we have learned today and we pray that you will constantly teach us how to pray more effectively. We remember the prayers of King Hezekiah who asked that his country be spared from invasion and strife and that he might live longer to serve you. We thank you that you answered his prayers and that you gave him and his nation your grace and blessing.

We pray for our country in its time of need that you will oversee the affairs of this nation and that truth and justice may prevail in all corners of our government. Be with our church with the many needs that confront it: a new pastor; the needs of members and friends with their personal, family, and spiritual concerns; those who are ill and in pain; youth who are resting during the summer and who will be returning to school in the fall, please protect them and their families. Teach us to pray as Jesus taught his disciples.

We pray for the family of Hazel that you will be with Craig, Kent, and Scott as they have lost their mother. May they turn to you as their source of comfort and guidance. We remember the family of Raymond that you will watch over Baldwin and Patricia and bring healing to their lives in this time of loss. We think also of the family of Diane and ask that you will be with Norma, Edward, Merrily, and other members of their extended family. May they find renewed faith and trust in the Lord. Please be with Risa who is slowly regaining movement and strength as she battles to overcome the effects of her stroke. We also pray for Melanie and for her coming heart valve repair surgery that you will guide the doctors who operate on her and that you will heal Melanie. For all those in our church who suffer pain and discomfort, help us who are strong and healthy minister to those who are ill and weak. In his name, Amen.

CHAPTER 12

A VOICE CRYING IN THE WILDERNESS

Isaiah 40:1–11 (July 5, 2020)

Scripture Reading. Comfort, O comfort my people, says your God. Speak tenderly to Jerusalem, and cry to her that she has served her term, that her penalty is paid, that she has received from the LORD's hand double for all her sins.

    A voice cries out: "In the wilderness prepare the way of the LORD, make straight in the desert a highway for our God. Every valley shall be lifted up, and every mountain and hill be made low; the uneven ground shall become level, and the rough places a plain. Then the glory of the LORD shall be revealed, and all people shall see it together, for the mouth of the LORD has spoken."

    A voice says, "Cry out!" And I said. "What shall I cry?" All people are grass, their constancy is like the flower of the field. The grass withers, the flower fades, when the breath of the LORD blows upon it; surely the people are grass. The grass withers, the flower fades, but the word of our God will stand forever. Get you up to a high mountain, O Zion, herald of good tidings; lift up your voice with strength. O Jerusalem, herald of good tidings, lift it up, do not fear; say to the cities of Judah, "Here is your God!" See, the Lord GOD comes with might, and his arm rules for him; his reward is with him, and his recompense before him. He will feed his flock like a shepherd, he will gather the lambs in his arms, and carry them in his bosom, and gently lead the mother sheep.

We are in the midst of celebrating the July Fourth weekend which commemorates the birthdate of the founding of the United States of America. In the whole history of the United States we have never experienced such a national and international pandemic of COVID-19 during the Fourth of July celebration. Unfortunately during this historical day there has been a resurgence of COVID-19 where several states (Texas, Florida, Arizona, and California) have experienced the doubling and tripling of virus cases during the last two weeks. Hospital beds in these states, particularly in ICU units, are filled to capacity.

Governors throughout the country are holding or scaling back reopening phase plans. The nation is bracing for a pandemic with ten times more of the present number of cases predicted by the Centers for Disease Control if people continue not to heed the warnings and not take precautions such as wearing a mask and maintaining social distancing. Dr. Anthony Fauci, Chief of Infectious Disease, at the Centers for Disease Control, Atlanta, Georgia, predicted 100,000 new cases per day if the American public continues at this pace. Historians will write about this American public health virus and decades later those of us who remain will tell our children and grandchildren what it was like to live in the Great Pandemic of 2020.

There will be chapters written on the disease, prevention, and treatment of COVID-19; the economic and political fallout; and the devastating implications of loss of life. But how will the church and church leaders and theologians address the impact of this coronavirus on the lives of people and the spiritual truths which we have learned from this disease? Personally I have found the messages from the Prophets series have spoken to the needs of the people of Israel and this generation of Americans who are seeking answers and turning to God.

THE PROPHECY ABOUT THE PROPHET

Isaiah 40:1–11 is a prophecy of the One who is to come, the Prophet who is a voice crying in the wilderness: Prepare ye the way of the LORD. For centuries the people of Israel waited for the fulfillment of this prophecy and for the Prophet to come. Many so-called prophets came and went and the expectations of the people were dashed with disappointment and disillusionment.

Finally the Prophet appeared in the wilderness of Israel (the rural backcountry, the hills around the river Jordan). He was a man with long hair and a beard with camel-skin clothes who was preaching a fiery message of repentance and calling people: "You brood of vipers" (You bunch of snakes). His name was John the Baptist, the forerunner of Jesus Christ.

When a person repented of his/her sins John baptized with water. He believed in full immersion of the body in the river Jordan. To this day the Baptist Church around the world practices the kind of baptism that John the Baptist performed in the time of Jesus.

John was the one who was foreseen by the prophet Isaiah in Isa 40. Luke 3:1–22 recorded the actions of John the Baptist and the reactions of the believers who followed him on his evangelistic tours. It was quite a sight to see and many throughout the country flocked to hear his message, believing that he was the One who is to come predicted by the prophet Isaiah centuries ago. In this sermon we want to examine this voice crying in the wilderness, believing that we need many voices crying in the wilderness who are preparing the way of the LORD. At the present time there is no strong voice today who is calling people to come to Christ to receive him as LORD and Savior. No Billy Graham, Charles E. Fuller, Karl Barth, or Reinhold Niebuhr. We need a modern-day John the Baptist to call America back to repentance and to the kingdom of God.

There was also another voice in the wilderness of racism crying out in our lifetime: Please, I can't breathe; Mama, help me; I can't breathe. His name was George Floyd and he was pleading for his life before every citizen in America who heard his cry for help and who responded to his plea. Since his death, thousands of people in the United States from every race and walk of life have come forward with conviction, courage, and resolve to end racism and police brutality and to reform the police and justice system of this country. George Floyd was like John the Baptist: a forerunner of conflict and change who was preparing the way for liberty and justice for all. But let us return to the mission of John who was preparing the way of the Lord foretold by the prophet Isaiah.

In this passage, Isa 40:1–11, we will focus on the following points: a comforting voice (40:1–2), a crying voice (40:3–8), and an uplifting voice (40:9–11).

A COMFORTING VOICE

The human voice is a remarkable gift from God our Creator. A newborn baby gurgles and cries to communicate needs to parents. Gradually a toddler makes sounds, forms words, and speaks in sentence as he/she listens to the conversations of parents and intuits these sounds and thoughts into one's psyche. The pitch of our voice is high, medium, or low. We use our voices in many ways: speaking words, singing melodies, making sounds and noises, listening and responding, thinking and speaking, knowing and communicating, remembering and sharing, and laughing and crying. When we want to train our voices for serious singing or speaking, we take voice lessons and speech classes. Our voice is such an important part of our life. We lead our life through and with our voice.

It is a reassuring thought that Isa 40:1 and 2 begins with a comforting voice: "Comfort, O comfort my people, says your God. Speak tenderly to Jerusalem . . ." God's voice is a voice of comfort in the midst of destruction, separation, and loneliness. Isaiah foresees that the people of Judah will be captured and taken into Babylonian exile, many never to see their homeland again. Comfort is the message from God.

Remember the times when we needed comfort as a child: waking from a bad dream, scared of the night, injured and scraped up after falling from our bike in the street, and receiving racist slurs from mean individuals. Recall our adolescent and adult years when comfort was so valued: losing a job, failing to get a promotion, being rejected by our boyfriend or girlfriend, recovering from a major operation or illness, loss of a parent or sibling, or separation due to divorce or death. All of us need comfort and it is readily available from our family, friends, and God

As we undergo the stress of the coronavirus, particularly if we are elderly or are parents worried about the health and well-being of our children, we need the comfort of God and the immediate actions of our doctors and nurses. Comforting ourselves and others is so important during this pandemic, particularly comforting the families of those who have persons stricken with this illness and comforting the exhausted healthcare workers who are on the frontlines of care in our hospitals and medical centers. Being a voice of comfort is so important today.

A CRYING VOICE

It is okay to cry. Women cry easily because it is a natural emotion for them. Men have a hard time crying because they are taught that crying is not manly and is a sign of weakness. Crying is important because it is an expression of human emotion. However, the crying voice in this passage is not so much a voice of crying but a crying out voice unto God and to the people of Israel. Isaiah 40:3–8 is a crying out regarding the glory of the LORD and the endurance and guarantee of the Word of God: "A voice cries out in the wilderness prepare the way of the LORD, make straight in the desert a highway for our God" (Isa 40:3). "Then the glory of the LORD shall be revealed, and all people shall see it together . . ." (Isa 40:5). ". . . the word of our God will stand forever" (Isa 40:8).

When John the Baptist appeared in the wilderness preaching and proclaiming, Luke 3:3-6 quotes this passage in Isaiah and asserts that this prophecy was fulfilled with the coming of John who was the voice crying in the wilderness, preparing the way of the Lord. John was a crying out voice who was announcing the coming of the LORD, Jesus Christ, into the lives of the people of Israel and all nations of the world. John the Baptist was the announcer. Jesus of Nazareth was the main attraction and star.

It is okay to cry out good news. The meaning of gospel is good news. The Christian hymn, "O Zion Haste," says: "Publish glad tidings, tidings of peace, Tidings of Jesus, Redemption and Release." We cry out the good news of the coming of Christ and we cry out and ask God to protect us from the virus and to heal those who are afflicted of it.

God's voice and our voices are important because God hears our voices through prayer and we hear the voice of God as we read the Scriptures. God speaks to us through the written Word of God. In the midst of this coronavirus we cry out to God for help and he answers us. We cry out to the LORD when a relative or friend is ill or dying because we have a friend in Jesus. As the hymn, "What a Friend We Have in Jesus," says: "What a Friend we have in Jesus, All our sins and griefs to bear. What a privilege to carry, Everything to God in prayer."

He is good and knows the Father who is in heaven. Why has this virus come into the world and why has it taken so many people? We do not know the answer, but we can cope and find a vaccine to overcome it. The best medical research minds and centers of the world are racing to find an antidote. We will find a cure. We shall overcome. We are more than conquerors through Christ who loved us and gave himself for us.

AN UPLIFTING VOICE

Isaiah 40:9-11 is an uplifting message of good tidings and news: "O Jerusalem, herald of good tidings . . . 'Here is your God!' See, the Lord GOD comes with might, and his arm rules for him; his reward is with him, and his recompense before him. He will feed his flock like a shepherd, he will gather the lambs in his arms, and carry them in his bosom and gently lead the mother sheep." It is an announcement of the mighty reign of God in the midst of Israel and the tender touch of God as a loving and gentle shepherd, folding Israel in his arms. Good news from the prophet Isaiah to a nation in need of uplifting, assistance, and help.

Jesus said in John 10:14 and 15: "I am the good shepherd. I know my own and my own know me, just as the Father knows me and I know the

Father. And I lay down my life for the sheep." Moreover the prophet Isaiah says: ". . . lift up your voice with strength . . . lift it up, do not fear . . ." (Isa 40:9). He has an uplifting voice as he heralds the message of the Lord as king and shepherd. These two figures point to the majesty of God on his throne and the tenderness and nearness of the protective and loving shepherd. God is near and far according to Isaiah.

We need uplifting when we are low and discouraged. Isaiah lends an uplifting voice to help us in our low moments. The Christian hymn, "Love Lifted Me," gives us an uplifting thought: "I was sinking deep in sin, Far from the peaceful shore, Very deeply stained within, Sinking to rise no more, But the Master of the sea heard my despairing cry, From the water lifted me, Now safe am I, Love lifted me, Love lifted me, When nothing else would help, Love lifted me; Love lifted me, Love lifted me, When nothing else would help, Love lifted me."

If you have an opportunity, lift someone up with an encouraging phone call; an email filled with news, humor, and music; or a funny greeting card. Brighten a person's day in a small but meaningful way. You will receive a blessing in return. The greatest thrill in life is to do something for someone else.

PASTORAL PRAYER

O God our Heavenly Father, we lift up our voices to you this day, thanking you for everything that you do for us everyday. You give us life so that we can wake up in the morning and start our day of work and responsibilities for our family, loved ones, community, and nation. We cry out to you for the injustices that we see daily in our streets and country and ask you for calm and peace. We cry out when people hurt each other and ask you to bring love and banish hate from this situation. We cry out because we know that people need Jesus Christ as Savior and Lord and that all of us need to kneel at the cross, asking your forgiveness of our sins and your cleansing of our lives.

Be with our nation on this Fourth of July weekend as we celebrate the birthday of our nation. Guide us back to the meaning of America: the land of the free and the home of the brave. Help us to live the meaning of our flag: One nation under God, indivisible, with liberty and justice for all. Bring us back from division. Help us to seek you again. Free us from harm and hate. Let us affirm liberty and liberate us from prejudice and discrimination. Keep us in the arms and scales of justice.

We remember our church and long for communion and fellowship with our brothers and sisters in Christ. Keep us safe and healthy. Bring us back so that we may see each other and became a visible fellowship again. Be with each member and friend of our congregation. We uphold all those in need, illness, and want that you will provide for their daily needs. We want to remember the families and friends of Hazel, Diane, and Raymond as they grieve their loss and ask that you will bring them your love and comfort. We remember Risa as she slowly recovers from her stroke. Be with her family as they minister and care for her. Prepare Melanie as she undergoes her heart valve repair surgery. In the name of our Lord Jesus, we pray. Amen.

CHAPTER 13

THE SUFFERING SERVANT
Isaiah 53:1–12 (July 12, 2020)

Scripture Reading. Who has believed what we have heard? And to whom has the arm of the LORD been revealed? For he grew up before him like a young plant, and like a root out of dry ground; he had no form or majesty that we should look at him, nothing in his appearance that we should desire him. He was despised and rejected by others, a man of suffering and acquainted with infirmity; and as one from whom others hide their faces he was despised, and we held him of no account.

Surely he has borne our infirmities and carried our diseases; yet we accounted him stricken, struck down by God, and afflicted. But he was wounded for our transgressions, crushed for our iniquities; upon him was the punishment that made us whole, and by his bruises we are healed. All we like sheep have gone astray; we have all turned to our own way, and the LORD has laid on him the iniquity of us all.

He was oppressed, and he was afflicted, yet he did not open his mouth; like a lamb that is led to the slaughter, and like sheep before its shearers is silent, so he did not open his mouth. By a perversion of justice he was taken away. Who could have imagined his future? For he was cut off from the land of the living, stricken for the transgressions of my people. They made his grave with the wicked and his tomb with the rich, although he had done no violence, and there was no deceit in his mouth.

Yet it was the will of the LORD to crush him with pain. When you make his life an offering for sin, he shall see his offspring, and shall prolong his days; through him the will of the LORD shall prosper. Out of his anguish he shall see light; he shall find satisfaction through his knowledge. The righteous one, my servant, shall make many righteous, and he shall bear their iniquities. Therefore I shall allot him a portion with the great, and he shall divide the spoil with the strong; because he poured out himself to death, and was numbered with the transgressors; yet he bore the sin of many, and made intercession for the transgressors.

With the urging of President Trump and the follow-through of many Republican governors in mid-May 2020 various states opened up their businesses to the public in order to recoup their financial losses. There were CDC guidelines on various phases of the opening to assist governors and state health departments. Georgia was the first state to reopen and Florida, Texas, and Arizona took minimal precautions during this phase of the COVID-19 crisis. New York and California slowly reopened their business economy county by county with detailed guidelines due to their large populations and major cities.

Despite the precautions taken by the governors of the states by the end of June 2020, there was a resurgence of coronavirus outbreak illness cases reported in Texas, Florida, Arizona, and California where the case numbers doubled and even tripled in a 24–48-hour period. COVID-19 cases were reported heavy in the 18–45-year age group, and bars and beaches were closed for a period in the affected states. Medical centers and ICU beds in these four states were impacted and filled to capacity. Governor Andrew Cuomo stated that this coronavirus resurgence was part of the first wave of the illness rather than the beginning of a second wave. The people of our nation were urged to wear masks, keep social distancing, and shelter in their homes rather than socialize in restaurants and other public places.

As we think about the Suffering Servant depicted in Isa 53:1–12 and the coronavirus striking the nation with strong revenge I would like to draw a parallel between the sufferings of Jesus and the sufferings of many virus patients who endured body aches, difficult breathing, loss of consciousness, and related trauma. News reporters interviewed countless recovered patients who described the agony that they underwent at the peak of their illness and their slow recovery.

We turn now to a careful analysis of the identity of Jesus (Who was Jesus according to New Testament scholars who write about the life of Christ?) and his connection with the Suffering Servant of Isa 53.

WHO WAS JESUS?

For two centuries New Testament biblical scholars have asked the questions: How did Jesus of Nazareth identify himself? Was the Jesus of history really the Christ of faith? Did the Gospel writers (Matthew, Mark, Luke, and John) portray Jesus after his death and resurrection as someone different from what he was while he was on earth? Why did Jesus avoid the designation as the Messiah or the Son of God? Did Jesus have a messianic consciousness or did he not believe himself to be the Messiah? Was Jesus divine or another human being? Volumes have been written to answer these questions by biblical scholars in Germany, the United Kingdom, and the United States.

A critical and careful reading of the New Testament Gospels reveals that Jesus identified himself as the Son of Man and the Suffering Servant. His mission on earth was to die for our sins. The former term, the Son of Man, comes from Dan 7:13–14 and refers to the apocalyptic figure appearing in the last days and is connected to the Suffering Servant (Luke 17:22–25). The latter designation, the Suffering Servant, is the accurate term for the mission of Jesus: Christ died for our sins in accordance with the Scriptures (1 Cor 15: 3).

In this sermon on the Suffering Servant we will explore: the Rejected One (Isa 53:1–3), the Wounded One (Isa 53:4–6), Silent One (Isa 53:7–9), and the Righteous One (Isa 53:10–12). Isaiah 53 is a wonderful passage to preach on Good Friday. However, it has implications for us who are suffering with COVID-19. People who are sick with this virus often feel the isolation and loneliness of rejection, deep wounds, and silent suffering. This passage speaks to their pain and offers in the end the Righteous One, Jesus Christ, who has experienced the suffering that we are enduring in this illness.

THE REJECTED ONE

Rejection is a cruel reaction and feeling. It means being cut off from the love and relationship we so desperately need as human beings. We may have been cut off from the care of our parents, rejected by a boyfriend or girlfriend, or have undergone a separation or divorce. Reports from recovered COVID-19 patients reveal difficulty with breathing, feelings of being cut off, and extreme isolation.

Isaiah 53:1–3 portrays the Rejected One: ". . . he had no form or majesty that we should look at him, nothing in his appearance that we should desire him. He was despised and rejected by others; a man of suffering and acquainted with infirmity; and as one from whom others hide their faces

..." The Christian hymn, "Man of Sorrows," says: "Man of Sorrows, What a name, for the Son of God He became. . . . Hallelujah, What a Savior!" The description of the Suffering Servant is the Rejected One: you would not want to look at him; he was despised and rejected; he was suffering and ill with sickness; people shielded their faces from him. Jesus on the cross must have felt this way: alone, rejected, forsaken, and suffering. A person in a COVID-19 coma may have had a similar experience, only to feel a sense of relief after recovering and being reunited with family and loved ones.

Being rejected by a myriad of circumstances is an awful experience to encounter and to work through for a person. The grace of our Lord Jesus Christ, the love of God, and the fellowship of the Holy Spirit enfold the life of a person who has been rejected along with our love and company.

THE WOUNDED ONE

Isaiah 53:4–6 describes the wounds of the Suffering Servant: ". . . he has borne our infirmities and carried our diseases; yet we accounted him stricken, struck down by God, and afflicted . . . he was wounded for our transgressions, crushed for our iniquities; upon him was the punishment that made us whole, and by his bruises we are healed . . . and the LORD has laid on him the iniquity of us all." A careful analysis of this passage reveals that the Suffering Servant is the substitute for our sins (our spiritual infirmities and disease, our transgressions and iniquities, our punishment) which he took upon himself. As a result, through the Wounded One we are made whole and are healed. Jesus took the punishment of our sins upon himself that we might be free. First Peter 2:24 reinforces this truth: "He himself bore our sins in his body on the cross, so that, free from sins, we might live for righteousness; by his wounds you have been healed." Christian systematic theologians call this the substitutionary atonement of Christ.

Wounds are physical but also psychological and spiritual. Trauma can reach beyond the moment and haunt us for years. PTSD (Post-Traumatic Stress Syndrome) is a current example of psychological wounds which fester in our psyche. We encountered this in wounded veterans who recovered from wounds and psychological trauma in the First and Second World Wars, the Korean War, the Vietnam War, and the Gulf War. Survivor's guilt, flashbacks of trauma, death, and loss, and suicide by the police are expressions of PTSD trauma which we hear about and are being treated in our community mental health centers.

At the same time all of us carry around old wounds: past events and experiences which still haunt us in our psyche. We are able to pull up painful memories of instances which have wounded us to this day. What should we do about all of these old wounds? We share them with a friend and confidante. We go further and work them through with a qualified therapist (a social worker, psychologist, a psychiatrist) and in group therapy with those who also share wounds so that the group helps each other. We come out on the other end with more insight, wisdom, and ability to cope the next time.

THE SILENT ONE

Isaiah 53:7–9 says: "He was oppressed, and he was afflicted, yet he did not open his mouth; . . . he was taken away . . . he was cut off . . . although he had done no violence, and there was no deceit in his mouth." The sound of silence reminds us that silence has a noise and a vibrance to it. Being silent and remaining silent speak volumes to us. It may mean that we are mad and angry but are unwilling to communicate our feelings in words. It also is an indicator of how deep our pain is to the point that we are unable to utter our feelings. Further silence may communicate that we want to talk about it later, not now. The Suffering Servant endured silence in the midst of his oppression, affliction, isolation, and innocence.

Often we seek solitude because in the silence we can think about our problems, self-problem-solve them, and pray to the Lord for help and guidance. It is okay to steal away to Jesus as the spiritual hymn tells us. Sometimes in the midst of the silence of solitude we find answers to our problems as we hear that small still voice of God speak to us and supply us with some simple answers which make sense to us and our particular situation. Go to your spiritual closet. Shut the door. Leave the distractions. Hear the voice of God who loves you and gave himself for us.

THE RIGHTEOUS ONE

There is an upswing in Isa 53 when the prophet declares: "Yet it was the will of the LORD . . . he shall see his offspring, and shall prolong his days; through him the will of the LORD shall prosper . . . he shall find satisfaction through his knowledge. The righteous one, my servant, shall make many righteous . . . I will allot him a portion with the great . . . he poured out himself to death . . . he bore the sin of many . . ." (Isa 53:10–12). Isaiah 53 is a passage which descends into the valley of despair and raises to the heights of ecstasy. The end point is that the Suffering Servant becomes the Righteous One who sees his offspring and lives a full life of prosperity and satisfaction, blessings to others, and inheritance. The Suffering Servant is the Righteous

One because he bore the sin of the people. In the end the trials of the Suffering Servant are worth the pain and sorrow because he substituted his life for the sins of the many. There is daylight at the end of the tunnel.

Often when we go through the trials and tribulations of life we are purified through the experiences which we endure as frail human vessels. How will we come out when the coronavirus ends and we find a vaccine that we can use to free ourselves from this disease? We recall the Salk vaccine which was a cure from polio. I remember that President Franklin Delano Roosevelt was a polio victim and that polio afflicted so many people, especially children who could not walk without crutches. When as a young child we went to the movies, there was an intermission. The lights came on in the theater and we contributed ten cents to The March of Dimes to find a cure for infantile paralysis. The can was passed around to those in the movie house and you could hear the cling of the dimes as each person gave to this worthy cause. President Roosevelt was a victim of this disease. One day we shall discover a COVID-19 vaccine and we will look back on 2019 and 2020 and wonder at the suffering and loss that the world went through as we encountered this killer, coped as best we could, mourned our losses, and achieved the victory.

SUFFERING SERVANTS

We have a friend who recently called us to tell us that she just found out that she has lung cancer. All her life she has been a person who has given herself to others in her community. She has minimized her own personal time and the normal pleasures in life to devote herself to the causes in her community which have contributed to the well-being of others. From early in the morning to the evening she has put in twelve-hour days, seven days per week on behalf of causes rather than spend the time with her personal and family life. She has lived a clean and decent life and has practiced good healthcare. Why would such a wonderful and caring person be inflicted with lung cancer to the point of not being able to breathe in a normal manner?

She is like the Suffering Servant of Isa 53. She has been a public servant for her whole life. She could have enjoyed her upscale lifestyle, but she wanted to devote her life in the service of others in her city and state. Why now must she have to suffer and prepare herself and her family with the possibility of leaving her loved ones behind in light of her illness? There are no easy answers to the life dilemma that she faces in her immediate future. All we can do for her is to love and support her and pray to the Lord for comfort and guidance. There are many suffering servants who bear the weight of concerns in this world and we must uphold them in prayer and supplication.

PASTORAL PRAYER

O God our Father. We thank you for the life and lessons of Jesus Christ, our Suffering Servant, who came to earth to save us from our sins and who bore the sins of the world upon himself. As we remember Isa 53, we pray for our friend who has received the news of having lung cancer that you will be with her and her family. For all of her doctors who form her team of healing be with them as they endeavor to treat her condition that your guidance will be with them. Strengthen her faith in you as she is treated for her illness and may you by your grace heal her and restore her to good health and well-being.

We pray for all those who are in pain and who suffer that your presence as the Great Physician will be there to heal their bodies and their souls. We thank you for the healing power of the Lord. Continue to be with our church and those who support it. We miss the fellowship and support of our brothers and sisters in Christ and pray that you will be with all of us as we make plans for opening our church. Help us to realize that it may take many more months before we can gather together in a safe and healthy manner. Give us patience as we recognize this fact.

We remember our seniors who need your strength and help. Help them through their loneliness and isolation. Give them friends who call and support. Sensitize the families of the elderly to their grocery, cooking, and cleaning needs. Be with those who are ill and are bed-ridden. Help them to maintain their nutrition. Healing them so that they can eat and find their will to live again. Be with our families as we relate as fathers and mothers, brothers and sisters, uncles and aunties, and cousins to cousins that we will all love and support each other as we live and cope with the many challenges and mini-crises that we face each day.

Be with us in the coming days ahead. For thine is the power and the glory forever and ever. Amen.

CHAPTER 14

THIRST, MONEY, AND SEEKING THE LORD

Isaiah 55:1–11 (July 19, 2020)

Scripture Reading. Ho, everyone who thirsts, come to the waters; and you that have no money, come, buy and eat! Come, buy wine and milk without money and without price. Why do you spend your money for that which is not bread, and your labor for that which does not satisfy? Listen carefully to me, and eat what is good, and delight yourselves in rich food. Incline your ear, and come to me, listen, so that you may live. I will make an everlasting covenant, my steadfast, sure love for David. See, I made him a witness to the peoples, a leader and commander for the peoples. See, you shall call nations that you do not know, and nations that do not know shall run to you, because of the LORD your God, the Holy One of Israel, for he has glorified you.

Seek the LORD while he may be found, call upon him while he is near; let the wicked forsake their way, and the unrighteous their thoughts; let them return to the LORD, that he may have mercy on them, and to our God, for he will abundantly pardon. For my thoughts are not your thoughts, nor are your ways my ways, says the LORD. For as the heavens are higher than the earth, so are my ways higher than your ways and my thoughts than your thoughts.

For as the rain and the snow come down from heaven, and do not return there until they have watered the earth, making it bring forth and sprout, giving seed to the sower and bread to the eater, so shall my word be that goes out from my mouth; it shall not return to me empty, but it shall accomplish that which I purpose, and succeed in the thing for which I sent it.

As we reflect on the murder of George Floyd and the mass rallies and demonstrations for Black Lives Matter and changes in the policing of America, there are multiple crises and dramas playing out during the summer of 2020. Will the national legislative proposals debated in Congress and the police reform of major American cities be sufficient to meet the concerns of the protestors and the rest of American society? What is the fallout from the rise in coronavirus cases as a result of the reopening of American businesses and the spread of the virus from the mass demonstrations and their participants? How have President Trump and former Vice President Biden responded to each other and to the needs of the American people as the presidential election and the November voting deadline loom in the next three months? How can we safely open our schools so that teachers and students will be protected from COVID-19? There are multiple crises and dramas that we are witnessing and we have yet to see how all of these events might resolve themselves during the coming months of 2020.

In the midst of these questions, our sermon is about thirst, money, and seeking the LORD. These three thoughts seem contradictory at first glance. But there are connecting points which we shall make during the sermon. Thirsting after righteousness, giving away free gifts without money, and seeking the LORD are the themes which we will weave together during the sermon. But before we do this, let us consider a spiritual puzzle.

A SPIRITUAL PUZZLE

What do thirst, money, and seeking God have to do with each other? When we are thirsty we search for the nearest water to drink in order to quench our thirst. When we want to buy an item in the grocery store or shopping mall, we reach for our wallet and pull out a credit card or pay with cash. When we run short of money we go to the bank or credit union and draw out cash. We earn our money from working at our job. But again, how are being thirsty and spending money connected to seeking God?

Isaiah 55:1–11 makes the connection between these three entities: thirst (55:1), money (55:1 and 2), and seeking the LORD by hearing (55:3), seeing (55:4 and 5), seeking (55:6 and 7), thinking (55:8 and 9), and speaking (55:10 and 11). This passage is a puzzle which somehow comes together in a unique and meaningful way and yet at first glance seems to be incredibly disjointed. Isaiah is inviting everyone to come to claim some freebies.

It is an open invitation that he makes to the people of Israel who are in spiritual need. Isaiah is like an announcer who travels in the neighborhood with a loud speaker and calls everyone to come out of their homes and get free water, free food and drink, and a free God without any strings attached. He gets our attention and has a message that we want to hear.

THIRST

When we go for our annual physical check-up the doctor reminds us that we need to drink at least eight glasses of water daily. Water is essential to our intake and helps to enrich our blood which contains water in its flow. Water is crucial to our life itself. We can die if we do not have enough water. When should we drink water? During our breakfast, lunch, and dinner; times when we are thirsty; during a hot day; during a cold day when hot water warms our body; and during the night when we awaken and are thirsty. Isaiah 55:1 says: "Ho, everyone who thirsts, come to the waters." Isaiah was making an important public announcement: If you are thirsty, come to the waters. Was Isaiah talking about physical thirst? Or was he alluding to spiritual thirst? Why did he say "waters" rather than "water"? Was he referring to a multiple source of water such as a spring or an oasis? Or was he asking us to go to the sea or ocean to enjoy the refreshing coolness of water? Interesting to speculate on what Isaiah meant when he invited the thirsty person to come to the waters.

Jesus says: "Blessed are those who hunger and thirst for righteousness, for they will be filled" in the Sermon on the Mount which is one of the Beatitudes (Matt 5:6). He also said to the woman of Samaria: "Everyone who drinks of this water will be thirsty again, but those who drink of the water that I will give them will never be thirsty" (John 4:13 and 14). Addressing the crowds that followed him, Jesus said: "I am the bread of life. Whoever comes to me will never be hungry, and whoever believes in me will never be thirsty" (John 6:35). Our LORD was talking about a spiritual thirst which is satisfied by coming to Christ who quenches our spiritual thirst for righteousness. As Isaiah first talked about those who are spiritually thirsty, Jesus is the answer to the invitation raised by Isaiah many centuries before the coming of Christ.

So if we are spiritually thirsty, the God of Isaiah in the Old Testament and Jesus Christ in the New Testament have water that will quench our thirst, even the waters of eternal life that are available to those who come in repentance and faith to the cross. We are human beings who need water to satisfy our physical and spiritual cravings which are called thirst. Come to Christ and he will satisfy your thirst.

MONEY

Isaiah invites those who have no money (the poor) to come and eat and buy wine and milk without needing money. He says: ". . . eat what is good, and delight yourselves in rich food" (Isa 55:2). Isaiah is talking about the feast that God has prepared for those who love and honor him. First Peter 2:2 and 3 remind us about the nurturing nature of God: "Like newborn infants, long for the pure, spiritual milk, so that by it you may grow into salvation—if indeed you have tasted that the Lord is good." All that God provides is ". . . without money and without price . . ." (Isa 55:1).

Isaiah is saying that we do not need money to buy all the bounty that are available from the provisions that God has stored up for us. It is available if we come to him. Jesus told his disciples: "Cure the sick, raise the dead, cleanse the lepers, cast out demons. You received without payment, give without payment" (Matt 10:8). Money is an important source of power to obtain the resources needed to survive and thrive. But Jesus encountered a wealthy man and said to him: "You lack one thing; go, sell what you own, and give the money to the poor, and you will have treasure in heaven; then come, follow me" (Mark 10:21). The reaction of the rich man was: "When he heard this, he was shocked and went away grieving, for he had many possessions" (Mark 10:22). Isaiah sets aside money and invites all to come to the free meal that God has prepare for those who follow him.

Bill Gates is an example of a wealthy man who have devoted his financial resources to eliminate world poverty in Third World countries. Recently he has taken up the cause of funding medical research to find a vaccine for COVID-19. I do not know whether Bill Gates has a spiritual faith but he is a great example of a person who has used his money (not for himself) but for others. The invitation of Isaiah stands: O taste and see the goodness of God.

Are you rich or do you just have enough funds to cover your expenses with minimal savings in the bank for a rainy day? You have heard the expression, "We are only a pay check away from homeless," and with people out of work and the coronavirus pandemic running rampant in the country, money and adequate living are crucial issues facing many Americans. Regardless of our wealth or lack of physical resources, we are able to be spiritually wealthy in the riches of Christ Jesus. Paul marvels in the riches that he has in Christ: ". . . with the eyes of your heart enlightened, you may know what is the hope to which he has called you, what are the riches of his glorious inheritance among the saints . . ." (Eph 1:18) and ". . . my God will fully satisfy every need of yours according to his riches in glory in Christ Jesus" (Phil 4:19). Being wealthy and rich may mean living another day in good health and safety under the guidance and protection of the Lord. Leading a rich life in this sense is worth more than our wealth in the bank account.

SEEKING THE LORD

Isaiah asks us to seek the LORD with our total faculties: hearing, seeing, seeking, thinking, and speaking. Regarding *hearing* Isaiah states: "Incline your ear, and come to me; listen, so that you may live . . ." (Isa 55:3). Isaiah wants us to hear and listen to what God will do: make an everlasting covenant with us (the new covenant in my blood, said Jesus). Hebrews 12:24 states: ". . . to Jesus, the mediator of a new covenant, and to the sprinkled blood that speaks a better word than the blood of Abel." Concerning *seeing* Isaiah predicts that Israel will be ". . . a witness to the peoples; a leader and commander for the people . . . who shall call nations . . ." (Isa 55:4 and 5). Was Isaiah referring back to the promise of Abraham that ". . . in you all the families of the earth shall be blessed"? (Gen 12:3). If this is so, both Genesis and Isaiah foresaw the coming of Christ (the incarnation) who will bless both Jew and Gentile in all the nations of the world.

For *seeking*, Isaiah urges: "Seek the LORD while he may be found, call upon him while he is near; let the wicked forsake their way, and the unrighteous their thoughts; let them return to the LORD . . ." (Isa 55:6 and 7). Isaiah calls for total repentance and a turning back to God. He mobilizes the people of Israel to action and asks them to seek the LORD while he is still available. About *thinking* Isaiah is profound: "For my thoughts are not your thoughts, nor are your ways my ways, . . . For as the heavens are higher than the earth, so are my ways higher than your ways and my thoughts than your thoughts" (Isa 55:8 and 9). Don't try to fathom my thinking and my ways. They are far higher and superior to yours. You can not outthink me, saith the Lord God.

Concerning *speaking* the LORD says: ". . . my word . . . that goes out from my mouth; it shall not return to me empty, but it shall accomplish that which I purpose, and succeed in the thing for which I sent it" (Isa 55:10 and 11). The Word of God speaks with sure certainty and authority. The Gospel of John starts out: "In the beginning was the Word, and the Word was with God, and the Word was God" (John 1:1). Karl Barth, the greatest systematic theologian of the twentieth century, begins his twelve volume work, *Church*

Dogmatics, with the concept of the Word of God in the tradition of Isaiah and John. Barth distinguishes three Words of God: the proclaimed Word of God (preaching of the Word which is the chief task of the minister each Sunday), the written Word of God (the Scriptures of the Old and New Testaments, the Bible), and the revealed Word of God (the revelation of God in the person of Jesus Christ).[1] Interesting how important the Word of God is to Barth at the start of his theology.

Isaiah is making the point that when we earnestly seek the LORD we must come to him with all our senses and with our whole being and becoming. Are you seeking the LORD as much as he is earnestly seeking you? Seek him out. Find him as your LORD and Savior. Possess him and you will never thirst or be destitute again, according to Isa 55:1–11.

A SEARCH FOR GOD

There is a Christian song which says; "If with all your heart, you truly seek me, you shall truly find me, thus saith the Lord, thus saith our God." Jesus said "Ask, and it will be given to you, seek and you will find; knock, and the door will be opened to you" (Matt 7:7) and ". . . seek first the kingdom of God and his righteousness, and all these things will be given to you as well" (Matt 6:33). Are you a seeker of God? Are you spiritually thirsty? Would you like the free grace and love of God, yours without spending money? These are the questions and answers posed by the prophet Isaiah many centuries ago which are still relevant today.

Certainly as a nation we need to correct the wrongs and illnesses of American society which have been played out during May and June 2020. But we also need to search for God and seek the LORD while he may be found and knock on his door which is always open to us. In a real sense, the COVID-19 crisis is an opportunity for you as an individual and for all of us as a nation to seek out the LORD in a new and meaningful way. Have we left God out of our life as persons, community, and nation? Now is the chance to return to him in faith and trust.

PASTORAL PRAYER

Dear God, In the midst of our busy life and the chaos which grip our nation, may we pause and seek you. May your wisdom flow into our mind so that we will know truth from falsehood. May your will be done as we vote

---

1. Barth, *Church Dogmatics*, I/1.

to elect our mayors, assembly persons, house of representatives, senators, and president. May your healing reach across America to help those who are afflicted by the coronavirus. May your intelligence guide our medical researchers as they are about to find a vaccine to combat COVID-19. May your invitation to come to the cross of Jesus be received and welcomed by those who hunger and thirst after righteousness. May your calling to ministry be answered by thousands of those who want to serve you in the Christian church. May your blessing be given to those who believe in Christ and who find a place in the local church. May you richly bless America and stand beside our country and guide our nation through the stormy seas of controversy and conflict.

We think of our church this day and ask that you will steady and preserve it. We know that we have not met for a long time, but we pray that you will strengthen the bond of faith and love which keep us together. As we chart out the direction and lay the path that we will walk in the coming months, we ask for your guidance. Be our compass so that we will walk with the LORD in the light of your Word. We pray that you will use our Sunday worship to deepen the lives of those who hear and see the Word of the Lord from the Old Testament and the Prophets. May the messages from the Prophets speak to the ills of this nation who have suffered loss of lives, been divided and torn asunder, and cried out for help and salvation. May your Word be a healing force in the life of this church. May our church go forward, strengthen by the power of your might and nourish by your spiritual truths of love and faithfulness.

Continue to be with our consistory as it considers the decision of a new pastor, the growth and welfare of this church, and the pastoral needs of its congregation. Help the consistory as elders to be wise in decision-making and as deacons to be servants of the needs of people. Be with those who are coping with their illnesses: Risa who is slowly recovering from her stroke, Melanie who is ready for her heart valve repair operation, Jan as she lives with Parkinson's disease, Lorrie in her rehabilitation with her stroke, and our seniors who need family care for grocery shopping and personal care.

Keep our country safe, strong, and true to the Word of God. In Jesus name we pray. Amen.

CHAPTER 15

I AM ONLY A BOY
Jeremiah 1:1–10 (August 2, 2020)

Scripture Reading. The words of Jeremiah, the son of Hilkiah, of the priests who were in Anathoth in the land of Benjamin, to whom the word of the LORD came in the days of King Josiah son of Amon of Judah, in the thirteenth year of his reign. It came also in the days of King Jehoiakim son of Josiah of Judah, and until the end of the eleventh year of King Zedekiah son of Josiah of Judah, until the captivity of Jerusalem in the fifth month.

Now the word of the LORD came to me saying, "Before I formed you in the womb I knew you, and before you were born I consecrated you; I appointed you a prophet before the nations."

Then I said, "Ah, Lord GOD! Truly I do not know how to speak, for I am only a boy." But the LORD said to me, "Do not say, 'I am only a boy'; for you shall go to all to whom I send you, and you shall speak whatever I command you. Do not be afraid of them, for I am with you to deliver you, says the LORD."

Then the LORD put out his hand and touched my mouth; and the LORD said to me, "Now I have put my words in your mouth. See, today I appoint you over nations and over kingdoms, to pluck up and to pull down, to destroy and to overthrow, to build and to plant.

Conversations are important to people, because we need to communicate thoughts and feelings to others. As we find out about another person we discover more about ourselves in the process.

A few weeks ago my grandson, Trevor, was listening to my July 5, 2020, sermon on "A Voice Crying in the Wilderness" (Isa 40:1–11) as he was eating breakfast with his mother and two brothers. He remembered the part of the sermon where I was talking about an uplifting voice and the need to lift people up who were down emotionally. After the sermon he got up from the kitchen table, ran toward his mother, our daughter-in-law Lisa, grabbed her waist, and tried to lift her up physically. "Trevor, what are you doing?" she cried out to him. He responded: "Well, the sermon said to lift people up and I thought that I should do that to you!" Trevor is a perfect example of someone who responded literally to lifting people up. Conversations and sermons are important vehicles.

Would you like to have a conversation with God and tell him how you feel about going through the coronavirus crisis? What would you say to the LORD? Would you complain about the inconvenience of wearing a mask and maintaining social distancing? Or being confined to your home and not being able to socialize with family and friends? Or would you thank God for keeping you healthy and safe and promise to help others who are struggling with this virus? Imagine talking to God about your thoughts and feelings.

What about a conversation with President Donald Trump on COVID-19? Would you ask him about the burdens that he carries as the president of the United States as he reads his daily briefing on the spread of the virus? Would you bring up his disappointments that the country is not experiencing the economic success and robust growth that he hoped for as the election looms near in November? Rather than criticize his leadership, would you offer to President Trump your sympathy and understanding of the political battles that he wages in the White House?

Perhaps you should realistically talk to a survivor of COVID-19 to piece together a history of his/her journey: when did he/she recognize the symptoms of his/her illness, how did he/she catch the virus, what medical emergency steps did he/she take for admission to the hospital, who were his/her doctors and nurses, what was the medical treatment, how long was the hospital stay, what was the aftercare at home, and how did he/she feel when returning to work? Taking a detailed history may reveal an interesting back-and-forth conversation with a former coronavirus patient.

Have a coronavirus conversation with God, Donald Trump, or a COVID-19 survivor. Which one would you select? Let me know your choice.

A CONVERSATION WITH GOD

Have you ever had a conversation with God when he talked with you and you conversed with him? We have the resources of prayer where we can talk to God and of the written Word of God, the Bible, where God speaks to us through the Scriptures. But I am talking about a real back-and-forth conversation between God and you. I often talk with God and he with me mentally in my own mind. Is this really God talking to me and I to him in a back-and-forth discussion or is this only in my imagination? I often wonder about this.

Jeremiah 1:1–10 captures a real conversation that Jeremiah had with the Lord. There is a back-and-forth dialogue between God and Jeremiah. God says to Jeremiah: "I formed you, I knew you, I consecrated you." Jeremiah answers God: "I don't know how to speak, I am only a boy." God responds to Jeremiah: "You shall go, You shall speak, I am with you, I have put words in your mouth, I appoint you." What do you make of this conversation between God and Jeremiah? Was God calling Jeremiah to spiritual service? Was Jeremiah willing to listen and obey the Lord? Or did Jeremiah have a good excuse regarding his inability to speak and his young age?

Jeremiah is called the weeping prophet. He laments over sins of Israel and the coming judgement of God. Along with the book of Jeremiah one must read the book of Lamentations which traditionally is ascribed to Jeremiah. He lived between 626 BC to 580 BC and was concerned about the religious corruption of his time (the lure of nature cults and Judah's spiritual insensitivity) as well as the imminent invasion from the north of Assyria and Babylonia. He interacts with King Josiah, King Jehoiakim, and King Zedekiah. His ministry spans the fall of Judah to the Babylonians, the deportation in 598 BC, the fall of Jerusalem in 587 BC, and his exile in Egypt.

Jeremiah 1:1–10 records the beginning of Jeremiah's ministry when he is called by the Lord to become a prophet who proclaims the Word of the Lord to Judah. The sermon is divided into the following parts: 1) the past (Jer 1:4 and 5), 2) the present (Jer 1:6–8), and 3) the future (Jer 1:9–10).

THE PAST

Jeremiah 1:5 says: "Before I formed you in the womb I knew you, and before you were born I consecrated you; I appointed you a prophet to the nations." We are discussing the omniscience (all-knowing character) of God. Does God have a plan and a career destiny for all of us? If God is omniscient does he know what we will do in our journey of faith as we live out our life? It seems this way as God reveals himself to Jeremiah. His past is the plan of God who knew what Jeremiah was going to accomplish as a consecrated prophet to all nations, not just Judah.

As you consider your life and your journey of faith, what has happened to you? Allow yourself to look back into your past and see the hand of God on you as you grew from a child through your youth and into your young adult and adult years. Can you detect the guidance of God in your life as you made life transitions and major decisions? Like Jeremiah, did God call and consecrate you to be a prophet or a messenger with a spiritual message? Think about the call of Jeremiah as the call to all spiritual believers to proclaim the message of God's love and faithfulness. Look back on your past life and try to discern the hand and will of God in your life. The same God who worked a work in you in the past is the same God who is available to you in your present life.

As I think about my past I see the hand of God guiding me through my life as he led me to this city. Sacramento will always be dear to my heart. I came here to join the social work faculty at California State University, Sacramento. We built and owned our beautiful home, raised our four children, found this church, and made new friends. In Sacramento I became a teacher, researcher, and writer of cultural diversity and healthcare policy. I was involved with the Commission on Accreditation and the Board of Directors of the Council on Social Work Education, our national accreditation body. I became a grandfather, a retiree, and an interim pastor. I was led by God to this community and have been so blessed by him.

Look at your past life in a new way. Discern the hand of God leading you in past decisions and directions that you made and took as you think about your past. This same God of your past is still available to you and is willing to lead you in the present if you let him. Would you take the hand of God and follow him?

THE PRESENT

God brings Jeremiah into his present life. Jeremiah has excuses: "Ah, Lord GOD! Truly I do not know how to speak, for I am only a boy" (Jer 1:6). But God has a comeback: "Do not say, 'I am only a boy'; for you shall go to all to whom I send you, and you shall speak whatever I command you. Do not be afraid of them, for I am with you to deliver you . . ." (Jer 1:7 and 8). When God calls us into his service we often have excuses about why we cannot serve him. Jeremiah gave two excuses: his lack of talent (I don't know how to speak) and his age (I am only a boy). But God answers Jeremiah with a resounding answer: I will give you my authority and I will speak for you with my presence.

When God calls us, he gives us his power, authority, and presence to those whom he sends. We may not be gifted speakers and we may be only a youth, but God compensates for our limitations and get the job done for his glory. As I write about this, I think of a young boy who was raised on a dairy farm in North Carolina during the Great Depression. He went to Bible college, got a bachelor's degree from Wheaton College, and rose to be the greatest evangelist who preached the gospel of Christ to more people in the world than anyone has ever reached before and after in the last century. His name was William Franklin Graham. Billy Graham was surely ordained and consecrated to God even before he was born. He practiced his preaching in the Florida Everglades while he was a young student in Bible college. He never went to theological seminary and often sought the counsel of Dr. John McKay, the former president of Princeton Theological Seminary, who said: "No, Billy, don't go back to school. You are too valuable with what you are doing now. God is using you."

He was a young man when he became pastor of a small church outside of Chicago and president of Northwest College in Minneapolis. He went to Los Angeles to hold evangelism meetings which opened the door for his Crusades for Christ. He was sent by God and spoke the message from the Bible. In his sermons he constantly said: "The Bible says..." And he preached from the written Word of God. He helped to found Fuller Theological Seminary and was on the board of trustees during its formative years. He started the religious periodical, *Christianity Today*, and held evangelistic meetings in the cities throughout the world bringing church leaders and members from all the major Protestant denominations together in ecumenical unity. Like Jeremiah, Billy Graham of our generation answered the call of God despite his limitations and was mightily used by the Lord to bring men and women, boys and girls of all races, colors, and creeds to Christ.

What is your spiritual gift in your life today? Is God calling you into Christian service to serve him in the church or the community as a minister or a layperson doing the Lord's work in a creative secular way? Will you make excuses to God and turn from his call like Jeremiah initially did when he was called by God? These are questions that you need to ponder and ask as you contemplate your future in this present moment.

THE FUTURE

God gave Jeremiah a future destination over nations and kingdoms: "Now I have put my words in your mouth. See, today I appoint you over nations and over kingdoms, to pluck up and to pull down, to destroy and to overthrow, to build and to plant" (Jer 1:9–10). This passage seems to indicate that before building and planting there is a time for pulling down, destroying, and overthrowing.

Revolution precedes positive change. Perhaps we are witnessing the destruction of racism, the pulling down of negative police behavior, and the overthrow of the *status quo* which hinder new policies and procedures. The process may take a long time to overcome our past history. But we must engage in this struggle. The future is bright for America as we are able to break through the storms that we find ourselves fighting during the midpoint of 2020. If we can weather the winds of change and steer the ship toward calmer waters and strong breezes, there will be smooth sailing ahead.

We must not give the excuses (I cannot speak; I am only a boy) that Jeremiah spoke to God. The Lord uses a host of unlikely persons to perform his acts of love, speak his Word of proclamation, and give us insight. We must submit to the will and call of God. He will supply the necessary strength, wisdom, and power that we need to serve him. Jeremiah was given the resources that made him a true prophet of God who was used to warn his people and write the messages from God in the books of Jeremiah and Lamentations.

As we look at the future of America, we are struck with the need to call many prophets like Jeremiah. Never before has our country faced so many challenges at the same time: coping with the coronavirus which has killed over 160,000 and sickened three million Americans; combating racism and police brutality and the need for major reform of our policing system so that it responds to the needs of American society; training and placing millions of unemployed in public works programs which will shape the restructuring of the American landscape; selecting new leaders to lead our cities, states, Congress, and the presidency; and related issues which accompany these major problems.

We need a new breed of theological leaders to teach and write a *theology of living* (how to get along with all people), *being* (who we are as persons and who we will become as a nation), and *acting* (what positive steps we will take to improve America) in the twenty-first century which permeates our theological seminaries, our denominations, our local churches, and our society. We need church social change agents, evangelists, pastoral counselors, biblical and theological scholars, ministers and pastors who will strike out in new and creative ways for the good of our country and our churches. We may need to abandon former ways which have destroyed the lives of people and seek new solutions to resolve social problems in an uplifting and resolute manner. This may mean abolishing old ways of suppression and introducing new avenues of affirmation. If we get people to work together, to cooperate, and to enact better ways of solving social evils and neglect, we will accomplish the meaning of "plucking up, pulling down, destroying and overthrowing in order to build up and plant a new seed of hope and justice for all" (Jer 1:10).

AMERICA ON THE BRINK OF SOCIAL CHANGE AND TRANSFORMATION

Is America on the brink of social change and transformation? Are we as a nation tired of division, falsehood, slander, and attack? Are we ready to vote out the old and bring in the new? Is there the dawning of a new America just around the corner? I truly hope so. God selected a youthful boy who felt that he was a poor speaker and infused him with the power of his might and with a prophetic message of destroying the old and building and planting the new. God is seeking new Jeremiahs who will become leaders of our churches, cities, states, and nation. Will you answer the call of the Lord and rise up as Jeremiah did many centuries ago with modesty, humility, and dependency on the power and authority of the Lord? I hope you will do so for God and country.

What does the future hold for you? Does God have great plans for you? Are you ready to have him lead you to the path of a future destiny that you could not have imagined which might become your life contribution to the world of people around you? As I think of my life and as it unfolded, I see the guidance of God as I journeyed through my life. Oftentimes it seemed undefined and uncertain, but as I look back, there were sign posts from God that were marked for me. As I followed his path I marvel now that God led me through challenges and obstacles to a broad way of dreams and fulfillments that only God knew would happen to me. Thank God I endeavored to walk with the LORD in the light of his Word and had his glory shed on my way.

PASTORAL PRAYER

Dear God, In the midst of this coronavirus confronting our community and nation we pray that you will speak and guide the leaders of our country who make important decisions affecting our political, social, and spiritual welfare. For our president, senators, and House members we pray that you will guide them to make sound legislation to ensure the public health of all citizens. For our governors and mayor, we pray that you will help them to protect all citizens from exposure to the virus by implementing safe practices in the communities. For our public health researchers, doctors, and nurses we pray that you will give them the wisdom and strength to conduct research on the virus vaccine and articulate the best healthcare practices as they treat the many patients that depend on them. For our theologians and ministers we pray that you will give them messages of comfort, love, and relief which they can share with the people who long to hear a Word from the Lord.

We thank you that you have guided our past and have plans for our present and our future. As you worked in the life of Jeremiah many centuries ago, may your presence permeate our lives in the present and for the future. We commit ourselves to you anew and afresh, trusting that you will lead us each step of the way in our family life, our schools, our jobs, and our relationships with others.

Be with our church as it comes together each Sunday to worship you in spirit and in truth. Although we are physically absent from one another, may you unite us together in prayer and in the reading of your written Word. May we feel a fellowship of unity and love although we are still sheltering apart in our homes. We continue to uphold in prayer Melanie and her heart surgery; Maybelle as she recovers from a fall; Risa in her stroke rehabilitation; Jan as she copes with her Parkinson's disease; Gordon and Merrily and their family as they mourn the loss of Gordon's sister, Lily; and all those who need your healing hand upon them.

Bless, O Lord, the many problems that we face in ourselves, our families, our community, and nation. Save us from our sins and bring us together in love and support. Amen.

CHAPTER 16

THE SPIRIT OF THE LORD IS UPON ME

Isaiah 61:1–4 (July 26, 2020)

Scripture Reading. The spirit of the Lord GOD is upon me, because the LORD has anointed me; he has sent me to bring new good news to the oppressed, to bind up the brokenhearted, to proclaim liberty to the captives, and release to the prisoners; to proclaim the year of the LORD's favor, and the day of vengeance of our God; to comfort all who mourn; to provide those who mourn in Zion—to give them a garland instead of ashes, the oil of gladness instead of mourning, the mantle of praise instead of a faint spirit. They will be called oaks of righteousness, the planting of the LORD, to display his glory. They shall build up the ancient ruins, they shall raise up the former devastations; they shall repair the ruined cities, the devastations of many generations.

On July 7, 2020, President Trump held a news conference to urge that schools should be opened for students in September. He indicated that he would ask governors to open schools in their states despite the fact that there was a coronavirus surge during the previous Fourth of July weekend where the United States reached three million cases, 130,000 deaths, and increasing rates among the 18–45 age group. His order seemed out of place with the fact that there was a marked increased spread of the virus growing rampant throughout the nation. Rather than pulling back, President Trump wanted us to expose children to the virus with the opening of school without providing a plan for dealing with the virus in a school setting.

One remembers after a two-month sheltering at home that in mid-May 2020 President Trump encouraged the opening up of the economy and businesses. As a result there was a lack of social distancing and face coverings with large crowds on Memorial Day and the Fourth of July triggering a virus surge. Beaches, resort pools, bars, and restaurants were crowded with young and middle-age persons. Rather than listening to President Trump, the country would have been better prepared to cope with the virus and flatten the curve if it extended its sheltering-at-home strategy and kept certain businesses closed.

If children return to school without national standards of care and caution, another COVID-19 surge might occur affecting the health and well-being of students in school. State superintendents of schools are at odds with President Trump's order without a nationwide implementation plan of public health for schools. At the same time they are working with local school superintendents and teachers to execute a safe plan of education and teaching for K-12 students. Without careful planning the same pattern of virus outbreak and surge will occur again, only this time the children and teachers of the United States of America will be victims of the coronavirus.

This is the latest news on the coronavirus which has afflicted our country, increased the disease victim count, and lost valuable ground gained in our previous efforts of coping with this disease. Stay tuned to the latest developments in America's efforts to fight COVID-19. As of July 13, 2020, there were 3.3 million cases of the coronavirus, 138,000 deaths, and sixty-two thousand new daily cases affecting the people of the United States. Unlike the European Union, China, and South Korea, the United States of America remains the leader in the spread of this public health illness.

POSITIVE NEWS

It is important for us to hear good news rather than bad news, particularly in the midst of a crisis. The old saying, "No news is good news," may not be necessarily true. Good news is great news. The prophet Isaiah offered good news with his message in Isa 61 regarding the presence of the Spirit of God. This classic passage has been preached in many ordination services where the ordained person is one who has the Spirit of the Lord descending on his/her being in the beginning of ministry. In a sense the ordained minister is following in the tradition of the prophets and in the ministry of Jesus who read these words as he began his ministry in his hometown of Nazareth. In this passage Isaiah is announcing the presence of the Spirit as he preaches good news to the people of Israel.

Isaiah 61:1–4 can be understood in three parts: to bring, bind up, and proclaim *good news* (61:1 and 2); to comfort, provide, and give *gladness* (62:3); and to build, raise up, and generate *construction* (61:4). In its immediate context it is a positive message to the exiled (those taken into captivity) and the oppressed (remnants of those who stayed in the destroyed cities) of Israel. All of the three themes, *good news-gladness-construction*, are positive signs that God's presence is indeed in the midst of the people of Israel and that God is performing mighty acts for them. In its far-reaching sense Isa 61 is an announcement of what it means to be a minister of God with a message from God. In this passage we are on holy ground as we study the meaning of these verses.

GOOD NEWS

Isaiah starts with a positive message that God has truly intervened on his behalf for his people and has bought them good news. Isaiah 61:1–2 states: "The Spirit of the Lord GOD is upon me . . . to bring good news to the oppressed. To bind up the brokenhearted, to proclaim liberty to the captives, and release to the prisoners; to proclaim the year of the LORD's favor, and the day of vengeance of our God. . . ." The beginning phrase, "the Spirit of the LORD is upon me," is the sign of a true Old Testament prophet. That is, the mantle of the prophet has been given by the LORD to declare the message from God. Passing and placing the mantle from one prophet to the next was the symbol that the Spirit of the Lord was upon a particular prophet.

Elijah did so when he passed his mantle on Elisha: "So he (Elijah) set out from there, and found Elisha son of Shaphat, who was plowing. There were twelve yoke of oxen ahead of him, and he was with the twelfth. Elijah passed by him and threw his mantle over him. He left the oxen, ran after Elijah . . ." (1 Kgs 19:19 and 20). The mantle had magical power as if it was infused with power from the Lord. To wear the mantle as a prophet was to be endowed by God himself: "He (Elisha) picked up the mantle of Elijah that had fallen from him, and went back and stood on the bank of the Jordan. He took the mantle of Elijah that had fallen from him, and struck the water, saying, 'Where is the LORD, the God of Elijah?' When he struck the water, the water was parted to the one side and to the other, and Elisha went over" (2 Kgs 2:13 and 14).

Furthermore, in the tradition of the Old Testament Prophets, Jesus himself at the beginning of his ministry reads Isa 61:1–2 at the synagogue in Nazareth (Luke 4:16–30) saying "Today this scripture has been fulfilled in your hearing" (Luke 4:21). How powerful is this passage in the prophetic tradition of the Prophets and in the mind and eyes of Jesus Christ who quoted from these verses.

The message is a positive one filled with prophetic meaning and available for those who are in bad situations (the oppressed, the brokenhearted, the captives and prisoners). Israel's military was defeated, its cities were in ruins, the leadership and the intelligentsia were taken out of the land and were in exile in a foreign country, the peasants remained, and a foreign nation now was in control and authority.

Yet in the midst of this plight Isaiah brings good news, liberty, and release. The present situation is bleak and dark but there is light at the end of the tunnel. The light is the Spirit of the Lord. Moreover, Jesus underscores the meaning of this passage as he begins his ministry with these words and message. There is a comparison between the times of Israel and Isaiah and the time that we faced with COVID-19. The present is dismal and people are in despair. The economy is in ruin, people have died but more people have recovered, emotions run high, and there is unemployment and hunger. But God through Isaiah gives good news in the midst of doom and gloom. God will bind up; God will give liberty and release; God will proclaim favor and vengeance. It is a promise from God that all will be right in Isaiah's time and the passage has meaning for the crisis that we are facing in 2020.

We are in desperate need of good news as we hear about the mounting numbers of new coronavirus cases and the increasing death toll. When will the American people have the discipline and the commitment to implement the CDC guidelines and flatten the curve in order to stem the tide of the COVID-19 surge? European Union countries have already surpassed America and are opening up their cities with minimum cases whereas the United States is barely able to cope with the increasing surge of new cases and deaths. We are in need of good news, but the requirement is for us to work hard to achieve it.

As the weeks pass and the people respond to the challenges of defeating this virus, we will have good news to share with each other as Americans. About a year ago in the June 24, 2019, issue of *People* magazine Mariska Hargitay and Peter Hermann shared their eighteen-year love story.[1] I was struck with the fact that both Mariska and Peter met on the set of *Law & Order: SUV*. Peter asked Mariska, the daughter of Jayne Mansfield and Mickey Hargitay, out on a date: to attend church with him. Mariska recalls: "We went to church together, and it was like getting hit with a lightning bolt, and I just started sobbing. Peter thought I was crying because I was so moved by the service. No, it was because I was just overwhelmed, realizing that he was

---

1. Coyne, "This is their Love Story." 42–48.

the one. After church we parted ways because I was moving that day, and I met my dearest friend, Ashley, and I remember we went around the corner into this Victoria's Secret. I told her, 'This is it. This is the man I'm going to marry.'" Good news for Mariska and Peter. Good news for all of us who love a love story. Good news for Americans who need to hear good news.

GLADNESS

There is a sense of gladness in the message of Isaiah. Out of mourning will come gladness and praise: "to provide for those who mourn in Zion—to give them a garland instead of ashes, the oil of gladness instead of mourning, the mantle of praise instead of a faint spirit. They will be called oaks of righteousness, the planting of the LORD, to display his glory" (Isa 61:3). The message is positive emotion: gladness, praise, righteousness, and the glory of God. Rather than suffer loss, Israel will experience gladness and all of the attributes which follow it.

Spiritual gladness comes from having God with us: "I keep the LORD always before me; because he is at my right hand, I shall not be moved. Therefore my heart is glad, and my soul rejoices; my body also rests secure" (Ps 16:8 and 9). Or gladness comes from being in the presence of the LORD: "Make a joyful noise to the LORD, all the earth. Worship the LORD with gladness; come into his presence with singing" (Ps 100:1).

Gladness comes from God from whom all blessings flow. I am thankful to God for:

- My wife, children, and grandchildren
- My counseling, teaching, and writing career
- My friends and mentors who helped me along the journey of life and faith
- My home with its front courtyard and flowers, bushes, and garden
- My pastoral church experiences
- My healthcare and safety
- My travels to various places around the world
- My food, clothes, and living
- The seasons of the year
- The surprises that come when you least expect them
- The beauty of living in California

- The ideal living city of Sacramento
- The presence, power, and healing of God for the future events in my life

I am sure that you can make a list even longer than I have and that you can voice gladness to the LORD for the way he has blessed your life, even when you face adversity and crisis. Serve the LORD with gladness.

Gladness and joy will return to this country when we achieve victory over the coronavirus which may only come when we find an effective vaccine for a cure. We want to have our family and friends come to our home and visit us and hear laughter and shouts and see happiness and joy on their faces. We long for the day when the virus is controlled and gladness is seen in our actions. We want to see our children jump with joy and relief. Personally I miss the noise and the hustle and bustle of grandchildren running hither and yon through the house.

We await that day, but in the meantime we must redouble our efforts toward containment through isolation and public health practices (the wearing of a mask, social distancing, washing hands, and avoidance of large gatherings). We will be glad when we practice these safeguards and protect ourselves from the virus. Gladness comes in the morning after working hard throughout the night.

CONSTRUCTION

Isaiah 61:4 recalls the destruction of Israel and Jerusalem and predicts its construction: "They shall build up the ancient ruins, they shall raise up the former devastations; they shall repair the ruined cities, the devastations of many generations." In the time of Isaiah, Israel and Judah were defeated nations which were crushed by the powers of Assyria and Babylon. The capital, Jerusalem, was in ruins, particularly the palace of the king and the temple of God. The population was depleted with forced exile and captivity.

There was "the abomination of desolation" mentioned in Daniel (Dan 11:31; 12:11) and in Matthew (24:15). Isaiah foresees construction: the building of the cities, the restoration of the temple of God, and the repair of torn-down Jerusalem. The books of Ezra and Nehemiah chronicle the construction process. Nehemiah 2:18 declares: "Then they said, 'Let us start building!' So they committed themselves to the common good."

Construction means the process of building a structure. It is a creative art of following a blueprint out of which comes a dwelling which is inhabited by people. Being a contractor involves committing one's self to a contract which is an agreement to erect a building. The analogy of rebuilding of Israel is much like the reconstruction of our lives. Often a person may say: "I'm ruined." Is it financial ruin, moral ruin, or a related area? Feeling ruin may feel like a person is fractured and hurting. Jesus the Great Physician or in this case the Great Reconstruction Contractor can come into our life and rebuild the ruins that we feel within us. The healing of our body, mind, soul, and spirit is the meaning of salvation (wholeness and healing).

Construction of our life may involve:

- Reworking our self-image and sense of selfhood
- Examining our value system
- Remaking our personality and behavior
- Remodeling our educational and career goals
- Linking our self to a set of new friends and mentors
- Moving to a new city and environment
- Teaching ourselves about God and self
- Meeting Jesus in a new way

Your list may be different from the one you see here. These are some thoughts on reconstructing one's life. You may have related directions that you may want to pursue in your life. I recall a time in my life when I was so down and out that I did not have the energy or will to do anything meaningful. I was in a slump and needed to get going. But I couldn't. My wife and a therapist were so helpful during this period and with their help I was able to make a slow recovery. I am back to normal now and feel good about myself. My productivity is back to full speed and I love life and feel that God was my contractor who rebuilt my life and set a new structure in place for me.

Just think about the persons who have recovered from COVID-19. Many former patients report trouble thinking, moving, and sleeping. Their families and loved ones must be patient caregivers in their slow and painful recovery. We must be helpful as patients rebuild their lives from the effects of this virus.

Moreover, we must construct a safety net around ourselves and our families, community, and nation to protect ourselves from the deadly effects of COVID-19. We need shelters from the virus: our homes, our health practices, our distant and virtual relationships with others, our demand for protecting our children as they venture to school, and our willingness to worship and fellowship with our church on Zoom conferencing. We must be contractors who construct safe structures in order for us to live in meaningful relationships during the duration of this pandemic.

SERVING THE LORD

How many of us can say along with Isaiah: The Spirit of the LORD is upon me . . . ? Do we feel the mantle of the prophets descending on us and clothing us with the righteousness of God? Do we sense that call to ministry as the Spirit tells us that we should serve? Are we willing to hear and answer the call of the LORD and to give ourselves to full-time Christian ministry which involves going to theological seminary and pursuing a pastoral, counseling, missionary, and/or teaching ministry in the Christian church? These are questions which may be occurring in the mind of a person.

There is a tremendous need for those who minister in the church today. Our ranks are depleting and there is a need for new and fresh talent. At the same time we serve the Lord where we are and in what we do. The mantle of the prophet descends on us in our career. Along with the professional ministry is the Christian laity who serve God in many ways: teaching a church school class, conducting individual and group Bible study, mentoring a young Christian life, serving as stewardship chair person, executing a financial strategy for Christian giving, pursuing an MA in biblical studies or theology for personal and professional enrichment, conducting population research as data for evangelism in a community, and other creative ways to serve the Lord.

Whatever creative way that you desire to serve the LORD, the Spirit of the LORD will be upon you to do wondrous things in the sight of God and in the eyes of others who are blessed by what you do for them in the name of Christ. In the sense we hope that the mantle of the prophet will descend upon you and that you will sense the power of God working through you to be a blessing to someone today.

Moreover, in this time of the pandemic we need new ministers who are able to deliver the message of the gospel of Christ in creative ways without physically gathering people together in large groups. Media becomes the vehicle for sending the Christian message out to people. Videos, emails, Zoom conferencing, mailouts, telephone calls, mini Bible study and preaching sessions on cell phones, and other innovative means must be implemented soon. I suspect that congregations will not be meeting in worship centers for a long time, perhaps for a year until it is totally safe to hold such meetings. In the meanwhile it is important for us to devise new visual ways to present the gospel to those who are under the pandemic quarantine.

PASTORAL PRAYER

Dear LORD, We pray for our country which is in the midst of a public health pandemic where we are overwhelmed with the coronavirus. Our hospitals are filled to capacity with COVID-19 patients. Our doctors and nurses are in need of additional staff. Our people require discipline of mind, strong wills, and spiritual convictions to fight the battle toward recovery and restoration. Please grant to all Americans the courage to listen and follow the counsel of our doctors and public health officials. Help us to wear our masks, maintain social distance, wash our hands, and shelter in place as long as it takes to defeat this virus.

We pray this day for the Christian church and the ministers who are called to serve the Lord. We ask that you will give these servants of God the message of comfort and love to those who suffer from this virus and the message of patience and courage to those who are unwilling to heed the warnings and advice of public health doctors and nurses. Unite all citizens in the defeat of the virus and the victory of this battle. Help those to realize that we are at war with an invisible enemy who does not discriminate and afflicts all victims. As you have helped our country in wartime, so discipline all Americans to fight this battle with the armor of care and caution. We ask that our ministers will be preachers of this gospel message and prophets of warning and judgement. Help all of us to read the handwriting on the wall.

May the Spirit of the LORD fall on each citizen of our country so that everyone will feel the presence of the LORD and will soberly respond to the duties and responsibilities that our healthcare leaders convey to us. We also pray for the needs of our church that you will sustain each member who loves you and want to serve Christ and his kingdom. Be with our church leaders as they minister and serve others in need, oversee the church programs, and make crucial decisions. Uplift those in our congregation who are seniors, sick, and ill and in need of care. We pray for Merrily and Gordon and the loss of his sister, Lily, that you will be with the family who mourns her passing; for Maybelle as she continues to recover from her fall; for Melanie and her heart valve repair surgery; for Risa and her slow recovery from her stroke; and for our church members and friends who are in need of care and healing that you will sustain them. Mobilize their families, friends, and neighbors in the task of being caregivers and caretakers.

Give us the dedication and desire to cope with our life and the challenges that each day brings to us. In his name we pray. Amen.

CHAPTER 17

THE POTTER AND THE CLAY
Jeremiah 18:1-12 (September 6, 2020)

Scripture Reading. The word that came to Jeremiah from the LORD. "Come, go down to the potter's house, and there I will let you hear my words. So I went down to the potter's house, and there he was working on his wheel. The vessel he was making of clay was spoiled in the potter's hand, and he was reworking it into another vessel, as seemed good to him.

Then the word of the LORD came to me: Can I not do to you, O house of Israel, just as this potter has done? Says the LORD. Just like the clay in the potter's hand, so are you in my hand, O house of Israel. At one moment I may declare concerning a nation or a kingdom, that I will pluck up and break down and destroy it, but if that nation, concerning which I have spoken, turns from its evil, I will change my mind about the disaster that I intended to bring on it. And at another moment I may declare on a nation or a kingdom that I will build and plant on it, but if it does evil in my sight, not listening to my voice, then I will change my mind about the good that I had intended to do to it.

Now, therefore, say to the people of Judah and the inhabitants of Jerusalem: Thus says the LORD: Look, I am a potter shaping evil against you and devising a plan against you. Turn now all of you from your evil way, and amend your ways and your doings.

But they say, "It is no use! We will follow our own plans, and each of us will act according to the stubbornness of our evil will."

As we realize that Summer 2020 is ending and fall of 2020 will soon begin, we are struck with what has happened to us in the last few months and what is in store for us in the coming months. We have endured a coronavirus surge which has increased the death toll and hospital capacities of COVID-19 patients. We have seen the valiant efforts of state governors who are intent on stemming the spread of the virus. We are a part of the American citizens who are fighting the virus by sheltering in place, wearing face masks, practicing social distance, and washing our hands. We are hopeful that the curve is flattening and that our public officials have a firm control over best community practices so that American citizens can gradually resume their lives in a new normal and cautious environment.

As we anticipate the fall of 2020 we are preparing for the opening of a new school year. It will be an extraordinary educational experience: smaller and staggered class size, wearing of face mask, desks six feet apart, minimal physical and social contact, virtual distance learning, and no group gatherings for sports and socials. Parents will readjust their schedules to work at home and to spend time at the office. They will spend part of their day working with their children on schoolwork. School students will be forced to become self-responsible for homework, house chores, and tasks for daily living.

The nation will be primed for the presidential election. After Labor Day President Trump and former Vice President Biden will be on the campaign trail speaking to the issues facing our country and offering a vision of America for the next four years. By the end of July 2020 Vice President Biden holds a double-digit lead over President Trump due to the coronavirus crisis and the economic downturn. Candidates for local, state, and national races will be visiting our towns and cities and addressing voters on their concerns and commitments for social change.

There will be a flurry of activities that will grab the imaginations of people in communities across the nation and we will be swept up in the grandeur of the moment. Yet in the midst of these events Jeremiah reminds us that God is still the potter and that we the American people are still the clay being molded on the great wheel of the potter's spindle.

THE POTTER AND THE CLAY

The summer of 2020 is a fateful period in the history of the United States of America. We have suffered a dreadful loss of life due to COVID-19, a staggering number of coronavirus illness, unemployment and the loss of jobs which will never return to millions of people, an economy which will take years to recover its vitality, racism-injustice-police brutality, presidential choice, and related social problems which are reported daily in our news.

There is a God who is watching over us. He is in control of the universe. In Jer 18 God is depicted as the potter who is shaping and reshaping the clay (our lives, community, and nation), molding and remolding it, taking out the flaws, and creating a beautiful vessel in the final end. God is on the move with the people of America (we the people in order to form a more perfect union) and has our country on the potter's wheel creating a more perfect nation.

We see this new creation in our medical researchers who are fashioning a vaccine to combat COVID-19. We feel it in the Black Lives Matter demonstrations in our cities calling for social change and police reform. We sense this in the presidential election where debate over issues, leadership directions, and human personalities are exposed for the American people to ponder, select, and vote in November 2020. We realize this as more Americans are returning to work and readying their children for the opening of school with virtual work and education. We are on the potter's wheel being reshaped into a new creation. As Paul declared: "So if anyone is in Christ, there is a new creation: everything old has passed away; see, everything has become new! All this is from God, who reconciled us to himself through Christ, and has given us the ministry of reconciliation" (2 Cor 5:17 and 18).

America can remerge as a new country and can leave behind those old patterns of hate, division, and strife. It can be that shining vessel high on the hill and a new creation. As Christians we believe that when we truly come to Christ, Jesus and the cross reconcile us to each other as spiritual brothers and sisters. But Paul says that we now have a ministry of reconciliation which means that we must start the hard task of working with every person who has prejudice and discrimination and helping that person work through those ugly belief systems, emotions, and behaviors and reconcile him/herself to others who have the same difficulties. This is part of being on the potter's wheel as he shapes and reshapes our country, smoothing the imperfections and creating a beautiful product in the end.

Our sermon reflects these thoughts and is divided into three parts: reworking the clay (Jer 18:1–4), remaking the nation (Jer 18:5–10), and turning and amending your ways (Jer 18:11 and 12).

REWORKING THE CLAY

A lump of clay has no shape or substance, but in the hands of a skilled potter, the clay *is* transformed into a majestic piece of art or a vessel which holds water and new life. Jeremiah 18:1–4 is an invitation from the LORD to Jeremiah to go to the potter's house to observe the touch of a master potter. Jeremiah 18:4 is crucial: "The vessel he was making of clay was spoiled in the potter's hand, and he reworked it into another vessel, as seemed good to him." Imagine yourself sitting in the potter's workshop on the wheel shaping a vessel when you feel a flaw (a bump, a foreign impediment) and you eliminate this matter and reshape it, according to what felt and looked good in your estimation as the potter.

So it is with God. He is the master potter and we are the clay. God is shaping your life and the life of the nation slowly, carefully, and lovingly. He finds a flaw, a defect, or a foreign matter and eliminates it as he shapes and reshapes us to perfection and into a marvelous work of art. Have you been aware of God as the Potter working in your life? Is God gradually identifying and smoothing out the flaws of this nation? Is America becoming a work of art that we can be proud of owning as citizens? God is reworking the clay.

Take, for example, the murder of George Floyd by the four ex-police officers in Minneapolis, Minnesota. Weeks of protest by citizens from all walks of life brought together by a human and social wrong followed which led cities and states banning police chokeholds and instituting police reform. Mayors, city councils, and police chiefs are taking their own action to address and correct the police practice issues facing their localities. National legislation speaking to these issues await a Senate vote and presidential approval. Vestiges of past racism and Civil War monuments and the naming of military bases after Confederate leaders have been highlighted and are being resolved. Perhaps behind these actions and reactions is the Lord God who is the master potter shaping and reshaping the landscape and living patterns of the American people. There is the Christian hymn: "Have Thine Own Way, LORD, Have Thine Own Way; Thou art The Potter, I am the clay; Mold me and make me, after thy Will, while I am waiting, yielded and still." God is doing a great work in the life of individuals and of the nation. He is reworking the clay of our lives and the fortune of our nation.

REMAKING THE NATION

Jeremiah 18:5–10 immediately turns the narrative to the national spotlight. God's intention is for the nation of Israel which has direct implications for our country: "Just like the clay in the potter's hand, so are you in my hand, O house of Israel. At one moment I may declare concerning a nation or a kingdom, that I will pluck up and break down and destroy it, but if that nation, . . . turns from its evil, I will change my mind . . . (and) I will build and plant it . . ." (Jer 18:6–9). God's warning and ultimatum are stern and direct: turn from your evil ways, listen to my voice, and I will perform the good of my intention and build and plant you and your nation on solid ground. Do evil in my sight, turn a deaf ear to my pleas and I will pluck you up, break you down, and utterly destroy you.

God has an invitation and a warning for the nation of Israel which is applicable to our country. Turn from your evil ways: the hate, the accusations, the lies, the insults, the narcissism, the brutality, the murders, the destruction and looting of property, the chaos, the division, and related expressions of upheaval and suffering. Come unto me all you that are heavy-laden and I will give you rest: I will reshape you on the potter's wheel, I will eliminate the flaws of your being, I will build you up and plant the seeds of righteousness, fairness, justice, and faithfulness in the vessel that I am creating in my workshop.

I see a better United States of America high on the hill of liberty and justice for all, leading the rest of the nations with truth, faith, and power for all of its citizens particularly the least advantaged. I see European Americans, African Americans, Latino Americans, Asian Americans and Pacific Islanders, Native Americans, Muslim Americans, and other ethnic groups sharing political power, economic resources, and representative government together and with each other. I witness justice, fairness, and protection with service among our police for communities. I long for the president of the United States to be a person of integrity, truth, compassion, and vision who will lead our nation wisely and with humility and God's help. I anticipate landmark legislation which flows from the halls of Congress to the main streets of communities and states which are in great need. I want to see a great revival of faith and trust in God from our ministers and churches and the people of this country which will create a deep sense of spirituality. I await great opportunities to educate all citizens in our community colleges and universities so that the leaders of tomorrow will receive the best education to prepare them to confront and solve the problems which loom in the distant future. I wish for the remaking of the nation as Jeremiah wrote so many centuries ago.

TURNING AND AMENDING OUR WAYS

Jeremiah 18:11 and 12 has a startling end which is a rude awakening: "Thus says the LORD: . . . Turn now, all of you from your evil way, and amend your ways and your doings. But they say 'It is no use! We will follow our own plans, and each of us will act according to the stubbornness of our evil will.'" God's invitation is rejected. Rather than turning and amending their evil ways, the people decide to follow their own selfish plans and exhibit the stubbornness of being set in their ways. It is not the outcome that is anticipated by the prophet Jeremiah who is spurred on to fight for the right and the righteousness of God.

What does one do when an individual will not change his/her own selfish and destructive lifestyle or when a nation which is on the path of self-destruction refuses to turn from it? There is an old adage: "People do not change." They are set in their ways. It is hard to make incremental and gradual changes in people's lives and in the life of a community, state, and nation. Jeremiah faced this hardness of heart to God who promised building and planting. But we can never give up. We must try to work with those who will change and will respond to the Lord. Spiritual breakthroughs are few and far between, but we must keep trying as Jeremiah did as he faced rejection and stiffness.

WE ARE ON THE POTTER'S WHEEL

We as individuals and as a nation are on the potter's wheel. We are being shaped and molded by God the master potter daily in our lives. God is able to create a wonderful piece of art in us if we will allow him to perform his work. If we surrender to the Lord and let him have his way we move as individuals and as a country toward the paths of justice and righteousness. But if we resist as self-centered and stubborn beings, we risk the judgement of God and the decline of our country and civilization.

Will you act now to allow the LORD to shape us on the potter's wheel? Will you let him mold us into an individual and a nation that allow God in our human and civic life? Can we live out our pledge of allegiance: one nation under God? In the coming days, months, and years we shall see how our individual and corporate lives play out as the master potter and his wheel mold us. It is an exciting time in our life and the American life. What does God have in store for you? What will happen to the United States of America? After God finishes molding our country, what will the nation become in a year or in four years? Will it still be that city shining on the hill beckoning for all to come to its shores of liberty and justice for all? We truly hope and pray that the United States of America will recover from the coronavirus and be that beacon of light which blesses and guides all who stand beside her.

There was a man who lived in Wailua, Hawaii, on the island of Oahu which is on the way to the north shore where surfers love to catch extraordinary high waves. Eddie Rodriguez had a bad temper and would get drunk every weekend. He would come out of his house and yell and cuss and cause a scene. The local police knew him quite well. Everyone thought that he would never change. One day young John Kalili who grew up in Wailua returned home from Moody Bible Institute. John befriended Eddie and eventually he became a Christian. Eddie was a changed man who was transformed by the power of Christ. John and Eddie travelled throughout Oahu, speaking at various churches. Eddie would give his testimony of his life change and John would give the sermon on the good news of Christ. John would refer to Eddie as "a trophy of God's grace." I was a young high school student when John and Eddie came to my church youthgroup. I was moved and never forgot their words of faith and trust in Jesus Christ. John Kalili was the first man of Hawaiian ancestry to graduate from Princeton Theological Seminary. He returned to Honolulu to serve as pastor of a Hawaiian congregation.

The changed life of Eddie Rodriguez is a reminder that contrary to the reality that Jeremiah faced in his day, a person can respond to the Word of the Lord and make a moral and behavioral change toward a spiritual redirection. Allow the LORD to mold you and remake you on the potter's wheel.

PASTORAL PRAYER

O God of the heavens and the earth we come to you this day filled with the awareness of your power and might. Please help our country in the midst of illness, death, turmoil, and strife. We need your wisdom to sort out the mess that we face on many fronts.

We acknowledge that you are the master potter and that we are the clay in your hands. Mold us, shape us, and take out the flaws in our lives and the life of our nation. Make us into a vessel that comes from you, our Creator. We realize that it may take time on the wheel of the potter but we know that in the end we will be better as a nation.

Bless, O LORD God, our church as it seeks to minister to its people. Help us to reach out to our community through the video ministry as the Word of the Lord is proclaimed every Sunday. Make the messages that are sent be vessels of comfort and encouragement to those who hear and listen to the good news of Christ. We pray for our seniors, our sick, and those who are raising their families that you will be with all of us. Grant your guidance to those who care and nurture those who are dependent and in need. Grant to those who care your patience and love in the midst of need and demand.

We especially pray for Martin and his heart condition that you will guide his doctors; for Roseann's father and for Risa as they recover from their strokes that you will help them to exercise and recover; for Melanie and her heart surgery that you will be with her physicians; and for all those who are in need of healing and comfort.

In the name of Christ, we pray. Amen.

CHAPTER 18

THE NEW COVENANT
Jeremiah 31:31–34 (September 20, 2020)

Scripture Reading. The days are surely coming, says the LORD, when I will make a new covenant with the house of Israel and the house of Judah. It will not be like the covenant that I made with their ancestors when I took them by the hand to bring them out of the land of Egypt—a covenant that they broke, though I was their husband, says the LORD. But this is the covenant that I will make with the house of Israel after those days, says the LORD; I will put my law within them, and I will write it on their hearts; and I will be their God, and they shall be my people. No longer shall they teach one another, or say to each other, "Know the LORD," for they shall all know me, from the least of them to the greatest, says the LORD; for I will forgive their iniquity, and remember their sin no more.

Where are we as the closing days of summer come to an end and we return to our homes and ready our children for school and the coming fall months? The summer has been quiet for us as we have sheltered at home, worked away from our offices, and have our children in our midst. We have ventured out to the grocery store and the shopping malls but have been cautious and heeding the CDC requirements for coping with the pandemic. Most of us have not taken a summer vacation and flown on airplanes to Europe, Asia, or South America or taken a boat cruise due to the coronavirus. Now it is time to get ready for the start of school and a return to our normal schedule.

We do not know what to expect. Will our children be safe at school? If they remain home and participate in distance learning are we as parents able to help them with their homework and check their answers? Or are we too involved with our own work at our jobs to have enough time to help our children with their studies? Will it be a safe start of the school year or will there be other crises in the community to warrant our attention and concern? How will the presidential election between Trump and Biden play out as they campaign and face each other in the presidential debates? Will it be a close election or will Biden sweep the votes of an overwhelming majority of states? Will President Trump contest the election if he loses and will we face a constitutional crisis which may involve a vote of the United States Supreme Court much like the Florida vote involved George W. Bush and Al Gore? It will be an interesting fall season. Where are we and where will we be in the beginning of fall 2020?

Regardless of what happens to the United States of America, we want to focus on the covenant that God made with his people in the book of Genesis and throughout the history of Israel and the Christian church. In a sense the founding fathers believed in the separation of church and state so that no one religion would dominate and control the course of events in our country. At the same time there was a strong belief in the presence and blessing of God who would watch over and protect the United States of America. Hence the motto, "In God We Trust," a reference to the Creator in our primary documents, and later the inclusion, "one nation under God," in our pledge of allegiance. The thought of a covenant between God and country are implied in the establishment of the United States of America and are a backdrop to our sermon on the new covenant. We turn to the first covenant in the Bible between God and Noah.

AFTER THE FLOOD THE RAINBOW COVENANT

We read in Gen 6 that God brought a great flood over the earth to wash away the sins of the world. God saw corruption and violence and chose Noah and his family who walked with God as survivors (Gen 6:8 and 9). Genesis 6:11–13 makes this observation: "Now the earth was corrupt in God's sight, and the earth was filled with violence. And God saw that the earth was corrupt; for all flesh had corrupted its ways upon the earth. And God said to Noah, 'I have determined to make an end of all flesh, for the earth is filled with violence . . .'" We know the rest of the story: Noah builds an ark of cypress wood after the instructions of the Lord, saves his family and two of every living creatures (birds and animals), endures a rain of forty days and forty nights, and survives the great flood (Gen 6–8). At the end of the ordeal God makes the rainbow covenant with Noah and with the rest of the human race: "When the (rain) bow is in the clouds, I will see it and remember the everlasting covenant between God and every living creature of all flesh that is on the earth. God said to Noah, 'This is a sign of the covenant that I have established between me and all flesh that is on the earth'" (Gen 9:16 and 17).

The rainbow covenant is the first covenant that God makes with human persons. It precedes the covenant that God makes with Abraham, the father of the nation of Israel, in Gen 12:1–3. It is a reminder that when we see the rainbow in the sky after a rain that God established a covenant with us and has cleansed us from corruption and violence. As we pass through the ordeal of the coronavirus we need to reflect on the spiritual lessons of the Great Coronavirus Pandemic. As a result we must make a new covenant with the LORD as Americans and Christian believers. I believe that it is crucial for us to formulate a new pledge and agreement and recommit ourselves to the Lord.

What would be the terms of this new covenant after the coronavirus? Noah was confounded by the corruption and violence (Gen 6:11) in his day to the extent that God said: "... I am sorry that I have made them" (Gen 6:8). Has the level of the present corruption and violence in the United States reached that of Noah's society? I pray that this is not the case. Perhaps our new covenant should be that we will honor and be faithful to the Lord and that he will guard and guide us from harm and danger in light of future pandemics.

COVENANT THEOLOGY

A covenant is a compact or a binding agreement between two parties which involves an undertaking which benefits both and solidifies a relationship. In the Bible there are covenants made between God and his people. The Old Testament covenant begins with Abraham, the father of Israel, from whom will come the Messiah, Jesus Christ (Gen 17:4). Later God made a covenant with the people of Israel (the Ten Commandments) on Mount Sinai with Moses as the mediator (Exod 34:28 and 29). In the New Testament God established a covenant with the church. The death and resurrection of Christ is the new covenant written in the blood of Christ (Mark 14:24; Heb 12:24).

Later the Protestant reformers, Luther and Calvin, formulated covenant theology to explain the covenant of works and the covenant of grace. The covenant of works describes the Old Testament where Israel is to obey the Torah (the Law) and offer sacrifices to God which is a prefigure of the atoning death of Christ. The covenant of grace is the New Testament redemption where Christ offers himself as the sacrifice for sin and faith in Christ and the promise of eternal life is the response of the believer. In infant baptism the church establishes a covenant with the parents of the child to raise and teach the Christian faith so that when a person reaches the age of discretion, he/she will affirm his/her faith in Christ and will participate in the confirmation service as a Christian believer. Covenant theology was brought to the thirteen colonies by the pilgrims who settled in Massachusetts and established local autonomous congregations. These churches became the Congregational Churches of America which later merged into the United Church of Christ today.

Jeremiah 31:31–34 talks about the covenant that God made with Israel and Judah at Mount Sinai. That was the old covenant. Here God is announcing a new covenant that he will make which will be a transformative agreement of the heart. Our sermon involves: 1) the old covenant of the Law (Jer 31:31 and 32), 2) the new covenant of the heart (Jer 31:33), and 3) he covenant of knowledge and forgiveness of the Lord (Jer 31:34).

THE OLD COVENANT OF THE LAW

If you read the books of Leviticus, Numbers, and Deuteronomy in the Old Testament, one is struck with the multitude of laws pertaining to individual, interpersonal, and community behavioral rules and regulations of worship and sacrifice. The law was there not only to regulate the behavior of the people of Israel but also to keep them faithful and obedient to the LORD God. The law was not an end unto itself, although it became such in the time of Jesus because Israel underwent the exile due to its disobedience to the law and the worship of idols rather than to the One True God. The Pharisees were intent on strict obedience to the law as a demonstration that God would never cast Israel aside and send them into another exile, although by then Israel was no longer an independent nation but rather annexed to powerful nations as conquerors over her.

The LORD announces that he will make a new covenant with the house of Israel and Judah that will be different from the Old Testament covenant (Jer 31:31). Jeremiah 31:32 recalls the covenant made by God with the people who left Egypt became a broken covenant. It was an external covenant of laws (thou shalt and thou shalt not) which did not work out for the people in their faith relationship with God. The old covenant of the Old Testament was inadequate for the needs of the people of Israel. Beyond strict regulatory rules the old covenant stressed the loving faithful relationship between God and his people of Israel.

The apostle Paul writes the entire book of Galatians in the New Testament explaining the shortcomings of the law (the old covenant) and the dawning of the new covenant of faith. If you have time, read the book of Galatians, and follow Paul's logic and argument about the law and faith. His essential argument is: "We ourselves are Jews by birth and not Gentile sinners; yet we know that a person is justified not by the works of the law but through faith in Jesus Christ. And we have come to believe in Christ Jesus, so that we might be justified by faith in Christ, and not by doing the works of the law, because no one will be justified by the works of the law" (Gal 2:15 and 16). Jeremiah in his day speaks about another new covenant which foreshadows the faith covenant.

THE NEW COVENANT OF THE HEART

Jeremiah 31:33 announces the covenant of the heart: ". . . I will put my law within them, and I will write it on their hearts; and I will be their God. And they shall be my people." God says that he will take the external law and make it an internal belief of the heart. What is the meaning of this verse? The heart is the center of affection and being. We use the metaphor (I love you with all my heart) to mean that from our very essential being comes our love for another person. When we say the pledge of allegiance to our flag we place our hand over our heart which symbolizes that these words are uttered from our innermost self.

The placing of the law in the hearts of the people of Israel means that the essence of the law of love (the greatest commandment: Love the LORD your God with all your heart, soul and might and love your neighbor as you would love yourself and your family) would now be placed in us. God's intention for establishing the law was to form a relationship between himself and his people (I will be their God and they shall be my people). This is the meaning of the new covenant of the heart.

When a person comes to Christ and accept him as Savior and LORD, that individual receives Christ into his/her life and is guided by him. Jesus Christ enters the being of that person's life. John 1:12 declares: "But to all who received him, who believed in his name, he gave power to become children of God, . . ." The decision to become a Christian and to follow Jesus is a matter of the heart.

THE COVENANT OF KNOWLEDGE AND FORGIVENESS OF THE LORD

Jeremiah 31:34 concludes: "No longer shall they teach one another, or say to each other, 'Know the LORD,' for they shall all know me, from the least of them to the greatest, says the LORD; for I will forgive their iniquity, and remember their sin no more." When faith becomes a matter of the heart and flourishes within a person, a transformation occurs according to this verse. An individual and indeed all the people truly have a deep knowledge of God. That knowledge is transferred from the mind to the heart. Religion is no longer an external act of worship. It becomes a vibrant knowledge of the heart (the spirit and the soul). From the core of one's being God dwells within the person. It becomes a living force which governs a person's life. If an individual is directed inwardly by the heart and faith, one does not have to worry about sinning against another. God truly forgives his/her iniquity. Sin becomes a thing of the past. Behold, all things have become new (2 Cor 5:17). A person has become a new creation and creature in God's sight.

God truly forgives that person when there is the new covenant of the heart which transfers and translates itself into the covenant of knowledge and forgiveness of the LORD. Jeremiah saw these connections and penned these verses inspired by the Word of the LORD many centuries ago. These truths are still with us today.

THE FLOW OF THE COVENANTS

The changing of the old covenant into the new covenant of the heart which leads us into the covenant of knowledge and forgiveness of the LORD were foreshadows of the new covenant of the body and blood of Jesus Christ (This is my body which is broken for you, This is my blood which is shed for you, Do this in remembrance of me). It flows from the Old Testament history of the old covenant to Abraham and Moses through the covenant of the heart proclaimed by Jeremiah to the new covenant of Christ in his death and resurrection in the New Testament.

These historical connections are a part of the signposts which we find in the Old and New Testaments. They are markers in our journey of faith. The author of the book of Hebrews surveys the grandeur of those persons of faith starting with Abel through Abraham and Moses and ending with those who suffered for their faith. His conclusion is: "Therefore, since we are surrounded by so great a cloud of witnesses, let us also lay aside every weight and the sin that clings so closely, and let us run with perseverance the race that is set before us, looking to Jesus the pioneer and perfecter of our faith, who for the sake of the joy that was set before him endured the cross, disregarding its shame, and has taken his seat at the right hand of the throne of God" (Heb 12:1 and 2). Thanks be to God who made a covenant with us.

God makes a series of covenants in the Old Testament: the rainbow covenant (Gen 9), the Abrahamic covenant (Gen 12: 1–3), and the Mosaic covenant of the Law (Ex 20). Jeremiah 31 predicts the new covenant of the heart and the covenant of the knowledge and forgiveness of the Lord which are a foretaste of the New Testament. In Jesus Christ is the full knowledge of God. As Paul declares: "For in him the whole fullness of deity dwells bodily, and you have come to fullness in him, who is the head of every ruler and authority" (Col 2:9 and 10). Jesus talks about the new covenant of the heart when he said in the Sermon on the Mount: "Blessed are the pure in heart, for they will see God" (Matt 5:8) and offers the forgiveness of our sins: "In him we have redemption through his blood, the forgiveness of our trespasses, according to the riches of his grace" (Eph 1:7). It is amazing that Jeremiah foresaw the essence of the New Testament covenant of the body and blood of Christ which is attested in these verses.

COVENANT MAKING, MAKERS, AND KEEPERS

This sermon on the new covenant is an opportunity for us to make a personal covenant with God. A covenant is an agreement and understanding between two persons and covers areas of our lives that are important for us to stake out. Is there a part of your life that you would like to dedicate to God and reserve for him? Make a covenant with God regarding a decision in your life.

Many years ago we were having trouble with starting our family as a young married couple. Together we were struggling with medical problems which caused infertility. We both underwent surgery to correct our infertility problems but nothing seemed to work for us. Often I would read the story of Abraham and Sarah and identify with their lack of children. Privately I made an informal covenant with God to love and obey him and asked that he would provide a family for us. After leaving Hawaii and returning to graduate school in Ohio God brought our first child, Lori, from Taiwan and before moving to Sacramento my wife, Joyce, was pregnant with our son, Jonathan. Amy and Matthew followed several years later and we have four children and nine grandchildren. Making a covenant with God brought blessings into our lives as father and mother and as grandfather and grandmother. Blessed be the name of the Lord.

There are covenants that you can make with others. In the Old Testament we read about the covenant that David and Jonathan, two close friends, made with each other: ". . . the soul of Jonathan was bound to the soul of David, and Jonathan loved him as his own soul. . . . Then Jonathan made a covenant with David, because he loved him as his own soul" (1 Sam 18:1, 3). Would you like to make a covenant with a friend or confidante: your husband or wife, a close friend from your childhood, a school or college friend, or a friend from work or from your tight circle of acquaintances? Identify an area of agreement and understanding and make a personal covenant with that person. Become a covenant maker and holder with God and with others.

WHERE SHALL WE GO?

What would happen if we made a series of covenant agreements with the primary persons of our lives? There may be a rippling effect which will cause us to see that covenant-making has possibilities for resolving differences between larger entities such as neighborhood disputes; practical solutions to social problems; the interplay between gang violence, the reaction of the local community, and the action of the police; and Black Lives Matter and police brutality. Maybe covenant-making (much like the steps toward peace-making) is a vehicle for problem resolution and the direction that we need to pursue as we grapple with the problems facing our cities. Where shall we go? is a meaningful question as we wind down the year 2020 which has been a volatile and chaotic season.

PASTORAL PRAYER

O God of the covenant, we come to you this day thanking you that you made covenants with Noah, Abraham, Moses, and Israel and that you make a new covenant with us in the blood and body of Jesus Christ. We thank you that Jeremiah foresaw that covenant of the heart and the knowledge and forgiveness of God and that your Son, Jesus, came to fulfill and embody this new covenant.

As we are in the midst of this grave pandemic, we pray that you will protect and heal those who are suffering from the coronavirus. May we make a new covenant with you in the midst of this pandemic to remember the Lord God and to be faithful unto you and just and fair with our neighbors who live in our community. We also pray that you will teach us to be covenant makers and keepers with others and that we will bond with them in a covenant agreement to seek love, mercy, and justice to those who are oppressed in our community.

We remember our church this morning and ask your presence and guidance as we seek your will for our future. Be with our members and friends who support us in prayer, giving, and commitment that all of us will shoulder the load and work together as one body in Christ. Lead us as we covenant with you for our present and our future: our decision to seek and select a new pastor for our church, our planning to have video worship services, our tithes and offerings for the ministries of our fellowship, and our members and friends who need you in their journey of faith. Continue to be with those who are in pain and suffering as the Great Physician. We pray for our church school which will open in October that you will be with our teachers in their planning and preparation process. We pray for those who are ill: Roseann's father and Risa as they recover from their strokes, Martin and his heart condition that you will strengthen him every day, and Melanie and her heart surgery. We thank you that Martin has been released from the hospital and for Roseann's father and his recovery from his stroke. Continue to be with them. Strengthen their bodies, minds, and spirits. Be with our seniors as they mature in their years. Be with us all. In the name of Christ, we pray. Amen.

CHAPTER 19

ONE SHEPHERD, A COVENANT, AND VEGETATION

Ezekiel 34:23–31 (October 4, 2020)

Scripture Reading. I will set up over them one shepherd, my servant David, and he shall feed them, he shall feed them and be their shepherd. And I, the LORD, will be their God, and my servant David shall be prince among them. I, the LORD, have spoken.

I will make with them a covenant of peace and banish wild animals from the land, so that they may live in the wild and sleep in the woods securely. I will make them and the region around my hill a blessing; and I will send down the showers in their season; they shall be showers of blessing. The trees of the field shall yield their fruit, and the earth shall yield its increase. They shall be secure on their soil; and they shall know that I am the LORD, when I break the bars of their yoke, and save them from the hands of those who enslave them. They shall no more be plunder for the nations nor shall the animals of the land devour them; they shall live in safety, and no one shall make them afraid. I will provide for them a splendid vegetation so that they shall no more be consumed with hunger in the land, and no longer suffer the insults of the nations. They shall know that I, the LORD their God, am with them, and that they, the house of Israel, are my people, says the Lord GOD. You are my sheep, the sheep of my pasture and I am your God, says the Lord GOD.

We are at a pivotal moment in the calendar of our nation as we transition from the end of summer to the beginning of fall. The year 2020 has not been a good year. People have gotten sick and many have recovered from COVID-19. We thank our public health researchers and our doctors and nurses in the hospitals and medical centers across the country for their endurance and assistance. But there have been countless deaths from the coronavirus with the largest number occurring in the United States. How can a country with our size, our knowledge of medicine and science, and our unlimited resources be the world's greatest victim of this pandemic? As we move into the fall with the opening of school, we pray that all our children and teachers will be protected from the affliction of this illness in the classrooms across our nation. We pray for all the candidates for public office from the president of the United States to the local city council that they will be safe from illness and harm as they campaign for the votes of the American people.

We also mourn the loss of Ruth Bader Ginsburg and her work for women's rights and watch closely that her successor on the court will maintain the rights and freedom of all Americans. We think of the family of Breonna Taylor, those who have demonstrated on her behalf, and the decision of the grand jury of her peers who weighed the facts of the case and rendered a ruling. What a difficult situation for all who are involved with this tragic accident.

As we consider the message of Ezek 34:23–31 we are reminded that God is the good shepherd who watches over us, that the promises of God are available to everyone who calls on the name of the Lord, and that vegetation and growth shall come in due season. As we make this seasonal transition from summer to fall, let us be mindful of the presence of God who watches over us and cares about our needs.

THE PROMISES OF GOD

Ezekiel was both a prophet and a priest whose ministry was from 593 BC to 563 BC. He was instrumental in bringing back to Jerusalem the people who were in exile and were returning to their land. The temple of God in Jerusalem was destroyed in 587 BC. Ezekiel's ministry involved infusing faith, hope, and new life into the lives of a defeated and shattered people as returning exiles. Ezekiel, Ezra, and Nehemiah were the prophets of the post-exile period who led the people back from captivity to a nation and cities which were destroyed and in ruin. The people faced recovery and rebuilding, much like our nation where we find ourselves in need of finding our true self and restoring health, vigor, and unity. Ezekiel 34:23–31 contains three promises of God which uplifted the aspirations of the people who were starting over in the midst of the ruins of their nation.

Picture the scene which is before Ezekiel as he leads his exiled people from Babylonian captivity back to Jerusalem which is no longer a thriving city. Jerusalem lays in waste and desolation. Most of the former inhabitants have been either killed or taken away to other lands. There is no food, job, or economy to sustain adequate living. Government and social services are limited and unreliable. There is much rebuilding of houses, businesses, and landmark structures required for the population to function as a living and viable entity. There has been major disruption.

Ezekiel returns and preaches the promises of God. He offers hope in the midst of doom and gloom. He turns the people back to the glory days of David and reminds them of the shepherd role of the young David (Ps 23). He emphasizes that God will give them a covenant of peace which will bring solace and security to rebuild without the threat of invasion and war. He promises that there will be the planting and harvesting of crops so that people will eat and not be hungry and that God will reaffirm his relationship with his people as the shepherd and his sheep.

America has also undergone a period of death and destruction although most of its people and city buildings remain standing. Our wounds are deep and filled with loss over lives, racism and brutality, lack of leadership, division and strife, chaos and lies, ridicule and deceit, isolation and corruption, and a host of social problems which require immediate attention and major solutions. Like Ezekiel we need leaders who can bring order out of disorder, sanity out of insanity, and vision out of blindness. Let us rise up and rebuild, said Ezekiel, Ezra, and Nehemiah who were the prophets of the post-exile period and charged with inspiring the people with spiritual encouragement when the country was at its lowest point and was beginning the painful and tedious task of reconstruction. We as a nation are in need of the promises of God. We are facing landmark rebuilding of our identity as one nation under God with liberty and justice for all. We reaffirm this truth, but we realize that it is difficult to achieve in our daily life.

God speaks to the returning people and offers three promises: 1) one shepherd over them (Ezek 34:23 and 24), 2) a covenant of peace (Ezek 34:25–28), and 3) vegetation, plenty, and spiritual relationships (Ezek 34:29–31).

ONE SHEPHERD OVER THEM

Ezekiel 34:23 and 24 declare: "I will set up over them one shepherd, my servant David, and he shall feed them: he shall feed them and be their shepherd. And I, the LORD, will be their God, and my servant David shall be prince among them; I, the LORD, have spoken." It is interesting that this passage of Scripture starts with the shepherd motif. The shepherd and sheep are common to the people of Israel who remembered that King David was once a shepherd boy in his youth and also wrote Ps 23 as their ruler. God promises the people of Israel that David will again rule as prince and will be a nurturing and kind shepherd of the flock. Why was this so important for the people to hear and believe this promise from God? Because the people were without leadership and were faced with an enormous rebuilding process. They had no resources except their bare hands, faith in God, and sheer willpower.

How would you start over if all your belongings were destroyed and your house and community laid in ruin? I often wonder how the people of the South, Midwest, and West have the will to rebuild when I see the destruction of a tornado, hurricane, or forest fire demolish homes and businesses in communities. People have the will and the fortitude to pick up the pieces, clean up their towns, reconstruct their dwellings, and reorder their lives. In parts of this country the people have not only worried about the coronavirus but have lost their homes, businesses, schools, and communities to natural disasters. Yet they persevere and move forward as people convinced that their existence and being are important to their family and community.

America needs a good shepherd who watches over the flock, feeding them, leading them in the path of righteousness, and restoring their souls. King David was the good shepherd of his people in the Old Testament. In the New Testament Jesus was the Good Shepherd who said: "I am the good shepherd. The good shepherd lays down his life for the sheep" (John 10:11). Now we look to our leaders to shepherd us through stormy waters and treacherous roads as our country moves from crisis to more crises. God promises one shepherd over us in the book of Ezekiel.

A COVENANT OF PEACE

Ezekiel 34:25–28 talks about a covenant of peace: "I will make with them a covenant of peace. . . . I will make them . . . a blessing . . . they shall be showers of blessing . . . they shall know that I am the LORD . . . they shall live in safety, and no one shall make them afraid." The people of Israel longed for peace from war, destruction, and disaster. God promises a covenant of peace free from strife and conflict and with a guarantee of safety and the absence of fear.

We abhor war as the American people but we have fought many wars during the twentieth and twenty-first centuries: World War I (1917–1918), World War II (1941–1945), the Korean War (1950–1953), the Vietnam War (1955–1975), the Gulf War (1990–1991), Afghanistan (2001-present), and the Iraq War (2003–2011). President Woodrow Wilson described the First World War as "a war to end all wars" but it did not happen that way. We still have US military troops stationed in various parts of Europe, Asia, and the Middle East. We are a peaceful nation and are a part of the United Nations and NATO which seek to ensure peace.

This passage in Ezekiel promises a covenant of peace which opposes war and conflict. It has much relevance for us today as we witness the strife and conflict in our city streets. We know why there are demonstrations and partial symbolic takeovers of a Seattle city district and the steps of a state capitol building. Demonstrators want to call attention to social injustice and police brutality. How do we negotiate with demonstrators, act with swift justice, defuse the volatile situation, and bring calm to the streets of our cities? How do we right the wrongs that have taken place for many years on our city streets? Do we offer a more protective and serve-the-community police force? Do we send out clinical social workers and mental health counselors with police officers and calm down mentally ill and homeless individuals rather than shoot them? Do we penetrate a low income area with youth outreach workers and offer youth drop-in centers rather than more police presence?

These are some proposals (Defund The Police) (Refund Social Services) which are being discussed by city leaders and community activists which may reduce killing and work for the good of communities which are now under siege. Perhaps this is the content of a covenant of peace where mayors, police chiefs, city council members, health and mental health resources, community organizers, and even urban gang leaders come together to plan and execute social programs which will ease the tension in major cities of the United States. America, turn to Ezek 34:25 and read and learn about a covenant of peace and then implement it in your city.

VEGETATION, PLENTY, AND SOCIAL RELATIONSHIPS

Ezekiel 34:29-31 promises: "I will provide for them a splendid vegetation so that they shall no more be consumed with hunger in the land, and no longer suffer the insults of the nations. They shall know that I, the LORD their God, am with them, and that they, the house of Israel, are my people, says the Lord GOD. You are my sheep, the sheep of my pasture and I am your God, says the Lord GOD." God's promise to the returning exiles is that they will be able to plant and harvest crops so that they will not be hungry and will become one people and nation again. God will reestablish his covenant relationship with Israel as the people of God and the shepherd of his sheep.

God leads us back into our torn up and ruined cities and offers a bounty of plenty and an absence of want. God wants us to reclaim the meaning of one nation under God and longs to be our shepherd who nurtures and protects all of his sheep which includes all people regardless of race, color, and creed. Many have lost their jobs, have experienced hunger, and have gone to food distribution centers. The United States of America has endured the criticisms and insults of nations for pulling back from treaties and agreements and for chaos in the streets which have been reported on news programs around the world. Yet God calls out to us to return to our broken and downtrodden cities where he can give us rest. Come unto Me all you who are heavy laden and I will give you rest (Matt 11:28). He is our God and the shepherd of us all. Come to him for comfort, understanding, wisdom, and union with him and one another.

There will come a time when our nation shall recover from this coronavirus pandemic. We shall blossom as a nation. Our citizens, young and old, man and woman, rich and poor, shall come forth as healthy and strong people. Like the returnees from the Babylonian captivity there shall be a slow recovery and the rebuilding of cities and lives. The pandemic may flare up in hot spots from time to time, but we shall experience the gradual vegetation of our lives, the plenty from our restored economy, and the resumption of social relationships, as predicted by Ezekiel.

Like the remnant survivors of Israel who picked up the pieces, so we as Americans shall resume our lives, wiser, cautious, and circumspect in our awareness of a public health outbreak. This was the destiny of Israel envisioned by Ezekiel as he assured Israel of the shepherding protection and love of God and his covenant of faithfulness over his people. God's promises remain true and available to the American people if they return to the Lord and remain faithful to him.

Second Chronicles 7:14 reminds the American people of God's invitation: "if my people who are called by my name humble themselves, pray, seek my face, and turn from their wicked ways, then I will hear from heaven, and will forgive their sin and heal their land." This verse has relevance for the pandemic facing us. The need of God's people for humility, prayer, seeking, turning, and the forgiveness and healing of God in the land. How touching and real is the need for our nation under God to seek the Lord anew and again in a land of disease, illness, and death. Seek the LORD while he may be found, call on his name, and return to the LORD God Almighty.

SPIRITUAL LONGINGS

I long for a spirituality which will sweep across America and be infused in the hearts and lives of our people as the pastor of a church One shepherd to guide and protect us, a covenant of peace between neighbors in our communities, and vegetation, plenty, and social relationships. I live in Sacramento, California, which was once called the most diverse city in America by *Time* magazine in 2002. We have a home in the South Sacramento Greenhaven-Pocket area of the city. It is populated with European Americans, Asian Americans, African Americans, and Latino Americans who relate well to each other. We greet and talk on our daily walks along the green belt, help one another as neighbors, have a neighborhood watch and news alert on our internet, and the mayor of the city lives several blocks from us. We are a tight knit community which has been responsive to Black Lives Matter, the coronavirus pandemic, and police reform. There are a number of churches in our area: St. Anthony's Catholic Church, Greenhaven Neighborhood Church, The River's Edge Church, Faith Presbyterian Church, Greenhaven Lutheran Church, Chinese Community Church, Sacramento Buddhist Church, Japanese United Methodist Church, and many others. We believe and practice spiritual values in our lives with each other.

There are tensions and disagreements, crime and violence, and other conflicts which are a part of city life. There are improvements needed in the community: police reform, sheltering the homeless, job loss and unemployment, and other related matters which the mayor, the city council, and concerned citizens need to address and resolve as we move together as a community However, by and large, the ethnic diverse people of this city have respected each other and lived together in neighborhoods. For this we should be thankful and grateful that there is a harmony and acceptance of each other as persons.

Let us hope that we will recognize that God is our shepherd, that we need to abide and maintain a covenant of peace with each other, and that vegetation, plenty, and supportive social relationships will be seen in our midst. Ezekiel foresaw these three resources in the midst of destruction and rebuilding. He mobilized the remnant people of Israel as a single force and they retuned to their land with a renewed faith and commitment to God and to each other. I pray that in the midst of this coronavirus pandemic when we are discouraged, disheartened, and down that we will remember that God has not forgotten us and has given us spiritual resources to draw strength, determination, and courage.

PASTORAL PRAYER

Dear God, In the midst of uncertain and perilous times we come to you as our shepherd. We need your guidance and protection as we face the COVID-19 pandemic. As the good shepherd, lead us beside the still water and the paths of righteousness and restore our souls. Help us to make a new covenant with you as individuals and as a country who needs to hear and see the Word of the LORD. Plant new vegetation in our lives so that we may grow and blossom with good fruit and plenty for those who are starving and hunger for a Word from God. Help us to embody your love, comfort, and provision as we seek to help those who are ill and in need of our friendship and listening and support.

As we enter the fall months we pray that all citizens of this great country will wear masks, shelter at home, wash hands, and avoid large crowds and by so doing will flatten the curve and help to suppress this COVID-19 virus. Be with the medical researchers and public health officials who are working with the development of a vaccine that you will oversee the testing period of this drug and swiftly bring it to the end of clinical trails so that it may be distributed and save lives. Bear down on the discipline and resolve of our people that we may fight this virus with your wisdom and diligence. Help us to make with you and with our nation a covenant of cooperation and commitment to follow the guidelines of the Centers for Disease Control.

We think of the many people in our country who need you as their Savior and LORD and pray that men and women, boys and girls, family and friends will be brought to the foot of the cross and find Jesus as their friend. Deliver us from our arrogance and our self-sufficiency and humble us with the awareness that we are vulnerable and frail and in need of you. Help us to cope with our daily struggles of living: the challenges of relating to our spouse in a healthy and supportive way, raising our children with wisdom and love, going to our jobs with energy and creativity, working around our home and yard, helping our friends, relatives and neighbors who are our support system, and keeping us all safe and secure. Be with our communities and our nation as we endure this great pandemic. Help us to practice wise and safe protocols.

We remember Danny and Patty and pray for Patty's father, Mr. C., who is in the Asian Community Center Nursing Home that you will comfort him. We pray for our dear brother, Martin, that you will provide him strength and courage as he faces each day. May your grace sustain him. Be with Roseann's father and Risa as they recover from their strokes. Support Melanie as she awaits her heart surgery. Guard and guide us, Dear LORD. Amen.

CHAPTER 20

FROM DRY BONES TO LIVE BONES
Ezekiel 37:1–14 (October 18, 2020)

Scripture Reading. The hand of the LORD came upon me, and he brought me out by the spirit of the LORD and set me down in the middle of a valley; it was full of bones. He led me all around them; there were very many lying in the valley, and they were very dry. He said to me, "Mortal, can these bones live?" I answered, "O Lord GOD, you know." Then he said to me, "Prophesy to these bones, and say to them: O dry bones, hear the word of the LORD. Thus says the Lord GOD to these bones: I will cause breath to enter you, and you shall live. I will lay sinew on you, and will cause flesh to come upon you, and cover you with skin, and put breath in you, and you shall live; and you shall know that I am the LORD."

So I prophesied as I had been commanded; and as I prophesied, suddenly there was a noise, a rattling, and the bones came together, bone to its bone. I looked, and there was sinew on them, and flesh had come upon them, and skin had covered them; but there was no breath in them. Then he said to me, "Prophesy to the breath, prophesy, mortal, and say to the breath; Thus says the Lord GOD: Come from the four winds, O breath, and breathe upon these slain, that they may live." I prophesied as he commanded me, and the breath came into them, and they lived, and stood on their feet, a vast multitude.

Then he said to me, "Mortal, these bones are the whole house of Israel. They say, 'Our bones are dried up, and our hope is lost; we are cut off completely.' Therefore prophesy, and say to them, Thus says the Lord GOD; I am going to open your graves. And bring you up from your graves, O my people; and I will bring you back to the land of Israel. And you shall know that I am the LORD, when I open your graves, and bring you up from your graves, O my people. I will put my spirit within you, and you shall live, and I will place you on your own soil; then you shall know that I, the LORD, have spoken and will act, says the LORD."

From March 2020 to August 28, 2020, there has been a marked increase, a movement toward flattening the curve, and then a surge of coronavirus illness and death since July 2020. By August 28, 2020, the statistics are one thousand deaths per day, 5.8 million cases of illness, and 180,000 deaths from COVID-19 in the United States. By October 15, 2020, the death toll in the United States will reach 215,000 and 7.8 million cases of coronavirus infections.

Dr. Anthony Fauci of the Presidential Coronavirus Task Force warned that by the end of 2020 400,000 Americans will die of COVID-19 if we do not heed the public health guidelines of the CDC. Never before in over a hundred years since the Spanish Flu epidemic of 1918 have we witnessed the outbreak of an invisible virus which has afflicted so many citizens of this country. It is ironic that given the medical scientific knowledge, the public health resources, the research arm of drug companies, and the most advanced medical schools in the world that we have been unable to stem the tide of this virus. We are months away from the distribution of an effective vaccine to curb the deadly effects of COVID-19. Can we hold on and exercise our containment strategy: shelter at home, wearing face mask, washing hands, and avoid large gatherings?

We focus on Ezek 37:1–14 which is a passage on the valley of dry bones (death) which is transformed by the Word of the LORD into the valley of live bones (new life). It is fitting for us to study and preach from these verses in light of the illness and death which we have faced for much of this year.

FROM THE VALLEY OF DEATH

Ezekiel 37:1–14 begins with the valley of death where there is an abundance of dead bones of people piled high on each other. It is a reminder of the abomination of desolation as spoken in the book of Daniel. Why is this the starting point of Ezekiel and the beginning of our sermon today? Perhaps this passage is here to remind us that we are passing through a pandemic which has created a valley of death and dead bones of innocent victims who succumbed to a mysterious and vengeful virus which swept over the world killing countless people regardless of social status, ethnic origin, or religious faith.

As we move toward the beginning of fall and the coming winter of 2020 the Centers for Disease Control warn us that this pandemic will destroy and harm us even more as the year comes to an end. Its fury has no end in sight and its sting will be felt in the waning days of 2020. Perhaps it is ironic that we are talking about dry and dead bones turning and reviving into live and vibrant bones. From death to life rather than from life to death. A resurrection from the reality of death to the miracle of new and real life. Maybe this is the real message and hope of Ezek 37:1–14 that the author of this book wants to convey to his readers: that resurgent life can come from lifeless bones through a miracle performed by the Word of the LORD.

If God has the power to bring life from death and restore the lives of men and women by his Word, surely he can work his works in the midst of this great coronavirus pandemic which has afflicted this nation and other countries around the world. This is the underlying truth of this passage for us to read and believe as we face the threat of COVID-19 in the midst of our lifetime. Listen and envision the valley of the dry bones which by the Word of the LORD turns into the valley of the live bones. We are witness to the power of God to bring new life from formless death.

THE SONG: DEM BONES

Few persons are familiar with the passage, Ezek 37:1–14, but they may have heard the song, "Dem Bones," which was written and composed by James Weldon Johnson and his brother, J. Rosamond Johnson. The song was first recorded by the Famous Myers Jubilee Singers (1928) and popularized by Fred Waring and The Pennsylvanians on April 30, 1947. "Dem Bones, Dem Bones Dem Dry Bones, Now Hear The Word of The Lord." Preaching from Ezek 37:1–14 is a challenge for any preacher because of the raw and graphic nature of this passage of Scripture. Ezekiel is guided by the LORD and taken to a huge valley of bones. He recalls that the hand and the spirit of the Lord transported him there. The scene is out of a mind-altering experience where Ezekiel sees the dry bones of dead people turn into live bones of living persons.

Our sermon is divided into three parts: valley of dry bones (Ezek 37:1–6), valley of live bones (Ezek 37:7–10), and dried up bones and God's Spirit (Ezek 37:11–14).

VALLEY OF DRY BONES

"The hand of the LORD came upon me, and he brought me out by the spirit of the LORD and set me down in the middle of a valley; it was full of bones. He led me all around them; there were very many lying in the valley, and they were very dry. He said to me, 'Mortal, can these bones live?' I answered. 'O Lord GOD, you know.' Then he said to me, 'Prophesy to these bones, and say to them: "O dry bones, hear the word of the LORD. Thus says the Lord GOD to these bones: I will cause breath to enter you, and you shall live. I will lay sinews on you, and will cause flesh to come upon you, and cover you with skin, and put breath in you, and you shall live; and you shall know that I am the LORD"'" (Ezek 37:1–6). What is the meaning and significance of the valley of dry bones? In one sense the LORD led Ezekiel to a mass graveyard of bones from dead people in order to demonstrate a miraculous event: the proclamation of the Word of the LORD which brings life back from death.

This is the message from the valley of dry bones: that God has the power to impart new life from death. Paul declares: "For the wages of sin is death but the free gift of God is eternal life through Jesus Christ our Lord" (Rom 6:23). This is the essence of the gospel of Christ to America: that in the midst of death, murder, and killing, God through Christ gives life and restoration from death to everyone who believes in Jesus. Those dry bones which we are carrying around in our lives can be transformed by the power of God through the death and resurrection of Christ. We can have new life for ourselves and our nation through Jesus Christ.

The Christian hymn, "The Day of Resurrection," reminds us that we have passed from death to life in Christ: "The day of resurrection! Earth, tell it out abroad; the Passover of gladness, the Passover of God. From death to life eternal, from earth unto the sky, our Christ hath brought us over, with hymns of victory."[1] We sing this hymn with the assurance that God brings life out of the dry dead bones in us and that we are transformed from death to life in Christ.

VALLEY OF LIVE BONES

"So I prophesied as I had been commanded; and as I prophesied, suddenly there was a noise, a rattling, and the bones came together, bone to its bone. I looked, and there was sinews on them, and flesh had come upon them, and skin had covered them, but there was no breath in them. Then he said

---

1. Hymn written by Saint John of Damascus, 750 AD.

to me, 'Prophesy to the breath, prophesy, mortal, and say to the breath: Thus says the Lord GOD: Come from the four winds, o breath, and breathe upon these slain, that they may live.' I prophesied as he commanded me, and the breath came into them, and they lived, and stood on their feet, a vast multitude" (Ezek 37:7-10).

As we read these verses, we are privy to the work of God through the role of the prophet Ezekiel. The prophet of God goes beyond his normal duties as a forth teller (messenger of repentance) and fore teller (messenger of coming judgement). Rather Ezekiel participates in the recreation of people on a parallel to the creation of man and woman. Genesis 2:7 says: "then the LORD God formed man from the dust of the ground, and breathed into his nostril the breathe of life; and the man became a living being." Ezekiel 37:7-10 describes the creation of muscle and flesh, pulse and movement, and the breath of life from the four corners of the wind coming from the creative hand of God. The prophet Ezekiel becomes the vehicle for such a recreation, turning dead people into living beings.

The thrust of reading about this valley of live bones is that God can actually perform a miracle and bring dead people back to life again. The valley of dry bones piled on top of each other becomes the valley of live bones where the bones have been brought together to form human beings who are moving and alive again by the power and creative might of the Lord. Remember 1 Cor 15:22: "for as all die in Adam, so all will be made alive in Christ." Can God take persons who are spiritually dead and perform a miracle of infusing new muscle, movement, and breath into a person's spiritual being? Are there dead (spiritually dead) persons walking around committing acts of violence and grief on other human beings and need to be recreated by the LORD God? We read about them in the newspaper and see them on the nightly television news. Individuals in the valley of dry bones can become part of the valley of live bones. They can be alive in Christ.

DRIED UP BONES AND GOD'S SPIRIT

"Then he said to me, 'Mortal, these bones are the whole house of Israel. They say, "Our bones are dried up, and our hope is lost; we are cut off completely." Therefore prophesy, and say to them, "Thus says the Lord GOD: I am going to open your graves, and bring you up from your graves, O my people; I will put my spirit within you, and you shall live, and I will place you on your soil; then you shall know that I, the LORD, have spoken and will act, says the LORD""" (Ezek 37:11-14).

The valley of dry bones and the valley of live bones are object lessons for the people of Israel who faced a grave predicament. The exiles have returned to death and ruin. Indeed their bones are dried and depleted of energy and life. Returning to their homeland has been comforting but starting again without resources is lost hope. The people needed the spirit of the LORD placed within them to begin to work, rebuild, and resettle the land. I recalled that after World War II many Jewish Europeans did not return to their former countries. Rather they migrated to Palestine and fought to establish the nation of Israel. After gaining their independence they transformed the desert into fertile land and build new villages and towns. The spirit of the LORD was invested in their efforts and today the nation of Israel thrives despite the displacement of the Palestinian refugees and the tension between these two people. The people of Israel were displaced and resettled twice in the time of the Babylonian captivity and the Second World War. They returned to their native Israel and picked up the pieces because the spirit of the LORD was with them.

The United States of America must be transformed from a valley of dried bones to a valley of vibrant and alive people who have been infused with the Spirit of God. Pick up the pieces of the dead and dry bones and transport them from the dead graves to the valley of the live bones to a place where there is life and hope. Yes, as we experience the transformation from death to life in a pandemic that is flattened by the efforts of all Americans who must act boldly and practice good common public health hygiene, we will be living again in the valley of live and healthy people.

Will you pledge yourself and your family to take your personal responsibility to act as a thoughtful citizen of the United States of America by wearing a mask, sheltering at home, practicing social distancing, and washing your hands? If everyone from the president to the common person will dedicate themselves to this public health practice we will be able to change our country from the valley of the dead bones to the valley of strong and healthy people.

This passage highlights the transformation from death (the valley of the dry bones) to life (movement and activity) (the valley of the live bones) by the power of the Word of God. God speaks and the dead bones are turned to living human beings. What a miracle and transformation! We have the same experience when we come to Christ, our Savior and LORD. He changes us from being spiritually dead to a new life in Christ. Moreover, in the midst of death which we see and hear on a daily basis due to the pandemic we need a transforming Word from the LORD which will give us new hope and life to our weary bodies and souls. We need to see that God can take us from the valley of death to the valley of life as he transforms us by the power of his might. As Paul declares: "So if anyone is in Christ, there is a new creation; everything old has passed away; see, everything has become new!" (2 Cor 5:17) and "So you also must consider yourselves dead to sin and alive to God in Christ Jesus" (Rom 6:11). This is the message behind the valleys of the dry bones and live bones which Ezekiel portrayed in Ezek 34:23–31.

Ken Burns has produced a documentary on *The War* which chronicles four cities in the United States and the citizens who left these towns to fight in World War II. George Frazier, a resident of Mobile, Alabama, was captured on Corregidor in the Philippines and was in the US Army under General Douglas MacArthur. He was reported missing in action and presumed dead by his family. George remained in a Japanese POW camp until the end of the war. When he returned to the United States he was allowed a telephone call and promptly called his family from San Francisco. His mother, aunt, and older sister all fainted in disbelief and his father poured a pitch of water on his wife to revive her. George Frazier passed from death to life in their hearts and lives that day. He returned from the dead, married and raised a family, but he struggled to cope with the horrors of war that he experienced as a soldier.

Psalm 23:4 describes the experience of passing through the valley of death to the valley of life: Even though I walk through the valley of the shadow of death, I fear no evil; for you are with me; your rod and your staff—they comfort me.

Will you listen and hear the Word of the LORD? He transforms your life from death to life by the power of his Word. Through Christ God makes us dead to sin and alive in Christ. We become this new creation in Christ. We move from the valley of death to the valley of life by the power of the Word from LORD who infuses life in the dry and dead bones and turns them into live bones and vibrant human beings.

PASTORAL PRAYER

Dear God, We have suffered a great loss of life as we have coped with this coronavirus pandemic. Please be with all the families who have lost loved ones and those who have been afflicted and are recovering. As Ezekiel witnessed life from the valley of the dead bones, we pray that you will bring new life to our families, communities, and nation. Help us to recover that which we have lost and experience newness of life from your creative hands.

As we enter this season of life protect our families and our children and teachers as they begin a year of learning. We pray for wisdom for those who oversee the education of our youth. Grant them the courage of leadership in their protective custody of guiding and guarding the health and vitality of those who enter the classroom. Give to our spiritual leaders the fortitude to speak out when they witness the wrong and point to the right. Guide our political leaders and the voters of America as they listen, evaluate, and select the people who will represent them in local, state, and national offices.

Be with our churches who are still sheltering in place that they may be a strong witness for Christ and for social and economic justice. Help us to work in our community although we may not be able to meet in our buildings of worship. Be with those who have suffered the loss of a loved one. Help us to reach out to those who need our help whether it be for food, shelter, and personal care. May the Spirit of the Lord be in our midst as a good neighbor and friend.

We pray for Joe who is recovering from a stroke and will be in a nursing home that you will be with him and support Mary Jane, his wife; for Melanie who is recovering from her heart surgery; for Martin in his journey of faith and his heart condition; and for Eddie and Yvonne as they mourn the loss of Eddie's brother, King. For all of us who need your presence in our time of crisis we pray in the name of Christ our Lord and Savior.

In the name of our Lord, Amen.

CHAPTER 21

JUDGEMENT AND CALLING ON THE NAME OF THE LORD

Joel 2:30–3:3; Malachi 3:1–4 (November 1, 2020)

Scripture Reading. I will show portents in the heavens and on the earth, blood and fire and columns of smoke. The sun shall be turned into darkness, and the moon to blood, before the great and terrible day of the LORD comes. Then everyone who calls on the name of the LORD shall be saved; for in Mount Zion and in Jerusalem there shall be those who escape, as the LORD has said, and among the survivors shall be those whom the LORD calls.

For then, in those days and at that time, when I restore the fortunes of Judah and Jerusalem, I will gather all the nations and bring them down to the valley of Jehoshaphat, and I will enter into judgment with them there, on account of my people and my heritage Israel, because they have scattered them among the nations. They have divided my land, and cast lots for my people, and traded boys for prostitutes, and sold girls for wine, and drunk it down.

See, I am sending my messenger to prepare the way before me, and the Lord whom you seek will suddenly come to his temple. The messenger of the covenant in whom you delight—indeed, he is coming, says the LORD of hosts. But who can endure the day of his coming, and who can stand when he appears?

For he is like a refiner's fire and like fullers' soap; he will sit as a refiner and purifier of silver, and he will purify the descendants of Levi and refine them like gold and silver, until they present offerings to the

LORD in righteousness. Then the offering of Judah and Jerusalem will be pleasing to the LORD as in the days of old and as in former years.

As we enter November 2020 we are aware that the COVID-19 crisis is still a part of our daily life. American families are back to their normal fall routines after a long and busy summer and children are back to school doing mostly virtual distance learning. Some parents have jobs which can be accomplished at home with occasional trips to the office. These parents are able to help their children with their homework while the whole family remains in their homes. Other parents and children must travel to the office and school in-person settings. Still others are unemployed and stay at home or one spouse is not working and stays home with children in virtual or in-person school arrangements. All American families are in the process of adjusting to a variety of work and school combinations which will take a period of adaptation.

In the meantime the coronavirus is still active in many parts of the country with surges of the first wave or the beginning of the second wave which may be combined with influenza toward the end of 2020. There is still the need to practice wearing masks, maintaining social distance, washing hands, and avoiding large crowds. The Centers for Disease Control and the Presidential Task Force are still in charge of directing the national response to the pandemic, while state governors and their health department counterparts are focused on local outbreaks and flattening the curve.

The testing and modification of an effective vaccine are still months away from becoming a reality. In early 2021 there may be a safe and effective vaccine available to vulnerable sections of the country where COVID-19 patients are most affected by the virus. The rest of Americans may have to wait until critical care COVID-19 patients are cared for by vaccine inoculation. Furthermore, to ensure the containment of virus spread, the rest of the world will require vaccines available to them. The process and outcome will be slow and gradual with economic recovery and return to the new normal taking months and even years before we reach a steady state of growth and restoration.

THE CLOSING MESSAGE OF THE PROPHETS

We are at the end of our preaching series, "Messages from The Prophets." When we first planned and started these sermons, I was not aware how relevant the writings of the Prophets would be to the national, state, and local problems that we are confronting: the COVID-19 pandemic and the mounting sickness and death in America, the killings and deaths of African Americans in Georgia, Kentucky, and Minnesota (particularly the murder of George Floyd by the Minneapolis police officers), and the Black Lives Matter demonstrations in cities across the country.

The prophets of Israel spoke to the social and spiritual problems facing the nation of Israel and preached the judgement of God and the repentance of sins to the king, the clergy, the wealthy, the middle class, and the poor. No one was exempted from the messages which came from God. As we have expounded the biblical prophetic messages Sunday after Sunday and applied them to similar issues facing the United States of America and as you have read these sermons and worshipped and prayed over them, my prayers are that you will connect the Old and New Testaments to your personal lives and our corporate life as American citizens. I hope that you will be alert and aware of how the biblical message is appropriate to the issues of today and that you will proclaim the good news of Christ with spiritual insights and social concern.

Our closing sermon of this series focuses on judgement and calling on the name of the Lord. Joel's message is the prophetic message of judgement and repentance, while Malachi foresees the coming of the messenger of the LORD and of the LORD himself. We look at: 1) coming judgement, 2) coming persons, and 3) coming salvation as we close out the prophets from Amos, Hosea, and Micah through Isaiah, Jeremiah, and Ezekiel to Joel and Malachi.

COMING JUDGEMENT

Joel's message is coming judgement on Israel: "I will show portents in the heavens and on the earth, blood and fire and columns of smoke. The sun shall be turned to darkness, and the moon to blood, before the great and terrible day of the LORD comes" (Joel 2:30). Joel is preaching about the last times and the day of the LORD which is part of Old Testament eschatology. Joel's description is akin to John's picture in the book of Revelation: ". . . I looked, and there came a great earthquake; the sun became black as sackcloth, the full moon became like blood, and the stars of the sky fell to the earth as the fig tree drops its winter fruit when shaken by a gale" (Rev 6:12 and 13). These signs and wonders in Joel and Revelation are a part of how nature announces the day of the LORD which foreshadows coming judgement.

What can we say about these passages in 2020? We certainly cannot put a fixed date on the end of the world or the coming of Christ who will judge the living and the dead (Mark 13:24–27, 29, 32; Acts 2:17–21; 1 Thess 5:1 and 2). There will be a judgement day for all, but the preaching of coming judgement was a way of turning people to the Lord before that event occurs in the lives of Israel and the rest of the world. The preaching of judgement confronts people and brings them back to God.

In the Black Lives Matter demonstrations there is a notable absence of the Christian church, particularly African American clergy. Martin Luther King Jr. drew his leadership base from the Black clergy and Black churches across the South through the Southern Leadership Conference. Using nonviolence, prayer, preaching, and hymns, Dr. King mobilized demonstrators which influenced the passage of the Civil Rights Act of 1965. However, one does not see the visible leadership of Black clergy in the 2020 demonstrations and marches. The people themselves have assumed leadership roles rather than clergy. It is a diverse people's march and movement which speak to its broad appeal.

However, unless we return to the LORD there will be coming judgement upon our nation. Let us heed the present signs of this reality: earthquakes, floods, tornados, hurricanes, epidemics and pandemics, wars and rumors of wars, and other natural and manmade disasters. But we cannot conclude that these are signs of the end of the world. The Bible teaches that there will not be an end of this world. Rather there will be a new heaven and a new earth: "Then I saw a new heaven and a new earth; for the first heaven and the first earth had passed away, . . ." (Rev 21:1). Let us judge ourselves each day so that we eliminate what is not pleasing in the eyes of the Lord and be the kind of person that God wants us to become in his sight.

COMING PERSONS

Malachi 3:1 prophesies the coming of my messenger and the LORD himself: "See, I am sending my messenger to prepare the way before me, and the Lord whom you seek will suddenly come to his temple," while the closing verses of Malachi declares: "Lo, I will send you the prophet Elijah before the great and terrible day of the LORD comes" (Mal 4:5). John the Baptist is the coming messenger and the prophet Elijah who is sent to prepare the way of the LORD, Jesus Christ (Matt 11:7–15; 17:10–13; Mark 6:14–16).

The New Testament Gospels mention the Old Testament verses from the prophets concerning John the Baptist and Jesus as the Messiah (Matt 3:3; Mark 1:2 and 3; Luke 3:4–6; John 1:23). These two personages were prophesied in the Old Testament and eagerly sought out in the previous centuries until John the Baptist and Jesus appeared on the scene.

Is America ready for the coming of the messenger and of the LORD himself in the *Parousia* (a Greek word meaning arrival or consequent presence and denoting the arrival of a king or a person of prominence; see Phil 1:26). The second coming of Christ is predicted in the New Testament (Acts 1:11; 1 Thess 4:16 and 17). In the civil and political strife of the streets of this country, are we ready for the coming of the LORD? What will be our condition when he comes to take us as believers and judge the sins of the world? We need to amend our lives and be ready and prepared for his coming.

COMING SALVATION

Joel 2:32 exhorts us: "Then everyone who calls on the name of the LORD shall be saved; . . ." Salvation (a Greek word meaning wholeness and healing) is the main doctrine of the Christian faith. It means turning from our sinful lifestyle and believing on the LORD Jesus Christ who died for our sins and rose again from the dead. Salvation is calling on the Lord and asking him to save us. In Acts 16:30–31 the jailer asked: "Sirs, what must I do to be saved?" Paul and Silas together answered him: "Believe on the Lord Jesus, and you will be saved, you and your household." Simple faith and belief in Jesus and salvation will come to you and all that live in your house.

The coming judgement, coming persons, and coming salvation remind us of the Battle of Normandy on June 6, 1944. The question which was asked for three years after the entrance of the United States into the Second World War was: When were the Allies coming to liberate Europe? Operation Overlord was the answer which was the coming of judgement on Nazi Germany, the coming persons of Allied forces, and the coming salvation of liberating Europe. There were 1,200 planes for the airborne assault, five thousand ships for the amphibious armada, 160,000 troops under the joint command of General Dwight D. Eisenhower and Field Marshall Bernard Montgomery. The landing was secured and the coming of this great army hastened the defeat of German forces and the end of the war in Europe.

As we close this preaching series, *The Great Coronavirus Pandemic and Messages from the Prophets*, it is fitting to remember the importance of calling on the name of the LORD. Perhaps this was the missing element which Israel lacked: an unwillingness or even forgetting to call on the name of the LORD. When one calls out to God, a person truly needs help from the LORD and believes that God will help in a situation. The role of the Old Testament prophet was to redirect the attention of the people of Israel back to the LORD so that people would call on his name. Calling on the name of the LORD brings salvation to the people. Salvation presupposes that a person has heard about the judgement of God and repentance. To repent means to have a contrite heart and turn from a course of self-centeredness to a direction of following the LORD. If an individual, family, community, state, and nation have gotten this spiritual message in light of the pandemic and the Old and New Testaments Scriptures, then we have succeeded in our efforts.

As we have striven to preach selected passages from the Prophets of the Old Testament we hope that you have seen how the Old Testament feeds into the New Testament and how the New Testament reinforces and fulfills the whole of Holy Scriptures.

As the Christian hymn, "Make Me a Blessing," declares: "Out in the highways and byways of life, many are weary and sad; Carry the sunshine where darkness is rife, Making the sorrowing glad: Make me a Blessing, Make me a Blessing, Out of my life, may Jesus shine; Make me a Blessing, O Savior, I pray Thee my Savior; make me a Blessing to someone today!"

May the Blessings of God the Father, God the Son, and God the Holy Spirit be with you, both now and forevermore. Amen!

PASTORAL PRAYER

Dear LORD: As we finish this preaching series on *The Great Coronavirus Pandemic and the Messages from the Prophets* we thank you for the wondrous Old Testament passages from the books of the prophets which speak to our situation in 2020. We know that we are engaged in a great pandemic which has affected the lives of Americans and our economic, social, and political life. We thank you for speaking through the written Word of God which has addressed our needs and given us comfort and direction as we face the unknowns of this virus. May we call upon the name of the Lord constantly and seek the presence of God in this time of crisis. May our spiritual resources be more than sufficient to meet whatever befall us.

As we are still in the eye of the storm see us through to calmness and peace. May the LORD be our Refuge in this time of trouble. May we listen to our public health leaders as they seek to inform and educate us in our responses to the coronavirus. Be with us and protect and safeguard us.

We pray for Joe and his wife, Mary Jane, that you will help them as Joe recovers from his stroke; for Martin and the strength of the Lord in his heart condition; for Melanie and her heart surgery; for Olivia and her stay in a care home; and for Danny and Patty and Patty's father, Dr. Gaing, who is at the Asian Nursing Home. Be with them all, Dear God. Amen.

CHAPTER 22

LESSONS FROM THE CORONAVIRUS

This book has taken you on a journey that started with the story of the coronavirus as it impacted the United States of America in early January 2020 and grew to become a national and international pandemic in the subsequent months. We began by building a weekly chronology of how COVID-19 gradually affected the lives of American citizens and how the biblical messages from the Old Testament prophets addressed this public health crisis. We are concerned that the Christian Church needed to speak to the spiritual, emotional, and behavioral dimensions of the coronavirus phenomenon. Rather than remain silent, the good news of Jesus must address this healthcare issue with compassion and love.

The messages of the Old Testament prophets encompassed the needs of COVID-19 sufferers: good and evil in the pandemic; justice, kindness, and humility in the face of economic survival; strength, trust, and peace as guideposts in the midst of infection and death; the amazing acts of God; how to pray in a threatening situation; how to be a suffering servant; crying out to God; calling on the Spirit of God; the new covenant between God and human beings; and other reassuring themes.

Rather than reiterate the essence of these themes we press on to an urgent issue: What are the lessons from the coronavirus crisis which we learn as citizens of our nation? This purpose of this closing chapter is to think with you about a number of themes which come to mind as we enter a second wave of the COVID-19 outbreak and to leave with you an agenda that you may take with you as you continue to cope with this disease. In the following sections we explore: lessons from the prophets, lessons from biblical theologians, and closing remarks. We hope that you will reflect on these issues and act on them in creative and life-saving ways.

LESSONS FROM THE PROPHETS

Old Testament biblical scholarship on the prophets revolves around three representative theologians of the twentieth century: R. B. Y. Scott, Abraham J. Heschel, and Gerhard von Rad. Together they laid a sound foundation for understanding the dynamic nature of the prophets and their actions and messages.

Scott explained the unique message of the prophets:

> Their message . . . was addressed to men of their own day, in the conditions and circumstances under which they lived, and in language which only men of their own nation and time could fully understand. It abounds in figures of speech and contemporary allusions which to us are obscure; not . . . because prophecy is a tongue of esoteric mystery, but mainly because our knowledge of that ancient time is so far from complete.[1]

A case in point is the analogies of the potter and the clay (God and the nation of Israel), the valley of the dry bones and the valley of live bones coming alive at the sound of the Word of the LORD, and the playing out of the unfaithfulness of Hosea's wife. These figures of speech or allusions are examples of *analogical prophetic preaching* when the prophets utilize a tangible life example, play it out before the people of Israel, and make a spiritual point in the process. We have seen these analogies in selected passages of our preaching series.

Scott further connected foretelling and the moral situation when he said:

> The prophets foretell doom . . . and deliverance . . . as an immediate consequence of their moral and spiritual condition. . . . What is about to happen is the necessary consequence of a moral situation . . .[2]

Amos 5:14–15 and the treatment of good and evil, Mic 6:8 and the rules of justice, kindness, and humility, Isa 1:1–9, 16–18 and the depiction of a sinful nation and changing scarlet into snow, Isa 6:1–13 and the choice of holiness and hollowness, and Isa 26:1–15 and the admonition of strength,

---

1. Scott, *The Relevance of the Prophets*, 1.
2. Scott, *The Relevance of the Prophets*, 10.

trust, and peace address the moral boundaries that the prophets conveyed to Israel and Judah.

The role of the prophet is depicted in clear terms:

> The prophet, not the priest or the teacher, is the voice of God in that moment. He is the spokesman who can articulate the meaning of an eternal order and a Divine reality. He discloses the moral crisis in which men stand unheeding. He declares which is the way of life and which the way of death.[3]

We have seen this in Isa 40:1–11 (a voice crying in the wilderness), Ezek 37:1–14 (from dry bones to live bones), and Joel 2:30–3:3 and Mal 3:1–4 (judgement and calling on the name of the Lord).

Central to the relationship between God and Israel was the concept of covenant. Scott declared:

> The covenant of Yahweh established a community with the characteristics of a great family, with a common interest, a common life and a common will. Israel became ideally a 'people' in the strict sense of the Hebrew word 'am,' which means those who together form an entity, a whole, and whose members are united by 'fellow-feeling' as brothers and comrades.[4]

We saw this in the new covenant Jer 32:3–34 (a covenant of the heart and the knowledge of God) and the concept of the covenant in Ezek 34:23–31. We pointed to the rainbow covenant with Noah, the covenant of the nation of Israel with Abraham, the covenant of the law with Moses, and the New Testament covenant of the body and blood of Jesus Christ.

The phrase, "Thus saith the Lord" or "The word of the LORD came upon me," underscored the transmission of that Word through the prophet to the people of Israel. Scott listed five forms of The Word:

> ... a *declaration* of the spiritual realities of past and present conditions, a *reproach* or an *exhortation* addressed to men in the present, and a *threat* or *promise* with regard to Yahweh's action in the imminent or more distant future.[5]

When Amos 5:14–15 said, "Hate Evil; Do Good," this is a *declaration*. Or when Isa 1:2 stated: "I reared children and brought them up, but they have rebelled against me," this is a *reproach*. *Exhortation* is seen in Isa 1:18: "Come now, let us argue it out, says the Lord, though your sins are like scarlet, they

---

3. Scott, *The Relevance of the Prophets*, 13.
4. Scott, *The Relevance of the Prophets*, 24.
5. Scott, *The Relevance of the Prophets*, 100.

shall be like snow; . . ." *Threat* is portrayed in Joel 2:31: "The sun shall be turned to darkness, and the moon to blood, before the great and terrible day of the LORD comes." Finally *promise* is found in Isa 9:7: "His authority shall grow continually, and there shall be endless peace for the throne of David and his kingdom. He will establish and uphold it with justice and with righteousness from this time forward and forevermore." Examples of these five forms of how the Word from God to the prophets abound in their writings.

Scott's analysis of Israeli society is built on materialism and human pride:

> The nation had set its heart on the wealth and buildings of its cities, its military power and alliances, the luxury of its court circle and the elaborateness of its sanctuaries. Kings and princes, judges and military officers, priests and official prophets, together formed the human framework of the social structure-its mainstays, . . . The community did not see that it shared the instability of leaders who were concerned with privilege rather than responsibility; since the foundations of society had been undermined by the corruption of justice and the neglect of truth and mercy, this human framework must collapse like a structure of wax before a fire.[6]

The description of Israel's society sounds familiar with the American society in 2020: material wealth, elite power, corruption, lying, and other forms of social decay.

Scott focuses on the judgement of God which is the precursor for the repentance of Israel and a return to the Lord. He explained:

> The impact of Yahweh's judgment . . . will be felt by every constituent element of the social order which Israel has erected, in neglect and defiance of the human values fundamental to her professed religion. The monarchy and the royal establishment, the temple priesthoods with all the paraphernalia of their cult-service, the cities and palaces which are the outward and visible sign of wealth and power, the judges and elders who had betrayed their trust, the army boastful of its prowess—each will be struck down in a way appropriate to rebuke its pride. The arrogance of power and possession is most hateful in the eyes of Yahweh, for it is the mark of a spirit in individuals and society which neither fears God nor has regard for man.[7]

---

6. Scott, *The Relevance of the Prophets*, 114.
7. Scott, *The Relevance of the Prophets*, 174.

In our preaching series we focused on good and evil (Amos 5:14–15), a sinful nation (Isa 1:1–9), darkness (Isa 9:2–7), and judgement (Joel 2:30—3:3) which express and reinforce the coming judgement of God and which culminated in the Assyrian and Babylonian captivity and exile.

Heschel wrote about the nature of the human condition. He states:

> Man is rebellious and full of iniquity, and yet so cherished is he that God, the Creator of heaven and earth, is saddened when forsaken by him. Profound and intimate is God's love for man, and yet harsh and dreadful can be His wrath. Of what paltry worth is human might—yet human compassion is divinely precious. Ugly though the behavior of man is—yet may man's return to God make of his way a highway of God.[8]

Heschel drew the paradox of God and the human person: God's love and wrath and man's sinfulness and possibility of returning to God. The prophets leave the door open: repentance and turning back to God and God's loving faithfulness (his *hesed*). Akin to this was Heschel's concept of divine pathos where the prophet feels and communicates God's feeling for the human person. He said:

> . . . the fundamental experience of the prophet is a fellowship with the feelings of God, a sympathy with the divine pathos, a communion with the divine consciousness which comes about through the prophet's reflection of, or participation in, the divine pathos.[9]

The prophet experienced the love and care of God and communicated this to the people. It was a total connection between God and the people of Israel through the prophet as the conduit.

Heschel highlighted the concept of historical justice which is bound up in the righteousness of God. He taught:

> The presence of God in history, the manifestation of His will in the affairs of the world, is the object of the prophet's longing. It is not mystical experience he yearns for in the night, but historical justice. Mystical experience is the illumination of an individual; historical justice is the illumination of all men, enabling the inhabitants of the world to learn righteousness.[10]

---

8. Heschel, *The Prophets*, 5 and 6.
9. Heschel, *The Prophets*, 26.
10. Heschel, *The Prophets*, 175.

We saw this in Mic 6:8 where we distinguished between social, economic, and distributive justice and where Micah connected justice to walking humbly with your God.

Heschel recognized that the prophet in the face of preaching the message of God is confronted and confounded with the hardness of heart and an unwillingness to change and heed the Word of the Lord. He confessed:

> With some qualification one might say in the spirit of the prophets that the history of the world with which they dealt was none other than the progress of the condition of hardness of heart.[11]

We saw this play out in the potter and the clay sermon (Jer 18:1–12) where despite of a wonderful analogy of God as the potter and Israel as the clay there was in the end rejection and hardness of heart on the part of the hearers. Jeremiah and the rest of the prophets faced this reality in the final analysis.

Von Rad analyzed the message structure of the prophet when he observed:

> As a rule, however, the prophets prefaced this messenger formula with another form of words whose purpose was to draw the recipient's attention to the message and which, indeed, gave the first precise designation of those for whom it was intended. In the case of a divine threat, what was prefixed was a 'diatribe',[12] in the case of a promise, an 'exhortation'. These two, the messenger formula and the prefaced clause, must both be present before we have the literary category 'prophetic oracle.'[13]

For readers to understand the prophetic message von Rad pointed us to looking for the divine threat (e.g., thus saith the LORD: a message of divine judgement) (the diatribe) and the promise and/or the exhortation (e.g., God's forgiveness and promise based on the covenant of the law). Look for either or both from von Rad's perspective.

Von Rad highlighted the importance of the prophet's call which has an impact on the people of Israel. He explained:

> The event of which the prophet tells burdened him with a commission, with knowledge and responsibility which placed him in complete isolation before God. It forced him to justify his exceptional status in the eyes of the majority. This makes clear

---

11. Heschel, *The Prophets*, 191.
12. A diatribe is a prolonged discourse, often a bitter and abusive speech of writing, satirical criticism.
13. von Rad, *The Message of the Prophets*, 19.

that the writing down of a call was something secondary to the call itself, and that it served a different end from the latter. The call commissioned the prophet: the act of writing down an account of it was aimed at those sections of the public in whose eyes he had to justify himself.[14]

Furthermore von Rad stressed the wholly other life that the prophet pursued in his calling from the Lord. He stated:

> So deep is the gulf which separates the prophets from their past that none of their previous social relationships are carried over into their new way of life.[15]

He further observed:

> This was more than a new profession: it was a totally new way of life, even at the sociological level, to the extent that a call meant relinquishing normal social life and all the social and economic securities which this offered, and changing over instead to a condition of dependence upon Yahweh and upon that security alone.[16]

In our preaching series we focused on the callings of Isaiah (the Spirit of the LORD is upon me [Isa 61:1–4]) and Jeremiah (I am only a boy [Jer 1:1–10]). These two major prophets had a significant impact on Israel and Judah, but they paid a price in their self sacrifice.

Von Rad pointed out that when a prophet responded to the calling from God he not only made a personal sacrifice but experienced a freedom in his role as prophet. He made this observation:

> As the result of this divine call he surrenders much of his freedom—occasionally he is completely overwhelmed by an external compulsion; but paradoxically, just because he has received this call he is able to enjoy an entirely new kind of freedom. Drawn into ever close and closer conversation with God, he is privy to the divine purposes and is thereby given the authority to enter into a unique kind of converse with man.[17]

This freedom to know the mind and the heart of God was the payoff for the prophet to make his human sacrifice of self so that he would be close to God and know his will.

14. von Rad, *The Message of the Prophets*, 34.
15. von Rad, *The Message of the Prophets*, 37.
16. von Rad, *The Message of the Prophets*, 37.
17. von Rad, *The Message of the Prophets*, 56 and 57.

Von Rad has the final word on the role and place of the prophets and summarized their essence. He wrote this tribute to the prophets:

> All the prophets share a common conviction that they stood exactly at that turning point in history which was crucial for the existence of God's people. This is the standpoint from which one has to understand their passionate demolition of the old. In particular of all false means of security before God, as well as what they say of the approach of entirely new and terrifying divine acts of salvation. Yet, they also shared a common certainty that the new thing which they expected was already prefigured in the old, and that the old would be present in the new in perfect form.[18]

The prophets were in a line of succession to each other where each prophet contributed the Word of the LORD in his time of history. As they demolished the old ways of the people's practices, the prophets offered a new Word of the LORD which added to the riches of the law of God.

Scott, Heschel, and von Rad together portray a broad perspective on how Old Testament studies on the prophets enriched our insights and preaching from the prophetic messages which apply to the contextual themes and events of the present COVID-19 crisis impacting our nation.

LESSONS FROM BIBLICAL THEOLOGIANS

Since the coronavirus outbreak in the United States which began in February 2020 there have been a steady stream of Christian books which have addressed this pandemic crisis. Hitchcock believed that the pandemic is a foreshadowing of what is to come but not a fulfillment of the apocalypse.[19] Bolsinger and Edington are concerned with how the church will survive and grow during and after the pandemic, particularly disruptions in the church and the need for adaptive leadership in the pandemic and how the church will gather after the pandemic.[20] Still a majority of writers are focused on individual and corporate responses to the coronavirus and the need for spiritual resources. Jeremiah discussed ways to worship and pray under pressure in the midst of the pandemic.[21] Mair and Cawley addressed overcoming challenges related to work, singleness, loneliness, grief, and death and dying

---

18. von Rad, *The Message of the Prophets*, 256 and 266.
19. Hitchcock, *Corona Crisis*.
20. Bolsinger, *Leadership for a Time*; Edington, *We Shall Be Changed*.
21. Jeremiah, *Shelter in God*.

during the coronavirus.[22] Piper reminded us of God's goodness and sovereignty, the fragility of the world amid COVID deaths, and the stability of faith.[23] Tomeo discussed Scripture and stories of the saints and healthcare workers as examples of courage and leadership.[24]

The coronavirus has disrupted the normal activities of the local church, but there are some practical ways for the church to cope now and when the crisis has passed (Bolsinger; Edington). Most Christian writers addressing the coronavirus have concentrated on the available spiritual resources to respond to the personal and family needs and losses (Jeremiah; Mair and Cawley; Piper; Tomeo). (See previous footnotes.)

However, two biblical theologians, N. T. Wright and Walter Brueggemann, have written biblical and theological books on the pandemic which have stood above the religious field of this new and growing literature: N. T. Wright, *God and the Pandemic: A Christian Reflection on the Coronavirus and Its Aftermath* (Zondervan, 2020), and Walter Brueggemann, *Virus as a Summons to Faith: Biblical Reflections in a Time of Loss, Grief, and Uncertainty* (Cascade Books, 2020).

N. T. Wright is Professor of New Testament and Senior Editor at The University of St Andrews (Scotland) and Research Professor at Oxford University, while Walter Brueggemann is Professor Emeritus of Old Testament, Columbia Theological Seminary (Decatur, Georgia). Both represent the wide spectrum of biblical and theological insights into the spiritual dimensions of the coronavirus pandemic and address a number of issues related to the Christian church and this public health crisis confronting countries around the world. We now turn to them for their perspectives on the spiritual dimensions of the coronavirus pandemic.

N. T. WRIGHT: *GOD AND THE PANDEMIC*

N. T. Wright (full name Nicholas Thomas Wright, working name Tom Wright) is regarded as the most recognized Protestant evangelical theologian and professor of the English speaking world today. He is acclaimed as an English New Testament scholar, Pauline authority, and Anglican Bishop of Durham. Wright holds the DPhil degree from the University of Oxford, Merton College, and wrote his doctoral dissertation on "The Messiah and the People of God: A Study in Pauline Theology with Particular Reference to the Argument of the Epistle to the Romans." He has used his subject matter

---

22. Mair and Cawley, *Healthy Faith and the Coronavirus Crisis*.
23. Piper, *Coronavirus and Christ*.
24. Tomeo, *Conquering Coronavirus*.

as a springboard to write over eighty books. Many are scholarly works which encompass the entirety of the critical issues of the New Testament for theologians and theological students but there are also Bible study guides and daily devotions for the laity of local church congregations who want to study and learn about the Scriptures. His *magnum opus* work which I prize in my modest theological office library is his four-volume book, *Paul and the Faithfulness of God*.

But Dr. Wright has not only distinguished himself as a prolific author and writer but has been a part of the parish life of the church as a pastor and the Anglican Bishop of Durham (2003–2009). Durham is a historic city and I imagined that Bishop Wright was not only involved with church duties but participated in the daily life of the town with its many social, economic, and political problems. From town to gown Tom Wright became Research Professor of New Testament and Early Christianity at the University of St Andrews (Scotland), St. Mary's College (2010–2019) (nearby the famous St Andrews golf course where the game of golf began several centuries ago), and worked with many doctoral students who would later teach in universities and theological seminaries around the world. He returned to the University of Oxford, Wycliffe Hall, as Senior Research Fellow and has come full circle, having studied there for the Anglican ministry from 1971–1973.

N. T. Wright has written a timely book in *God and The Pandemic*. It contains an opening quote from Justin Welby, Archbishop of Canterbury, entitled "Praise for God and the Pandemic." Written originally as an article for *Time* magazine in the early stage of the coronavirus pandemic as it struck Great Britain and the United States, Zondervan Publishing Company, Grand Rapids, Michigan, published his expanded book version which was one of the first pandemic religious analyses in the English speaking world.

Rather than summarize the contents of Wright's five brief chapters, I will critically comment on the content of Wright's discourse as he surveys the Old Testament and the New Testament. He argues for *the need to lament* for now as the coronavirus claims victims throughout the world. At the beginning of his book, Wright cautions: ". . . we need a time of lamenting, of restraint, of precisely not jumping to 'solutions.'"[25] But rather than expanding on the meaning of this thematic plea, Wright takes his readers on a trip throughout the Bible and demonstrates his knowledge of Scripture and biblical characters. His discourse is sometimes relevant when he relates biblical passages and characters to the pandemic and the theme of lamenting. But in other places he seems to go from topic to topic without a purposeful logic

---

25. Wright, *God and The Pandemic*, xi.

and strategy for concrete steps that Christians and non-Christians ought to pursue as they cope with loved ones who are victims.

In his opening chapter, "Where Do We Start," Wright talks about Greek philosophers, Christian conspiracy theories, and the famine, blight, and pestilence of the Old Testament. Then in chapter 2, "Reading the Old Testament," he discusses the Babylonian exile, several of the Psalms, and Job. In his third chapter on "Jesus and the Gospels" Wright stresses the need for a Christology which is central to our understanding of the pandemic. However he fails to show how a Christ-centered perspective could be useful as we hear about the daily numbers of new coronavirus sickness and death rates, the responses of President Donald Trump to the pandemic, and the demonstrations of the Black Lives Matter movement against Black killings and murders and police brutality.

His fourth and fifth chapters on "Reading the New Testament" and "Where Do We Go From Here?" show some improvement but take us through the Passover, the book of Acts and the travels of Paul, the Sermon on the Mount, more on Paul's journeys and letters, the groan of creation in Rom 8:22–27, the post-resurrection events, the response of Christians to sickness and plagues in early church history, the use or disuse of church buildings during the pandemic, and the healing presence of Jesus. In light of the worldwide pandemic outbreak, Wright's writings should be more focused on practical steps that we should take to lament and to act on a lamentation that provides Christian care and love in the community and nation.

Wright's parting suggestion in light of this public health crisis is: use this time of lamenting as a time of prayer and hope.[26] While this spiritual thought is comforting, the message of lamenting falls short of going beyond a sense of spirituality. Wright could have given us much more details about lamenting and the book of Lamentations which has applications to cope with the daily stressors of the coronavirus. My study of the book of Lamentations reveals the following states of lamenting in Lam 1–4: mourning, suffering, affliction, sorrow, weeping and tears, distress, destruction, ruin, brokenness, desolation, and hunger. Likewise Lam 2, 3 and 5 talk about the return to the Lord: turning to God, the steadfast love of God, the mercy of the Lord, the great faithfulness of the LORD God, the goodness of God, his compassion, and restoration.

If Wright could have written about these truths from Lamentations, practically applied them to the daily lives of people who are shocked and stressed by the pandemic, and offered a compass for future efforts to cope with illness, death, and loss, he would have made a great contribution to

---

26. Wright, *God and the Pandemic*, 75.

a world suffering with this grave crisis. Wright's book is a step in the right direction but his basic themes require much more development and practical applications. At the same time it must be noted that N. T. Wright wrote at the beginning of the pandemic while my remarks are made after the first wave and at the middle of the second wave in the United States. Wright's perspective is that of a theologian based in England whose instincts and reactions are toward lamenting the tragedy and impact of the pandemic. In this sense we thank him for his spiritual sensitivity and wisdom and his pastoral care and concern.

WALTER BRUEGGEMANN: *VIRUS AS A SUMMONS TO FAITH*

Walter Brueggemann has given his readers seven biblical reflections and summons about the virus. While he does not explain the demographics of the coronavirus called COVID-19, Brueggemann is concerned how critical faith may be understood through the lens of the current virus and how the community of faith, the church, may maintain its missional identity as it confronts this pandemic. Brueggemann draws structural boundaries for his readers which help to understand the content of his reflections or sermons: the virus is a serious crisis which challenges us to read carefully the biblical text; the virus is a summons to which we must respond; and from close textual work we must identify problems that arise to us. Keeping these three structural parameters in mind helps us to understand his reflective sermons.

In his "Reaping The Whirlwind" it is easy to judge Brueggemann as a punitive biblical theologian because he links the lingering impact of the virus on the coming of the plague in the Old Testament. The reality of divine judgement, the suffering of evil people, pestilence, indictment for disobedience, covenantal violation, God's destructive power, and God's holiness are his themes. Midpoint through his sermon Brueggemann talks about punishment for violators, mobilization of negative forces, and raw holiness. Walter, have you lost your mind? Where is your mercy and compassion for victims of the virus? Brueggemann concludes: "None of these interpretive options is of much use or interest in the midst of the virus."[27] Rather he points us to our own limitations, divine concealment, and human wonderment. Do we have all the answers to the causes and effects of the virus? Do we know the end results of the pandemic? Perhaps we need to wait and see how the virus plays out in divine time.

---

27. Brueggemann, *Virus as a Summons*, 14.

Brueggemann's sermon, "Pestilence... Mercy? Who Knew?" is a biblical exposition of 2 Sam 24:1–25. King David sins against God and is given three options of punishment for his sin: three years of famine, three months of sword, or three days of pestilence. He chooses the last and hopes for God's mercy. In the 2 Samuel passage God strikes down seventy thousand people but spares the city of Jerusalem. After sharing this story with his readers, Brueggemann says: "I do not think for one moment that there is any ready transfer from this narrative to our real life crisis with the virus."[28] He speculates that the virus may curb our worst habits, slow us down, and lead to gentler treatment and generosity.

"Until The Dancing Begins Again" is a reflection on the prophet Jeremiah who noted the end of weddings (Jer 7:34), no funerals (Jer 16:9), and ruined waste land (Jer 25:10) like the restrictions of the virus in our time. But Jeremiah envisioned the resumption of life (Jer 33:10 and 11), God's faithfulness, steadfast love, restoration, hope, and goodness. He recalls the life and ministry of pastor Martin Rinkart who wrote the hymn, "Now Thank We All Our God," in a time of war and pestilence.

In his "Praying Amid The Virus 1 Kings 8:23–53" Brueggemann is concerned about praying for rescue and well-being for ourselves and our world. Drawing on Old Testament passages on pestilence and prayer, he points to the prayer of Solomon at the dedication of the Jerusalem temple (1 Kgs 8:23–53) where Solomon petitions God in prayer regarding seven disasters. Israel must remain faithful to the covenant. Prayer provides a context for hope in the midst of every disaster. Second Chronicles 6:14–42 and 2 Chron 7:12–16 reiterate prayer and forgiveness. The connection between pestilence and prayer in ancient Israel is relevant for today's virus. The rule of God as creator presides over war, pestilence, and famine.

"The 'Turn' From Self to God Psalm 77" is a journey from a preoccupation with self to a submission to and reliance upon God. The speaker turns inward to self-pity and self-preoccupation. Psalm 77 reveals a quest to seek God (vv. 1–6), a series of rhetorical questions about God's faithfulness (vv. 7–9), grief, trouble and a changing God (v. 10), the mighty works of God (vv. 11–14), and a recitation of the great deeds of the past between God and Israel (vv. 15–20). Missing is a connection and application of these verses to the suffering of people who are victims of the coronavirus and the national and international plight of the world in the great pandemic.

In a short concise sermon, "God's New Thing Isaiah 43:18–19," Brueggemann addresses the virus and the new normal: the release of some prisoners who constitute no threat, generous financing for needy neighbors,

---

28. Brueggemann, *Virus as a Summons*, 25.

and provisions for students and their education debts. He envisions prophetic imagination as "the anticipation of new social possibility that is available from the intention of the God of the prophets."[29] God's gift to us is a new normal.

Finally "The Matrix Of Groan Isaiah 42:14–15" sermon picks up on the "all creation is groaning" theme of Paul in Rom 8:22. The phrase alludes to the dawning of the new creation willed by God which is intrigue to the birthing process. The concept of newness is a process of pain from protest and anguish, slavery, and oppression where old creation is groaning in expectation. It is the voice of Jesus groaning on the cross on Good Friday which takes us to newness of life on Easter Sunday.

Brueggemann wrote his book on the virus from early February 2020 to Palm Sunday, April 5, 2020. During this time he witnessed the outbreak of the coronavirus in Seattle, Washington, New York City, and Los Angeles, California; the reactions of President Trump to COVID-19; the creation of the Presidential Task Force on the Coronavirus; and the closing of businesses, schools, and churches. Yet in his book he mentions the word *virus* without any demographic and dynamic details of the impact of the coronavirus on the American people and the American church. In several of his chapters Brueggemann offers valuable spiritual perspectives on coping with the virus while in other sections there is no mention of the virus and application of biblical and theological resources on this crucial topic. Furthermore Brueggemann's chapters are not interconnected to each other as far as the unification of the theme of the virus as a summons to faith.

There is no theological strategy for reacting and responding to COVID-19 which emerges at the end of his book so that readers have a plan to deal with the virus as Christian believers in the church. Brueggemann would have done much better if he would have taken Paul Tillich's situational theology perspective.[30] Tillich started with his description of human predicament (estrangement, neurotic and ontological anxiety) and correlated the human as questions to the divine as answers. Using existential philosophical language Tillich spoke of being and non-being in the human psyche, God as the Ground of All Being, and Christ as the New Being. Brueggemann could have written a stronger book if he started with the human dilemma of the coronavirus (the fear, pain, suffering, and death of the American people; the collapse of the American economy; the responses of President Trump; and the killings and murders of African Americans) and moved his audience to the Old Testament passages which responded to this human situation.

29. Brueggemann, *Virus as a Summons*, 58.
30. Tillich, *Systematic Theology*, vol. 1, 2.

This is the situational theology of Paul Tillich as he crafted his theology in the twentieth century. Nevertheless we commend Walter Brueggemann for writing his book in the early stages of the coronavirus which conveyed his insights about this public health crisis.

CLOSING REMARKS

As we leave the subject of the great coronavirus pandemic and the messages from the prophets, we hope that you as readers have taken with you the richness of the passages from the Old Testament prophets who spoke about their own set of problems facing the nation of Israel. They articulated messages from God to address the religious, political, and social problems of their lives and times. Yet we have seen how relevant and appropriate were the prophets and their writings to the problems confronting us as we encounter the COVID-19 crisis which has befallen the United States of America and the rest of the world. We hope that you have learned that there are spiritual resources which you can draw on as you cope with the coronavirus.

Beyond the biblical and theological lessons are lessons on public response, public health, and government responsibility which have become apparent in our national discussion and deliberations concerning the coronavirus pandemic. Regarding *public response*, we have learned the importance of marshalling and forming:

the public commitment to the prevention and transmission of the virus (wearing a mask, maintaining social distance, avoiding large crowds, and washing your hands);

the reality of public crisis loss (the death of a loved one) *and public recovery* (the restoration to health of a COVID-19 patient); and

the acceptance of the new normal (working from home, Zoom conference meetings, online distance learning, takeout orders rather than indoor dining, home haircuts, outside walks rather than indoor gyms, television movies at home rather than movie theaters, elbow bumps rather than handshakes and hugs, and other safety measures).

Concerning *public health responses*, we share several prevention measures such as:

the importance of heeding protection, prevention, and research information from the Centers for Disease Control and the Food and Drug Administration which are reliable medical science institutions staffed by leading scientists;

the learning of public health epidemiology studies on COVID-19 from medical journals, university medical and public health schools, and major news networks which are translated into information which can be understood by the American public; and

the seeking out of esteemed infectious disease experts such as Dr. Anthony Fauci and his colleagues who are trusted by the American people.

Pertaining to *government responsibility*, we are concerned about who the American people elect as the president of the United States of America who shapes the policy, legislation, and programs which impact and lessen the threat of the coronavirus pandemic in the following ways:

the leadership of the president to prepare the medical resources (medical equipment, medical supplies, public and private research laboratories, and related areas to cope with a national healthcare threat and crisis), the will and determination of the American people for present and future pandemics, and the foresight to devise a national strategy and standards for primary, secondary, and tertiary prevention with public and private institutions such as the federal, state, and local government, businesses, schools, transportation carriers and systems, and related organizational entities;

the provision of relief to the victims of a pandemic in terms of unemployment relief, job training and placement into new career paths, and financial support for state and local governments to maintain first line responders and necessary resource supports;

and *the resumption of work and productivity* so that the economy grows again with employment in emerging fields such as electric cars, designing and building modern infrastructure, climate conservation enhancement and control, and related areas.

There is much to digest about these multiple dimensions which are related to each other. We hope that you will start local, state, and national conversations about ways to cope and solve present and future pandemics. I have presented spiritual and theological dimensions which are important in our deliberations. My education background has been in theology, pastoral counseling and psychology, public health, social policy and healthcare, social welfare, cultural diversity and culturally competent practice. I would like to participate in future interactions with you in light of these perspectives.

If you would like to share your responses to this book, please contact me at domanlum@gmail.com. We need to begin our dialogue on *The Great Coronavirus Pandemic and Messages from the Prophets* and the implications for public response, public health, and government responsibility. Let us continue to think together about ways to prevent future pandemic tragedies which have cost the lives of so many people during this year of loss and grief. Then let us act as one people to implement preventive measures and active health programs into our national fabric as Americans. May we unite together as the American people to ensure a quality of life characterized by public health and safety, the common good, and liberty and justice for all.

BIBLIOGRAPHY

Augustine. *City of God*. Translated by Marcus Dods. New York: Random House, 1958.
Barth, Karl. *Church Dogmatics* . Vol. 1, Part 1, *The Doctrine of the Word of God*. Translated by G. T. Thomson. Edinburgh: T. & T. Clark, 1960.
Bolsinger, Tod E. *Leadership for a Time of Pandemic: Practicing Resilience*. Downers Grove, IL: InterVarsity, 2020.
Brooks, Phillips. *Lectures on Preaching*. London: Allenson, 1877.
Brueggemann, Walter. *Virus as a Summons to Faith: Biblical Reflections in a Time of Loss, Grief, and Uncertainty*. Eugene, OR: Cascade, 2020.
Childs, Brevard S. *Introduction to the Old Testament as Scripture*. Philadelphia: Fortress, 1979.
Coyne, Kate. "This is their Love Story." *People*, June 24, 2019.
Edington, Mark D. W., ed. *We Shall Be Changed: Questions for the Post-Pandemic Church*. New York: Church Publishing, 2020.
Erikson, Erik H. *Identity and the Life Cycle*. New York: International Universities, 1959.
Heschel, Abraham J. *The Prophets*. New York: Harper & Row, 1962.
Hitchcock, Mark. *Corona Crisis: Plagues, Pandemics, and the Coming Apocalypse*. Nashville: Thomas Nelson, 2020.
Jeremiah, David. *Shelter in God: Your Refuge in Times of Trouble*. Nashville: Thomas Nelson, 2020.
Long, Thomas G. *The Witness of Preaching*. 3rd ed. Louisville: Westminster John Knox, 2016.
Mair, Kristi, and Luke Cawley, eds. *Healthy Faith and the Coronavirus Crisis: Thriving in the Covid-19 Pandemic*. London: SPCK, 2020.
Moltmann, Jürgen. "Religion, Revelation, and the Future." In *The Future of Hope*, edited by Walter H. Capps, 102–26. Philadelphia: Fortress, 1970.
———. *Theology of Hope: On the Ground and the Implications of a Christian Eschatology*. Translated by James W. Leitch. Minneapolis: Fortress. 1993.
Niebuhr, H. Richard, et al. *The Advancement of Theological Education*. New York: Harper, 1957.
Piper, John. *Coronavirus and Christ*. Wheaton, IL: Crossway, 2020.
Rawls, John. *A Theory of Justice*. Cambridge, MA: Belknap, 1970.
Schleiermacher, Friedrich. *Christian Faith*. Vols. 1–2. Translated by Terrence N. Tice et al. and edited by Catherine L. Kelsey and Terrence N. Tice. Louisville: Westminster John Knox, 2016.
Scott, R. B. Y. *The Relevance of the Prophets*. New York: Macmillan, 1961.

Tillich, Paul. *Systematic Theology*. Vols. 1–2. Digswell Place, England: Nisbet, 1960.

Tomeo, Teresa. *Conquering Coronavirus: How Faith Can Put Your Fears to Rest*. Nashua, NH: Sophia Institute, 2020.

von Rad, Gerhard. *The Message of the Prophets*. Translated by D. M. G. Stalker. San Francisco: HarperSanFrancisco, 1965.

Wright, G. Ernest. *God Who Acts: Biblical Theology as Recital*. Studies in Biblical Theology 8. London: SCM, 1962.

Wright, N. T. *God and the Pandemic: A Christian Reflection on the Coronavirus and Its Aftermath*. Grand Rapids: Zondervan, 2020.

———. "The Messiah and the People of God: A Study in Pauline Theology with Particular Reference to the Argument of the Epistle to the Romans." DPhil diss., University of Oxford, 1980.

———. *Paul and the Faithfulness of God*. Minneapolis: Fortress, 2013.

Index

African Americans
    coronavirus effects, 17
    killings and shootings, 6–7
amazing God, 79–80, 82–83
amazing grace, 80
Amos
    the message, 16
    the prophet, 13–14, 15
Augustine, Saint, 66

Barr, William, 4
Barrett, Amy Coney, 5, 9
Barth, Karl, xiv, 46, 114–15
Biden, Joe, 5, 7–8, 9, 10–11, 111, 135
Black Lives Matter, 6, 111, 149, 171
Blake, Jacob, 6
Blum, Arthur, 84
Bolsinger, Tod E., 181
Bromiley. Geoffrey, 83–84
Brooks, Phillips, xiv
Brueggemann, Walter, 185–88
Burns, Ken, 166

Cawley, Luke, 182
Centers for Disease Control, 2, 72, 162
Chauvin, Derek, 71
Childs, Brevard S., xv
China, Wuhan, 1
Clinebell, Howard J. Jr., 84
comfort, 98–99
construction, 130–32
covenant
    covenant of knowledge and forgiveness of the Lord, 147
    covenant making, makers, and keepers, 148–49
    covenant theology, 144–45
    flow of the covenants, 147–48
    new covenant of the heart, 146
    old covenant of the law, 145–46
    rainbow covenant, 143–44
COVID-19 pandemic, xiii, 2, 5, 11, 12, 13, 15, 16, 17, 26, 30, 41, 49, 56, 63, 64–65, 68, 71, 72, 81, 97, 108, 111, 118, 128, 131, 135, 136, 152, 162, 169–70, 174, 187

darkness, 50
dried up bones and God's spirit. 164–66

Edington, Mark D. W., 182
Eisenhower, Dwight David., 60
Erikson, Erik, 74
Ezekiel
    the prophet, 152–53

faithfulness of God, 81
family therapy, 24
Father's Day, 79
Fauci, Anthony, 10, 72, 97, 161
Flag Day, 63
Floyd, George, 6, 63, 71, 98, 111, 137
Frazier, George, 166

Garland, Merrick, 8
Ginsberg, Ruth Bader, 5, 8, 9, 152
gladness, 129–30
Goldberg, Jeffrey, 8

good, 15
good and evil, 13–14
good news, 53, 127–29
government response, 189
Graham, Billy, 11, 14, 46, 121

Hargitay, Mariska, 128–29
Harris, Kamala, 9–10
herald, 43–44
Hermann, Peter, 128–29
heilsgeschichte, 82
Heiser, Merill F., 83
Heschel, Abraham J., 178–79
Hitchcock, Mark, 182
holy city, 68
homiletics, xiii
hope, 49
Hosea
    the prophet, 21
    the restoration between Hosea and
        Gomer, 23–24
    the unfaithfulness of Hosea and
        Gomer, 21–23
Hough, Joseph, 84
Hubbard, David Alan, 83
humility, 30

Isaiah
    the book, 34–35
    the calling, 45–46
    the message, 37–38, 44
    the prophet, 34–35, 56–57
    the vision, 41–43

James, Letitia, 7
Jeremiah, 119, 120, 122
Jeremiah, David, 181
Jesus
    his identity, 105
John the Baptist, 97–98, 171
Johnson, J. Rosamond, 162
Johnson, James Weldon, 162
joy, 51
judgement, 170–71
justice
    distributive justice, 15, 28, 29
    economic justice, 28
    social justice, 27, 28

Kalili, John, 140
Kim, Daniel Dae, 44–45
kindness, 29
King, Martin Luther Jr., 11, 14, 46, 67, 171
kingdom of God, 67

Ladd, George Eldon, 83
Latino Americans, 17
leadership, 76
liberation, 51
light, 50
Lincoln, Abraham, 16–17, 48, 72
Liu, Gerald C., xii, xvii
Logan, John A., 48
Long, Thomas G., xvii
Lum, Doman, xvii

MacArthur, Douglas, 166
Mair, Kristi, 182
Memorial Day, 48–49, 71
Messiah, 52, 57–60, 171
messianic consciousness, 105
Micah
    the prophet, 27
Moderna vaccine, 2
Moltmann, Jürgen, 49–50
money, 113–14
Mother's Day, 33

Nagley, Winfield, 83
National Day of Prayer, 88–89
Newsom, Gavin, 12–13, 72
Newton, John, 80

Obama, Barack, 8, 30–31
O'Brien, Robert, 8
O'Brien, Gregory St. Lawrence, 84
Ogoshi, Ted, 84

parousia, 172
peace, 75–76, 154–55
Pelosi, Nancy, 10
Pence, Mike, 5, 9, 12
Piper, John, 182
post traumatic stress syndrome, 106
prayer, 89–90
prayers of King Hezekiah, 90–92
preaching xi-xii, xiii, xiv

Presidential Coronavirus Task Force, 2, 5, 12, 26
Prude, Daniel, 6–7
public health response, 188–89
public response, 188

Rad, Gerhard von, xv, 179–81
Rawls, John, 15
Rodriguez, Eddie, 140
Romney, Mitt, 4
Roosevelt, Franklin Delano, 34, 72, 74, 88, 108

salvation, 172–73
Schleiermacher, Friedrich, 29
Scott, R. B. Y., xv, 175–77
sermon, xiii, xiv
seeking the Lord, 114–15
serving the Lord, 132
shepherd, 154, 156, 157
Singletary, La'Ron, 7
Son of Man, 105
Song, Carol Chung, 83
Spanish Flu epidemic, xiii, 161
spirituality, 157
Steinberg, Darrell, 84
Stone, Roger J. Jr., 4

strength, 73
Suffering Servant, 104, 105–8
suffering servants, 108–9

Taketa, Gladys, 65
Taylor, Breonna, 6, 63
tears, 63–64, 66
thirst, 112–13
Tillich, Paul, 187–88
Tomeo, Teresa, 182
Trump, Donald, 1, 3–6, 7–11, 72, 104, 111, 118, 125–26, 135, 143
trust, 74–75

valley of death, 161–62
valley of dry bones, 163
valley of live bones, 163–64

Waring, Fred, 162
Warren, Lovely, 7
Wilson, Woodrow, 63
Woodward, Robert, 8
Word of God, xiv
World Health Organization, 1
Wright, G. Ernest, 82
Wright, N. T., 182–85

www.ingramcontent.com/pod-product-compliance
Lightning Source LLC
Chambersburg PA
CBHW070741160426
43192CB00009B/1531